From Idolatry to Advertising

From Idolatry to Advertising

VISUAL ART AND CONTEMPORARY CULTURE

Susan G. Josephson

M.E. Sharpe
Armonk, New York
London, England

Library of Congress Cataloging-in-Publication Data

Josephson, Susan G.
From idolatry to advertising : visual art and contemporary culture /
Susan G. Josephson.—1st ed.
p.   cm.
Includes bibliographical references and index.
ISBN 1-56324-875-1 (hardcover : alk. paper).—ISBN 1-56324-876-X (pbk. : alk. paper)
1. Postmodernism—Philosophy.
2. Popular culture.
3. Art and technology.
I. Title.
N6494.P66J67   1995
701-dc20
94-45412
CIP

Printed in the United States of America

The paper used in this publication meets the minimum requirements of the
American National Standard for Information Sciences—
Permanence of Paper for Printed Library Materials,
ANSI Z 39.48-1984.

♾

BM (c)   10   9   8   7   6   5   4   3   2   1
BM (p)   10   9   8   7   6   5   4   3   2   1

Contents

Preface

∼⊙──────────────────────────────────────

THIS BOOK TOOK SHAPE out of my many years teaching philosophy to professional art students at the Columbus College of Art and Design. There I have had many discussions about what is happening in art, and the future direction of culture with the advent of the computer and television. From these discussions an understanding of the cultural evolution of visual art in all its forms began to emerge. I found that there was no book which really told the philosophy behind all of the visual arts that I could use as a text in my classes. This was the beginning of this book in the form of long handouts to my students which attempted to fill in the gap between what I wanted to teach and the available textbooks.

This book records the conclusions that I came to as I thought through the cultural evolution of each of the different sorts of visual art and tried to piece together their story from the perspective of philosophy. Chapter 1 discusses how culture shapes art to be what it is from the outside, like a mold shapes clay, and the great power of art to affect the way we think and to promote cultural change. Chapter 2 discusses the evolution of Fine Art from its birth in the Renaissance to its present old age and decline. Chapter 3 discusses the institutional structures that make art for popular taste its own sort of art, and the culture wars over censorship and whether public art should be Fine Art, or art for popular taste. Chapters 4 and 5 discuss the life histories of design and advertising.

This book is also the story of how art interacts with technology. In my work in Artificial Intelligence research I saw that there is an intimate connection between the evolution of design in engineering and design in art. In both sorts of design there is a growing understanding of how to make and use levels of packaging, and how to approach things from the functional perspective of the artifact. This is discussed in Chapter 4. My talk in Chapter 1 of how art styles affect us also reflects this functional approach. That is, instead of approaching art styles in the traditional ways, I have approached them in terms of the tasks of vision and how art delivers information packaged to be understood at different levels of visual processing. Using this functional approach, I stress what art does for us rather than what art is.

I also tried to address the evolution of culture given the mass media and mass market, and the role of art in the growing marriage between television and computer. As I thought about computers in my work in Artificial Intelligence, I saw that a new sort of idolatry was arising where the computers were being asked to be infallible experts giving us advice on everything from taxes to marriage problems and our health. I saw that computers were being used not just as art tools and artists, but also as art objects like the ancient idols. This started me thinking about how other ancient functions of religion were being filled by advertising and the media. This is discussed in Chapters 5 and 6.

Because this book has taken so many years to write it is not possible to thank all the people from whom I have gotten insights and encouragement. However, I do want to thank the General Studies faculty at the Columbus College of Art and Design for their help, especially the art historians Margaret Seibert, Michael Swinger, and Beverly Orr for their help on getting the art history right, and George Felton for his help on understanding advertising. I also want to thank the faculty and graduate students at the Laboratory for Artificial Intelligence Research at the Ohio State University for their input into vision and style and the nature of thought from an information processing perspective, especially B. Chandrasekaran, John Josephson, Bill Punch, and Mike Weintraub. Also I would like to thank Will Smith and Alan Govenar for many useful conversations about art and its place in modern culture. And, of course, I must also thank all my many philosophy of art students without whom this book would never have come to be.

List of Illustrations

CHAPTER 1

The Cultural-Niche Theory of Art

THE EARLY TWENTIETH CENTURY artist Piet Mondrian (1937) wrote that he imagined a future where we no longer just had paintings hanging on walls, but lived in realized art. The items of domestic life would all be art. We would live in art. He wanted artists to make this art so balanced that people would live their lives in its harmonies. In a sense, that future has come to be. We live in realized art. We have art on our bed sheets and on our T-shirts. We make fashion choices of color and line, even on our towels and our toilet paper. We see art images everywhere. There is a diversity in the kinds of art that we see around us. There are advertising posters on the walls of stores. There are illustrations in magazines. There are streams of images broadcast to us over television. We are indeed living in realized art.

This realized art, however, is not in a harmonious universal style as Mondrian was envisaging. It consists mostly in forms of art considered banal, sentimental, and in bad taste by most in the Fine Art artworld. Further, because so many people have no interest in Fine Art, it is often thought that visual art has somehow lost its relevance and potency. People ask what the point of art is, and whether it is worthwhile spending public money on art. When people think of art, they think of Fine Art, and the influence of Fine Art seems to be in decline.

However, although Fine Art seems to be in decline as a cultural force, visual art has more power in culture now than it ever had. Visual art is not all Fine Art. There is a diversity of kinds of art in contemporary culture. Besides Fine Art, there is also Popular Art, Design Art, and advertising. What Fine Art does for us is just a small part of the total cultural value we get from art. As traditional culture recedes from memory, and technology changes our lifestyles, people look for new values and lifestyles. These new values and lifestyles are carried by the art broadcast to us over the mass media and on the products we buy. The mass-media arts define our heroes and tell us about the good. Advertisements define pleasure and lifestyle. With mass-market goods we dress our bodies and houses in art, thus using art to define who we are. These contemporary visual arts play a large part in shaping our values, fantasies, and lifestyles.

If we want to know what visual art is all about in contemporary culture, it seems a good idea to look at the causes for the existence of these different types of art. To understand what art is, we should ask ourselves not just the traditional question of what these art forms all have in common which makes them all art, but we should also ask questions about how these various visual art forms are different from each other, what social functions and agendas they serve, and why some people like one sort and some people another. In the following chapters we will try to answer such questions. We will discuss the social and historical forces that have shaped each sort of art. We will discuss the part each sort of art plays in shaping our current mentality. We will discuss what each sort of art does for people, and what its powers are. We will look at Fine Art's power for giving us an aesthetic emotion, and Popular Art's power for giving its viewers vicarious experiences and heightened emotion. We will discuss the power of Design Art to structure our identities, and of Advertising Art to give us desire. We will look at the overall effect of these various kinds of art on our mentalities. We will look at the dialectical evolution of visual art in Western culture, focusing on the life histories of these four kinds of art.

We will approach visual art from the perspective of the cultural-niche theory of art. This theory uses a biological metaphor, looking at the different kinds of art as cultural forms of life which each have certain constitutive features and personal history. We will look at the various kinds of art as entwined but separate forms of life evolving in relation to each other and to the surrounding culture. Looking at art this way gives us insight into the role of visual art in culture, and into the direction which culture and art are evolving. It gives us insight into why artists accept one stylistic dogma rather than another, and what sorts of cultural forces cause art to change. It gives us an approach to the problem of how to compare works of art cross-culturally and across time.

Giving a general idea of the cultural-niche theory will be the subject matter of this chapter, then in the following chapters we will look in detail at each of the main cultural niches of art in contemporary culture. We will discuss the life history of each type of art from a cultural-niche perspective, showing how each type of art has evolved to have its own concerns and powers, and the cultural needs that each type of art fills. In the last chapter we will discuss the evolution of culture and art, and the effect of visual art on the evolution of the way we think. We will discuss the cultural agendas carried by visual art in our new age of electronic media and mass market goods.

1. THE DIFFERENT VISUAL ARTS

Art and Social Class

As we look around in our contemporary world we see that there are several different types of visual art impinging upon us. As we said, we see Popular Art, Fine Art, Design, and advertising. The first question that comes up is the question of what differentiates these types of art. What makes something Popular Art, for example, and not Fine Art or Design Art?

Most commonly, people have differentiated types of visual art by what class they serve. The social historian Arnold Hauser (1958) writes that there are as many different art trends running parallel to each other in any given historical period as there are cultural strata in the society. These trends in art correspond to various lifestyles and levels of education. For Europe and the United States, the basic cultural strata have been the educated and aristocratic class, the middle class and urban masses, and the country folk. A different type of visual art corresponds to each of these cultural strata. According to his analysis of art along class lines, the major types of art are Fine Art (fig. 1.1), Popular Art (fig. 1.2), and Folk Art (fig. 1.3). Fine Art serves the educated upper class, Popular Art is the art of the middle classes and urban masses, and Folk Art is the art of the peasant classes.

As a first approximation, looking at art this way does tell us something about the difference between these types of art. As Hauser writes, it was the aristocratic class who supported the Renaissance and Enlight-

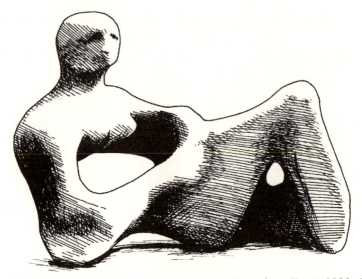

FIGURE 1.1 An example of Fine Art: Henry Moore, *Recumbent Figure*, 1938. Green Horton stone, length c. 54″. Tate Gallery, London.

enment academies and bought Fine Art for their collections. Fine Art was made from the beginning to reflect the tastes and serve the needs of this educated upper class. To serve the needs of the educated and aristocratic class, Fine Art is often critical of the status quo. It tends to grapple with fundamental human concerns, and challenge the viewer to change his or her perspective. This sort of art is meant to be mentally and aesthetically engaging.

In contrast to this, as Hauser writes, Popular Art is made by individual artists for popular taste. The artists that make art for popular taste are often professional artists who are themselves members of the elite classes with respect to art. Artists making art for popular taste are educated into the accumulated tradition of European Fine Art and culture. However, unlike elite artists who tend to express their own taste and life orientation in their art, the artists making Popular Art tend to pander to the taste of their clients.

The peasant classes, according to Hauser, are served by yet another form of art, Folk Art. The themes in Folk Art speak to what is common to all in the group. It is not thought of as having individual authors; rather it is passed down from one person to another, and no individual owns it. This sort of art is tightly constrained by fixed conventions. Folk Art is made by the folk for their own consumption. It is crafted art.

However, although there are different types of art, and these arts do have their origins in part in the needs of different classes, that is not

FIGURE 1.2 An example of traditional Popular Art: M.I. Hummel figurine, *The Photographer.* Hummel® and M.I. Hummel® are used under License from Goebel
© ARS AG, Zug/Switzerland.

what really distinguishes them in the modern context. Hauser's Marxist conception of class is less appropriate for differentiating the visual arts of today. In the modern context, what is more fundamental than class in differentiating various contemporary visual arts is their supporting institutions, ideologies, and distribution systems. Fine Art is displayed in museums and galleries, and tends to be individually hand-made items which are appreciated within the context of Fine Art ideology and history. Fine Art is art produced outside the mass-media and mass-market systems. Fine Art is art for art's sake, made for no other purpose than to be appreciated as art.

With respect to Popular Art, besides the older forms of Popular Art, paintings and sculptures produced for popular taste (fig.1.2), the majority of contemporary Popular Art is the commercial art that is broadcast on the mass media. Popular Art images are the illustrations in magazines and books, and on greeting cards and calendars. They are the images on television and in the movies. This art is made for a whole spectrum of class tastes, not just the tastes of the middle class. These mass-media arts are targeted to a range of ages, incomes, and ethnic groups.

The Folk Art of the European peasant classes was the craft objects of everyday life. These objects have been replaced by mass-market goods. For example, Figure 1.3 shows a hand-made quilt with a double ring pattern of the sort traditionally given to women at their wedding. Today factory produced mass-market quilts with the same pattern can be bought at the store. In general, we no longer make the things we use; we buy them, and most peasant craft knowledge has been forgotten. Thus,

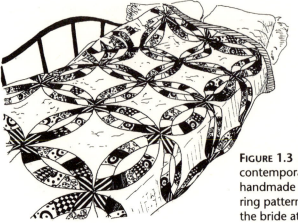

FIGURE 1.3 An example of contemporary traditional Folk Art: handmade quilt with a double ring pattern traditionally given to the bride at her wedding.

although there are still a few pockets of Folk Art here and there, for most of us the functions crafted goods once played in ordinary life are now played by mass-market manufactured goods. Thus, in Western society, Folk Art as the art of the peasant classes has been replaced by Design Art, targeted not just to the peasant class, but to all classes in society.

The Design Arts

The Design Arts are new forms of art created by the needs of the Industrial Revolution. Design Art is the art we see on the products we use. The flower decorations on sheets and tissue boxes are Design Art (fig. 1.4). The visual forms of our houses, cars, furniture, and clothes are all Design Art. The designs of efficiently operated machines in factories are also Design Art. The distinctions between the various Design Arts are distinctions of function. The Design Arts include such things as fashion design, package design, industrial design, interior decorating, and architecture. We can think of design as the creative act of shaping objects to be useful and attractive. Through their understanding of the consumer's psychology, designers try to make the product seem more desirable. The modern designer plays the roles of artist, engineer, and market researcher. The designer makes the styling of products and the form of new products.

   The Design Arts have different ideological concerns than those of Fine Art or Popular Art. With the Design Arts there isn't a concern with what makes something art. The ideological concerns for Design Art are what constitutes functional form and what the role of decoration should be. Design Art is concerned with function and with style. Putting

FIGURE 1.4 An example of Design Art : tissue box.

style on products makes them more attractive. It makes us buy more products as we throw out old ones, not because they are no longer usable, but because we no longer like their style. The consumer "decorates" his or her surroundings and person with this Design Art. Style sells, and designers sell style along with the primary function of the product.

Design Art is the art that is most married to industry. It participates in the most recent ideology of Western culture, the ideology of design. There are close conceptual similarities between the insights behind computer software technology and those embodied in Design Art, as we will discuss. We can find the ideology of design in both art and science, as both absorb technology and the philosophy of the artifactual.

Advertising

Advertising is often considered one of the Design Arts because marketing concerns are so important in the design of products. However, advertising has a distinctly different function from the rest of design. Advertising serves the function of creating desire for some product or promoting some cause. Of all the Design Arts, advertising has the most profound effect on our values and mentalities. Where Popular Art gives us media images, and design gives us art on the products we use, advertising uses the devices of Popular Art on the mass media to project a product image and to create desire for the product. The advertising image appears on the product, as well, to reinforce the identification between the media image of the product and the product itself. For example, Green Giant peas or asparagus have an advertisement on the mass media showing a lush cartoon valley with a jolly green giant who grows only the best vegetables, and the can of asparagus we find in the supermarket has a picture of the same green giant on it (fig. 1.5). Thus,

FIGURE 1.5 An example of Advertising Art : Can label for Green Giant asparagus. Copyright Pillsbury.

advertising is distinctly different in function from both Design Art and Popular Art. Advertising shares properties with both, and mediates between them.

The Four Main Visual Arts in Contemporary Culture

Visual art is not a single entity with one definition or ideological orientation. This idea that visual art is best understood as a plurality of approaches, institutions, functions, and ideologies is the central claim of the cultural-niche theory of art.

In general, we can best differentiate these arts, not by class but by distribution system and function. The mass media broadcasts Popular Art, and the products we buy project Design Art. Popular Art projects images — we look at them and have various responses to them as visual form and medium for messages, emotional stimulants, and so on. Design Art gives us attractive objects to use in everyday life. We use them to make aesthetic patterns in our houses and on our persons. We use the Design Arts to make our own art. Advertisement mediates between Popular Art images and Design Art products. It projects images of the products into the mass-media stream of art, and those images are then carried by the products. Fine Art acts as critic and counterpoint to these three arts and produces art for art's sake. It is produced by different forces than the others, and continues old traditions of art, including the traditional distribution system through museum and gallery shows first institutionalized in the Enlightenment French Royal Academy. It is made to be consumed by people who know something about art. Often Fine Artists also teach art to Popular and Design Artists as well as to non-artists.

Thus, Popular Art is mass-media art, Design Art is mass-market art, and advertising promotes a product in the media. Fine Art is distributed outside the mass market or media as one of a kind items to be appreciated in an art world context. Of course distinguishing these arts by the channels through which they reach us is not a completely clean way of distinguishing them. There are, for example, borderline cases like Fine Art that is sold in reproduction by museums in the mass market, or Fine Art images sold on mass-market calendars, or functional items sold as one of a kind items by galleries. So, although distribution system captures something about the difference between these arts, there is more to distinguish them than that, and there will always be borderline cases.

Although these major types of art dominate culture, there are also other sorts of art in contemporary culture. For example, there are also new studio-crafts that are distributed outside the mass-media, mass-market system at fairs, craft shows, and craft and consignment shops. This is potentially the beginning of another cultural niche for art. Where design is mass produced and carries mainstream values hand in hand with advertising, the studio-crafts are hand-made, individually crafted objects, and do not carry mainstream mass-culture values or advertising.

2. CULTURAL NICHES

From the perspective of the cultural-niche theory, there are many cultural niches within which visual arts are formed. These different visual arts are each the historical product of a different set of social needs. For example, when the Renaissance aristocracy needed a voice to propagandize for humanism, crafts people were trained to make Fine Art to help do so. When the Industrial Revolution changed people's lifestyles so that folk crafts became industrialized, the Bauhaus movement inspired a way of educating a new sort of craftsperson, and the Design Arts were born. When capitalism needed to make attractive packages and product announcements to stimulate demand, advertising and mass media came forth. Thus, Fine Art, Popular Art, Design Art, and advertising, can be thought of as forms of life serving externally defined functions.

Further, there are traditional functions of art around which a cultural niche for art might potentially be formed which have not been embraced by any of the art institutions. As we will discuss in chapter 6, idolatry is a function of this sort. Although art is used informally for this function, the advice-giving external authority function of idolatry is no longer being served by art. This function has begun to be served by non-art institutions. Engineers and computer scientists make computer systems that attempt to serve the function of being God-like advice givers. So, there are certain cultural functions which art is normally recruited to fill, but when there is no art available, as in the case of idolatry, something else is recruited to fill that function. This reinforces the biological niche metaphor for how art types are formed. Like the wolf niche which is normally filled with dog-like mammals, but in Australia is filled by a marsupial, the idolatry niche is normally filled by objects created by shaman-like artists. However, in contemporary Western culture, it is filled by objects created by engineers and computer scientists.

The niche of an animal in biology is its place in the ecosystem, that is, its relationship to its food, its habitat, its competitors and predators, and its partners within its niche. Either animals evolve so as to adapt more and more to their particular niches or they become extinct, and similar niches support similar adaptations. Also, there is a certain inertia to adaptation. Often animal behavior can be seen as coming from a previous adaptation to a different niche than the animals are now in.

We can see analogies between characteristics of a biological niche and the cultural niches of art. Analogous to food resources are economic resources which support the art of a particular niche. Food gathering strategy is analogous to the distribution systems for the art of a particular niche. Thus, when we differentiate art types by their distribution networks this is analogous to differentiating animals by whether they are carnivores, herbivores, or omnivores. Also, as we will discuss, there is competition between types of art for territory. For example, mass-market art competes with Folk Art, while Fine Art and Popular Art compete over which orientation will be displayed in public art. Also, cultural niches can overlap and interact with one another. Art evolves within each niche and adapts to the conditions it finds there.

Cultural niches are like containers which shape art to be what it is, like wax in a mold. Cultural niche is to art like a positive shape is to a negative shape. What we mean by cultural niche is the shaping interface between culture and art. Thus, the cultural niche is seen both in the outside conditions shaping art as well as in the art itself. A work of art looks the way it does because of the functions it was made for, the conditions surrounding its making, and its distribution. Art takes on the look of its niche. This too is analogous to biological niches where, for example, the marsupial that fills the wolf niche in one place looks quite a bit like the *Canis* mammal that fills the wolf niche in another place. Thus, the cultural niche is both the conditions forming art as well as the impressions those conditions have left on the art itself. If we put a Fine Art image into a Design function — like a Van Gogh painting on a coffee mug — it becomes Design Art and takes on the look of Design Art. What we mean by cultural niche, then, is this positive to negative shaping of art by cultural forces and their functional demands.

Besides institutions for distribution and training of artists, there are also ideologies of art. The ideologies of art structure art making and art evaluation. For a cultural niche to be successful, the artists need to have a sense of themselves and their mission as artists. There also need to be philosophies dictating value in art. These ideologies must cover all aspects of the artist's work. The artist's work is different in different niches, so the ideologies of different niches cover different aspects. For example, in the case of Fine Art the ideologies dictate subject matter, stylistic conventions, beauty, and artistic mission, all within the context of the general function of art which defines what Fine Art is. In the case of Design art, the ideologies dictate attitudes towards artistic mission, functional form, style and decoration, marketing, and craftsmanship.

Within each of these ideological slots, there can be replacement of one particular view with another. Thus, the orientation to art grows and changes within its niche. This is how art evolves within its niche. For example, within its own niche, Fine Art has evolved from neo-classicism where art was to teach and have a clearly defined style within which some grandiose subject matter was depicted. Its goals, among other things, was to be a non-objective art with no subject matter, and no clear stylistic conventions, whose mission is to give the viewer an aesthetic emotion. This range of orientations is all contained in the general function of Fine Art to produce unique objects to be collected and exhibited for their artistic qualities. This general function is then implemented by the institutions distributing the art and educating the artists. This is also analogous to biological niches where one set of conditions, like the climate, makes another set of conditions possible, like the animal's food sources and predators which then serve as the conditions to which the animal must adapt. In the cultural niche the general function is made possible by the availability of the necessary institutions, and within that general set of conditions (the institutions educating and defining who the artist is, the conditions under which the art is made, and how the art is distributed) the ideological structure, like the adapting animal, must then evolve.

This art ideology delivers a certain sort of art which then serves or does not serve the functions set up by these containing institutions. If the art ideology ceases producing art that serves these functions, then that ideology goes extinct, leaving its niche intact for some other ideology to take over. For example, in Fine Art, modernism ceased producing art objects that could be sold to collectors. The art had become too cynical and negative. Much of what was produced was not even in the form of art objects, but rather as happenings that could not be collected at all. This in part caused modernism to die, leaving room for postmodernism, a new ideology, to attempt to produce art that could serve the functions supported by the containing institutions. Sometimes the niche itself collapses; either the institutions disappear, or the culture no longer has any use for that function. As with biological niches, cultural niches can collapse and new ones will form.

Further, there is always pressure from the surrounding culture for the ideologies of art to reflect the general world view of the culture. For example, when the ancient Greek culture was rediscovered in the Renaissance it was appropriate for art to embody the classical ideology of Neoplatonism; and when romanticism swept through European culture, the ideology of Fine Art incorporated romanticism into its view of the artist's role and creativity. Thus, there are forces on the art niche to produce art for a certain function out of ideologies that resonate with the current world view of the culture. When this is not possible, the cultural niche loses its influence in the culture, as has happened with contemporary Fine Art. The competitors of that type of art then take over more territory, as for example, Popular Art has taken over many of the cultural resources once used by Fine Art.

With the cultural-niche theory we are not trying to define art as though it were some abstract concept, but trying to get some sense for what art in general *is* from looking at the whole collection of cultural niches of art. Looking at art across several cultural niches, we can see how it is shaped by ideology, institution, and cultural function. We can also see how the various types of art work together to support a certain cultural orientation, and shape the minds of their viewers. In the following chapters we will discuss each of these cultural niches of art, and the direction in which contemporary culture and thought are being pushed by these various arts.

Design Art, Popular Art, and advertising are part of the cultural pressure molding the popular mind into a more primitive mental orientation. These arts are creating desires in us, and giving us new mythologies and values. These arts make possible a new mythic level to culture. The technology of Artificial Intelligence is facilitating this as well. Popular

Art promotes a mental orientation antagonistic to critical thought, an orientation in which the popular mind loses its capacity to do complex rational problem solving. As this occurs those tasks requiring complex reasoning are being taken over by our pocket calculators and home computers. As this trend continues, computer systems are being created that could perform the functions of idols for modern people (see chapter 6). Idols are the most ancient form of art, and relating to machines as non-human advice-giving infallible authorities completes the archaic mind-set stimulated by mass-media and mass-market art. Through the mass media, television, and film a new "written language" for making permanent records of visual experience is being discovered. We are evolving a new relationship to artifacts, and preparing ourselves to use mass media and computers as external extensions of our minds. We are expanding with technology to a place where the non-rational parts of our mentalities can feel comfortable cocooned in human artifacts, with media images filling our minds and expanding our capacities for visual thought, while computers do rational problem solving for us.

Further, the various visual arts, as structured through these cultural niches, reinforce and structure cultural diversity in society. As old ethnic identities are slowly erased, new identities are shaped in part through participation in different art niches. We dress ourselves and surround ourselves with certain styles, and identify with different mass-media stereotypes and product ideologies. We also share habitual states of consciousness with people who consume the same type of art as we do. Thus, new identities are being formed through the power of art. Art in our culture is facilitating the evolution of the mind. It is creating new identities and reinforcing new mental skills.

3. DEFINING *ART*

The Institutional Theory of Art

The cultural-niche theory of art is in some ways really just an extension of the institutional theory of art. In "The Artworld" the philosopher Arthur Danto suggests that to see something as art requires seeing it in the context of the art world, that is in relation to art history and in an atmosphere of artistic theory. When an object is considered an artwork it becomes subject to an interpretation, writes Danto. That is, the difference between an artwork and a mere thing is that the artwork has an interpretation and the mere thing does not. The artwork's interpretation depends upon the artistic context of the work. This includes, but is not limited to, its art-historical context and its antecedents. It exists in an atmosphere of interpretation and the art world is a vehicle for interpretation. There is no art without there also being people who speak the language of the art world and interpret what the art *says* in that context.

Danto (1981) writes that being or not being a work of art is really a functional designation. Now the object is a snow shovel, and functions as such, now it is an art object, to be appreciated as such. Being an art object describes how one is to use the object, not what it is. To be appreciated as an art object, something must either look like an art object, be paint on canvas, for example, or be made by an artist who advocates that we accept it as such, like Picasso's *Bull* made out of handlebars and a bike seat. To be considered "art" something need only be picked out by the art world as art to be viewed or experienced under whatever theory then dominates the art world. We are not dealing with essences here, anymore than we are dealing with essences when we, say, designate an overturned box to be a chair. Being a chair does not designate an essence; it involves what we choose to do with the thing.

Along these same lines, the philosopher George Dickie (1971, p. 101) suggests as a definition of art: "A work of art in the classificatory sense is 1) an artifact, 2) upon which some person or persons acting on behalf of a certain social institution (the art world) has conferred the status of candidate for appreciation." Conferring status is like giving someone legal status, marriage, or an educational degree. A paradigm case of status conferring with art is being in a show or being played in a concert. The title on an art object is a badge of status. This view is what has been called the "institutional theory of art."

Differences Between Cultural-Niche and Institutional Theory

Like this institutional theory of art, the cultural-niche theory of art is also a functionalist theory. Something is art because it is chosen to be art by an art world and functions as art, not because of some intrinsic quality. However, the institutional theory, and most theories of art before it, all sought something that all objects designated as art have in common independent of their cultural setting. The cultural-niche theory defines art by its cultural setting. For the cultural-niche theory, art is not the individual objects picked out as art any more than, say, marriage is the individual married couples. What carries the constitutive essence of art is not the individual objects dubbed art, but the institutions that do the dubbing.

In terms of the cultural-niche theory of art, the distinction between kinds of art is not a matter of essential qualities. That is, although there are many images that are clearly one kind of art rather than another, in general there really is no unique quality about an image that can show us definitely which cultural niche the art belongs to. Is the *Mona Lisa* image Popular Art, Fine Art, or Design Art? If the image of the *Mona Lisa* is hung in a museum, it is surely Fine Art. If it is sold on a T-shirt in a clothing store it loses its high aesthetic value and gains a decorative joke value, thus counting as Design Art since it is a decoration on a T-shirt. It could be used as an advertising image or as a mass-media Popular Art image as well. The same image of *Mona Lisa* could be classed as Popular Art, Fine Art, advertising art, or Design Art, depending upon how it is displayed and marketed. Thus, we cannot really make a clear distinction between types of art on the level of a single image. Defining art as a particular kind must take into account its function and context. Art is not differentiated on the level of single images, but in terms of the institutions, ideologies, distribution systems, and functions that typically produce art of each sort.

The institutional theory of art, like almost all the attempts to define art before it, is really about what makes something "Fine Art," not just what makes something "art." That means that first of all, whatever characterizes art, it is assumed that it is something that the visual arts have in common with music, literature, theater, and dance. This collection has all been included in the set "Fine Art" since the Renaissance. Second, there is also agreement that "art" does not include things like cabinetwork, tissue boxes, blankets, dishes, or wallpaper, thus excluding from consideration those things that are normally excluded from the category of Fine Art. Third, generally art is something contemplated for its artistic qualities and is otherwise non-functional. This too is characteristic of Fine Art. So, when thinking about what "art" in general is, people tend to consider only Fine Art.

However, the cultural-niche theory is not concerned with just the visual arts that are Fine Art, but also with Popular Art, Folk Art, Design Art, advertising, studio-craft, and so on. From the perspective of the cultural-niche theory, any true definition of *art* would have to span all of these cultural niches. To say what visual art *is*, at least in our own culture, we look at the scope of its powers over all the art niches in our culture. First we see the distribution of function between the visual arts in our own culture as media art, product art, advertising, and "pure" art outside the mass-media market. Then we see within that structure what needs the various kinds of art fill, and what these arts do for us.

As we will discuss, among other things, Fine Art appeals to taste, Popular Art gives rise to vicarious experience and narrative thought, Design Art packages messages and functions, and advertising art engages desire. In our own culture, we might say that visual art is the capacity, the tool, with which thoughts and functions are packaged for various effects. However, these sorts of statements about art do not give a definition in the sense that the institutional theory gives a definition of art. They do not tell us what makes some object art rather than non-art, or tell us what to attend to in our critical responses to art. Indeed, as we've said, art is like a biological thing. We don't so much want a definition, giving us some sort of *a priori* designation of art essences, as we want empirical descriptions that tell us about each kind of art's typical life history and character.

4. OBJECTIVE STANDARDS FOR COMPARING ARTS

When people think about the nature of visual art they tend to look at the objects picked out as art in conventional art histories. However, conventional art histories tend not to treat the other powerful visual arts of our own time beyond Fine Art, namely, Popular Art, Design Art, and advertising. The Design Arts are not considered "art" because they are not functionless beyond being aesthetic. Also, the Design Arts do not typically show personal expressive creativity. So, the Design Arts are typically considered mere decoration. Popular Art is thought of as in bad taste, banal, sentimental, and so not worthy of consideration either. Since art histories are only looking at "good" art, they tend not to consider these other arts. Standing as they most often do within the Fine Art art world, art historians use the ideology and sense of artistic value of Fine Art to evaluate all art.

Conventional art histories, using Fine Art and its ideologies as their standards against which all art is viewed, blur distinctions which the cultural-niche theory wants to make. As we will discuss in chapter 2, Fine Art did not start until the Renaissance. Art objects before that, or in other cultural contexts should not be compared to Fine Art as though they shared the Fine Art ideologies of aesthetic form, expressiveness, and functionlessness (except to be collected and exhibited). From the perspective of the cultural-niche theory, Fine Art is only one cultural niche for art, and in contemporary Western civilization not the most important one.

The standards used to judge art cross-culturally and across niches ought not to be those of Fine Art, since that distorts our vision of these other arts and prevents us from seeing the true powers of art. Whatever art is, it is more than just what we have in Fine Art. For example, the ancestor figures of the Dogon of Mali in Black Africa (fig. 1.6) are valued in their own culture for their power to enact the ancestors. This power has nothing to do with excellence of execution, expression, or Aesthetic Form (see Armstrong, 1981). Yet, when they are hung in a Western art gallery or museum, they are displayed and appreciated for the way they conform to principles of aesthetics or show expressive excellence or virtuosity of execution. Looking at them in this way misses the essential nature of these objects as the conveyers of spiritual presence. Traditional art histories also discuss the archaic Greek statues in terms of their aesthetic contours and their degree of naturalism, thereby missing the power these art objects had as idols.

If we are not to be blind to the diversity of art, we need culturally independent standards that come from somewhere outside current ideologies of art. Such standards can be derived from perceptual psychology and cognitive science. These disciplines stand outside any cultural niche of art and its accompanying ideologies, and so can be "objective." From the perspective of these disciplines, there are cross cultural universals rooted in human psychology and the human nervous system. We can compare arts in different cultural niches by how they affect thought.

Viewing art in terms of cultural niches rather than in terms of individual objects of art, we can see that one of the main functions of art is to reinforce a certain mental attitude. That is, art helps us hold our minds with a certain focus. We look at art with a certain mental posture and expectation. For example, in certain situations we expect to be told a joke, to have a vicarious experience, or to have an aesthetic experience. Any individual art object reinforces just a particular instance of this mental posture. However, exposure to a particular type of art over and over again tends to make that mental posture into a general posture to events outside art as well.

One sort of mental state that contemporary advertising reinforces is a general state of suspended desire with cynicism and concern for our own self-interest. We approach advertising art with questions like: "What do I want to buy? What are they trying to sell me? What do I desire and what can I afford?" We ask ourselves such questions habitually in response to advertising art. We are exposed to such art many times each day on television, in magazines, newspapers, on products, in stores, and on highway billboards. This maintains within us a certain

FIGURE 1.6 An example of art with spiritual power: Ancestor figure on mask of the Dogon of Mali in Black Africa. Drawn after photograph from Robert Armstrong, *The Power of Presence, Consciousness, Myth, and Affecting Presence.* Philadelphia: University of Pennsylvania Press, 1981.

general mental attitude and state of expectation where we are concerned with the "bottom line," as well as an awareness of how our present lifestyle lacks things which would make it more comfortable or pleasurable. As we will discuss in chapter 5, this reinforces a restless striving to become more comfortable, which can come out as a cynical self-interest as well as a suspiciousness of other people's real motives. This state of mind is then constantly stimulated by exposure to advertising art and generalized beyond advertising through its constant repetition. In this way art not only affects us when we see it, but reinforces certain general approaches to life and hence, helps move culture in a certain direction.

Art's power to reinforce and stimulate certain mental postures is one way in which art is useful to cultures. Cultures maintain certain states of consciousness and mental attitudes with the help of art. In some cultures this is explicit. For example, medieval church art, Hindu art, and Zen art are all art forms promoting the state of consciousness of their religions. These states of consciousness are mental states useful to the culture, and art is created to maintain them and practice them.

One way we might determine how art of a certain sort is affecting thought is by researching how contemporaries within the context of the art's home culture and cultural niche reacted to the art (see Freedberg, 1989). Another aspect of a cognitive science of art is the study of mental states maintained by repeated exposure to art. It can be discovered how the modularities and regularities governing the geometry of a picture space (or three-dimensional forms) are used to resonate with our natural processes of perception so as to have different cognitive effects on us. This is the perceptual psychology of art. This sort of analysis is like that done by Rudolf Arnheim (1969 and 1982). Such approaches open the door to doing a cognitive science of art by promoting the discovery of principles governing what is possible for vision and cognition in relation to visual art. Because these sorts of concerns are from outside the ideologies of any particular art niche, they are objective. We can use them to compare arts across cultures and cultural niches without blinding ourselves to any of the powers of art.

Using Computer Programs to Test Theories

Evaluating art in terms of the principles governing what is possible for vision and cognition also opens the door to doing a cognitive science of art in which art is investigated by programming theories into computers. Through Artificial Intelligence research, a new science of art potentially opens up as we program computers to test our theories about art.

This sort of approach is suggested by the Aaron program of Harold Cohen (McCorduck, 1991). Harold Cohen designed an expert system called "Aaron" that independently composes pictures, and draws them in ink on paper. Cohen has programmed Aaron to make "representational" art by having it draw an outline around stick figures with the essentials of animals, humans or plants. This inner skeleton is not seen in the final drawing. Aaron has a knowledge base of possible figures, and possible relationships between them. For example, unlike rock figures, human figures cannot be upside down, or have rocks or other human figures on top of them. Thus, the program "understands" when it has drawn a human or a rock and treats each sort of shape differently.

Further, Aaron can be programmed with compositional rules. For example, for the "Eden" series it was programmed to compose using a variety of shapes, sizes, and spaces in each drawing (fig. 1.7). The program periodically scanned across the image it was composing to see if these compositional goals had been reached. It is this goal-directed behavior that distinguishes Aaron from normal computer software tools

FIGURE 1.7 An example of art which was entirely composed and drawn by a computer: computer-artist Aaron (H. Cohen), *Eden* series. India ink on paper, 22″ × 30″, 1987. Reprinted from *Aaron's Code, Meta-Art, Artificial Intelligence, and the Work of Harold Cohen* by Pamela McCorduck. Copyright © 1991, Pamela McCorduck. Used with permission of W.H. Freeman and Company.

for producing art. Each one of Aaron's drawings is unique and is composed and drawn by Aaron, not by Cohen.

By programming the computer with his own rules for producing representations, Cohen is discovering the rules and knowledge one needs for making representational art from the primitives up. Using Aaron, Cohen can see whether the principles he thinks he is using really result in the sorts of images he predicts. Thus, Aaron is a good expert system tool for investigating the knowledge and procedures involved in making art. Of course, Aaron is a simple program compared to other Artificial Intelligence programs. One can easily imagine more complex and cognitively interesting programs for producing art, or for appreciating art. However, looking at what has been done with even such a simple system suggests what is potentially possible. By following Cohen's lead and designing other expert systems that produce drawings, we could discover and test theories of composition and art's effect on mental states.

5. THE EVOLUTION OF VISUAL ART

Progress as Achieving Realism

The most common theories of progress in visual art focus on realism in art. These theories tell the history of art as a progression towards a truly illusionistic style. As the story goes, that illusionistic style was finally achieved with the big breakthrough during the Renaissance of systematic rules for perspective rendering. After that, this illusionistic style was further refined, until, in the nineteenth century, photography took over the job of making illusionistic art, and the artists were suddenly out of work. The artists were competing with the camera which could make better illusionistic art than the artists could, and so the artists changed style away from illusion so as to have something of value to do (Gibson, 1966, p. 231). This, then, according to this story, is the origin of "modernism" where the artists are making non-illusionistic and hence incomprehensible art. There is an evolution to art as there is to science, it is said. Within that process of evolution, perspective rendering is ahead of the other art styles. For example, Samuel Y. Edgerton, Jr. (1980) claims that the Renaissance discovery of perspectival rendering is a breakthrough much like modern science is a breakthrough. As soon as other cultures assimilate perspective rendering, he writes, it will replace their more primitive styles because it is more "realistic," just as science has replaced "folk" principles of physical nature. Further, according to this theory, if the art of a culture looks unrealistic to us, then it is unrealistic. Since artistic conventions communicate their representational content by giving us the same sort of information that we get in natural perception (Hagen, 1980), everyone with the same physical makeup will see art in the same way, independent of their culture. Realism or lack of realism in art is objective, and not culture-relative. The history of art should be seen as a progression toward the goal of achieving complete fidelity to nature, and when this goal was reached first in Renaissance perspective, and then finally with photography, artists had to abandon representation, since photography did it better.

There are several things wrong with this way of looking at the evolution of visual art. First of all, it is primarily the tradition of portraiture that has been affected by the camera, and it has not contracted the demand for art, but expanded it to include portraits for people of the middle and lower classes who in previous eras did not have the money to have their portraits painted. Now these classes can take a picture themselves, or go to a professional photographer to have it done. The camera has not taken jobs from artists, it has added to the sorts of things that an artist can do. Also, the camera has become a tool for making art, the goal of which is not just representation, but also sales. Advertising uses photography because it can be manipulated to show the whole range of things that paint on canvas can. But people think that what is photographed is literally real, and so it can be a more effective deception. Further, for reasons completely unrelated to the introduction of the camera, the ideology of Fine Art has moved away from an emphasis on subject matter, and hence realism. We will discuss this in chapter 2.

Second, and more fundamentally, this theory of progress in art presupposes that realism can be objectively determined. The alternative view is that the stylistic conventions in art are a language that we read. If artistic conventions are read like a language, then they communicate primarily by engaging our concepts. Since concepts are culture-bound, artistic conventions will be as well. And further if artistic conventions are like language, arbitrary systems of marks communicating only to those who have the cultural background to read them, then the same picture could look realistic to some and not to others. Thus, there is the claim that realism in art cannot be objectively determined (for example, Goodman, 1976) and a style like perspectival naturalism, which looks uniquely realistic to us in the West, is no more realistic than any other style.

Neither the view that all style reads like natural perception and so realism can be objectively determined, nor the view that all style reads like a language and so realism is relative to culture, is correct. Not all aspects of style communicate in the same way. That is, different levels of a composition are appealing to different levels of our visual system. Looking at vision from an information processing perspective, it becomes clear that visual perception is not a one step process, but occurs in a series of steps. We receive light patterns through our eyes and then do a series of calculations on them; each calculation serves as the input for the next calculation (Marr, 1982). This series of calculations occurs in two main stages: early vision and high-level vision. Early vision discovers the textures, shapes, volumes, and distances of objects from the viewer. It determines where things are in space. After this sort of information has been calculated from the light patterns on each retina, high-level vision, using concepts, then calculates what these objects are (Hurlbert and Poggio, 1988). Vision is organized around two basic tasks within which are various subtasks. The first basic task is discovering the spatial characteristics of things, and the second basic task is recognizing what things are.

FIGURE **1.8** Cartoon image of having a great idea. Reading this image is highly culture-bound since the viewer must know the depicting conventions of our culture to know that this image of a light bulb over someone's head represents a great idea.

Although people in all cultures process perception through the same visual mechanisms, the recognition task of high level vision is more culture-bound than the perception of volume and space of early vision. This is because high-level vision depends upon concepts. Different stylistic devices appeal to different levels of visual processing. Some stylistic devices communicate like a language, while other stylistic devices simulate natural perception.

Those aspects of style that are language-like are those used to make shapes recognizable. The representational shapes drawn in art are meant to be easy to match with our concepts (Arnheim, 1969, esp. pp. 27–37). For example, a picture of a duck needs to show its webbed feet or bill, or whatever feature allows us to recognize the shape as a duck. Early vision does not give us "duck," it gives us shapes and textures which we then recognize as "duck" with the help of our concepts. In early vision, the duck shape is just an oblong shape with two thinner shapes on the bottom, and a smaller roundish shape on top, it requires high-level visual processes to see those shapes as representing a particular object. These shapes, made to be recognized, are often culture-bound, although they do not need to be. For example, cartoonists draw "having a bright idea" as having a little light bulb go on over the person's head (fig. 1.8). Recognizing that the image represents a light bulb, and that a light bulb represents a bright idea requires the viewer to know the depicting

FIGURE 1.9 Drawing after wall painting from the tomb of Nakht at Thebes, eighteenth dynasty. The conventions used by the ancient Egyptians to indicate a family group showed the wife with her hand around her husband's waist and the daughter sitting between the father's legs with her hand around one leg. Even though reading the depicting conventions is culture-bound, we can still read the image because we share enough basic concepts about families.

conventions of the host culture. The ancient Egyptians represented a noble family group with the wife clinging to her husband's waist and their child between the man's legs clinging to his leg (fig. 1.9). (See fig. 6.4 for an equivalent modern convention for showing the family.) In such images viewers must know the depicting conventions as well as have equivalent concepts themselves in order to read the image. In the case of the Egyptians we still share enough basic concepts about families that we can read the conventional language of the image. While in the case of the cartoon having a bright idea, the required concepts are more culture-bound.

Although the stylistic conventions that give us recognition are like a language, potentially different from culture to culture, and in that sense arbitrary, the conventions which deliver the illusion of space are not. Since the early vision task of discovering the shapes, textures, volumes, and distances of objects from the viewer do not require concepts, they are not relative to culture. Proof that the third dimension is computed in early vision, and independently of concepts, is that we are able to see depth in Random Dot Stereograms (fig. 1.10). Random dot stereograms are pictures created by showing each eye a random dot pattern with a portion which is slightly displaced from that shown to the other eye.

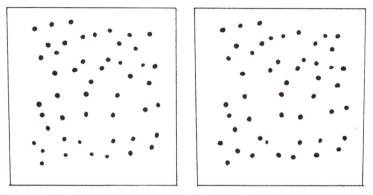

FIGURE 1.10 Random Dot Steriogram. The dots in the two images are displaced from one another just enough so that if we look at the right image with the right eye, while looking at the left image with the left eye, we can see a single image with depth. That we can see depth without representational content is proof that the third dimension is computed independently of concepts in early vision.

Even though these pictures have no representational or conceptual content, they are still perceived as displaying depth (Hurlbert and Poggio, 1988, p. 226). Thus, those aspects of style that deliver volume and depth are appealing to early vision and are not culture-bound, while those aspects of style delivering shapes for recognition appeal to high-level vision and concepts, and hence are culture-bound. In this way the same image can have both culture-bound and non-culture-bound aspects of its composition.

Illusionistic Realism

Perspectival naturalism in the Renaissance (fig. 2.3 on p. 47) was indeed a more universal style than that of the medieval in the sense that the conventions of perspectival naturalism work directly on the visual system without the mediation of concepts. Perspective is a system of geometric conventions that deliver information to the visual system like that which the viewer would get in one eye in one moment of viewing. In order to perceive perspectival representations as having depth, the viewer needs to compensate for the representation failing to change as a scene would when the viewing point changes (Rosinski and Farber, 1980). Thus, perspectival rendering does not simulate the complete complexity of natural perception, it only gives vision a few of the clues necessary to perceive space and volume.

Although perspective is illusionistic it is not perfect. For example,

FIGURE 1.11 Although perspective is illusionistic it is not perfectly so. For example, perspectively drawn convergence on tall buildings does not look quite realistic. This is because perspectival rendering does not simulate the complete complexity of natural perception.

we do not recognize extreme foreshortening or convergence at the tops of tall buildings as realistic (fig. 1.11); and "correctly" perspectivally distorted spheres are not perceived as spheres (Kubovy, 1986) even though in all these cases the rules of perspective are correctly followed. Thus, there are cases where rendering according to the laws of perspective does not produce realistic-looking pictures even to the Western viewer.

This imperfection of perspectival rendering is often taken to be a criticism of the view that Renaissance perspective is a universal illusionistic style. This is then taken as support for the claim that all artistic conventions are arbitrary and culture-bound, as is the case with language. On the contrary, these imperfections argue for the uniquely illusionistic quality of perspectival rendering. These imperfections show that under most conditions perspectival rendering is very well adapted to the workings of perception. Since, if it were just a case of reading the conventions, as for example Nelson Goodman claims (1976, pp. 14–16), then there would not be cases of "correct" rendering by the rules of projective geometry that did not "look right." If it were just a matter of conventions, all correct renderings by those conventions would look equally right to the Western viewer. Although Renaissance perspective is a system of stylistic conventions, these conventions are not arbitrary since they are constrained by what the visual system will find illusionistic, that is, by how we normally perceive depth. If what we mean by realism is this appeal to early vision, then perspectival art is uniquely realistic, and Renaissance perspectival art is more realistic than medieval art.

Even in perspectival art, however, some of the conventions — those that permit recognition of the figures represented in the art — are geared to disambiguate at a cognitive level and hence, are still culture-bound. Someone from a non-Western culture might be able to see that a perspectivally rendered painting is spatial without being able to read *what* is being represented in the art. The shapes drawn for recognition, such as a duck or an apple even in perspectival art, require knowledge of the culture and of the styles underlying the art. These images must match concepts to be understood.

Reading any image requires a perceptual posture. Seeing is task driven. We do not just see, we see with some purpose in mind. We are looking for the bathroom, watching out for dips in the sidewalk, or trying to recognize the person coming toward us. Because seeing is task driven, one must see with the right purpose in mind to see anything in art as well. So, only if the viewer is looking at the image with the purpose in mind of seeing a representation will they be able to read the picture as giving the illusion of depth. Someone from a culture that does not make representational art might look only at the surface itself and not through the surface at what is represented. In that case they would miss the illusionistic quality of perspectival drawing because they approach the art with the wrong set of expectations. Looking at flat surfaces as representational is not culturally universal, but once surfaces are looked at in that way, the third dimension is not read like a language, and is culturally universal, while the stylistic conventions carrying shapes for recognition are read like a language and are not culturally universal.

Realism of Recognition

Some cultures see art as realistic when it gives clear and complete recognition rather than when it simulates volume in space. For example, medieval art looks unnatural to modern Westerners because the figures look misproportioned, stiff, and flat. The medieval artist did not make art that read like perception. The medieval artist made art that had many levels of meaning including symbolic and allegorical meanings. For example, in the Romanesque miniature of St. John from the Gospel Book of Abbot Wedricus, St. John is shown sitting in the middle of the composition, with eight medallions surrounding him on the square border of the picture, each with a small picture in it (see fig. 2.2 on p. 44). There is no attempt to show a realistic space; rather all the figures are placed so as to express a symbolic message. The picture as a whole has meaning, and each small circle has meaning as well.

At one time this "lack of realism" in medieval art was explained as evidence that although its makers were aiming at realism, they were too unskilled to achieve it. Measuring art by the standard of how naturalistic it is, is common because this seems to be a culturally neutral standard. Because it takes skill to make art that gives the viewer the illusion of seeing a real scene, this is often used as a standard for judging the artist's skill.

A problem with this view is that the medievals themselves remark on how realistic and truthful their art looks to them (Gregg, 1984). What the medievals thought of as realism might very well have been clear and complete recognition rather than the illusion of spatiality. The art that looked realistic to them was art that clearly displayed their concepts. That is, their stylistic conventions allowed them to project a clear and complete image of the concept of a thing, and in that sense those images can be thought of as realistic representations. Thus, realism does not need to be associated just with perceptual illusion; it can also be associated with ease of recognition.

Even in our own culture some things are more appropriately presented in a style which supports realism of recognition. For example, a textbook or encyclopedia illustration would show realism of this sort (fig. 1.12). The realism of recognition depends upon shapes that allow clear and complete recognition. In this sense an encyclopedia illustration of a heart or an eye which shows a cut-away view with labeled parts can be thought of as realistic. These sorts of images do not show us what things look like in space, instead they appeal to our concepts of things. In realisms of recognition the style reads like a language because so much of the image is passed to high-level vision to disambiguate. These images require not just a language of forms, but also the help of a whole worldview and hence they are highly culture-bound. In the textbook illustration this need for a complex conceptual scheme to disambiguate the art is filled by the labels on the parts shown or a caption underneath. For the

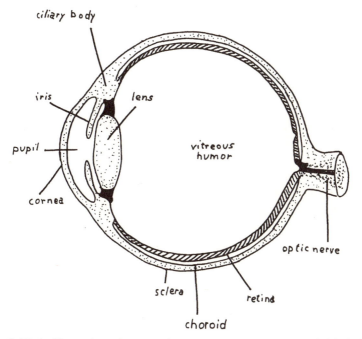

FIGURE 1.12 An illustration of an eye shown in a cut-away view with labeled parts can be thought of as realistic. However this is realism of recognition, not illusionistic realism, since this sort of image does not show us what this thing looks like in natural space. This sort of image is highly culture-bound since it requires a complex conceptual scheme to read it.

medievals, this complex conceptual scheme was given by the religious dogmas which the paintings express. Things like dogmas and captions are often needed for this sort of realism to help disambiguate the art by supplying the relevant complex conceptual scheme.

The Trade-off Between the Two Realisms

There are two basic ways to think of realism; there is realism with respect to recognition, and realism with respect to viewer-independent volumes in space. These realisms differ in which task of the viewer's visual processing dominates when reading the art image. They arise out of there being two basic tasks performed by the visual system in ordinary perception. Since we all have the same physical makeup, all cultures see in the same way. But, some cultures associate realism primarily with the recognition task and their art tends to use language-like conventions which must be read. Other cultures associate realism with the task of seeing viewer-independent objects in space, and their art tends to use clues which cause natural spatial perception. Perception and cognition are cross-culturally universal abilities, and art appeals to us by playing along the scale defined by the complexity of these visual tasks. Thus, we cannot use "realism" as a standard against which to compare styles, because each culture has its own sense of what is realistic. Judging progress in art by realism turns out to be a culture-bound standard.

Further there is a trade-off between making art with realism of recognition, and art that has strong realism as the illusion of natural perception. This trade-off reflects the natural modality in visual perception. This is a trade-off between showing the relationships between things as spatial or as conceptual. (A similar principle is suggested by Hefferman, 1985.) For example, it is quite common in non-perspectival art styles to show the most important person in a composition as larger than all the rest (fig. 1.13). If we read the picture as showing spatial relations then we do not see the larger person as more important, but just as closer to the viewer in the virtual space of the composition. Thus, an illusionistic style would introduce ambiguities. Also, the medievals, and the Japanese, for example, liked to show a succession of events, a series of happenings in a single painting. The illusionistic style constrains the artist to show a unified moment in time. Rendering things in a virtual three-dimensional space inhibits the range of meaning relationships that can be depicted in art.

Some styles have tried to get around the limitations due to this trade-off between conceptual and perceptual reading of art. These styles have tried to make a perceptual illusion which is still capable of carrying meaning in the way that realisms of recognition do, thus having some of the advantages of both sorts of realisms. For example, the neoclassical style used a deep Renaissance space into which they put highly idealized figures tightly constrained by a concise system of stylistic conventions (see fig. 2.5 on p. 53). These stylistic conventions made the gestures of the figures readable like a language so that they could communicate moral messages. Thus, neoclassicism was able to convey an illusionistic realism, and convey messages and meanings. However, the stylistic conventions that allowed them to convey meaning also greatly restricted their range of illusionistic realism. When the impressionists and others rebelled against neoclassicism by throwing out that system of stylistic conventions, their art became purely perceptual without meaning or message.

The development of European art is not a linear development from one type of realism to the next, but a shift back and forth between these two types of realism. The art of the archaic Greeks used a realism of recognition. Statues were sculpted to imitate the essence of their subject,

FIGURE 1.13 Drawing after gigantic statues of Rameses II at Abu Simbil. The ancient Egyptians showed the most important person as larger than everyone else. If we were to read this diversity of sizes as showing spatial relations we would not see the larger person as more important, but just as closer to the viewer.

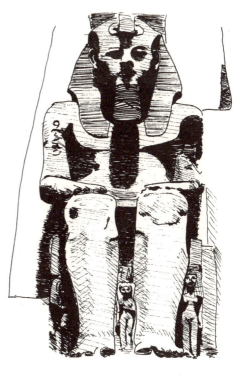

not the illusionistic appearances (Pollett, 1972). The classical Greeks broke away from this and made art using illusionistic realism. They even used perspective, although it was not as systematic as that of the Renaissance. The medievals used a realism of recognition again. Then the Renaissance artists rediscovered perspective and made illusionist realism in rebellion to medieval art. Thus European art has vacillated between these two types of realism. Neither is more advanced than the other, and the change from one to the other does not represent progress.

Basic Levels of Control

If we want a way to compare and judge progress across cultural niches we need standards which come from outside any given art cultural niche, and standards that let us compare across cultural niches. Standards that are derived from the effect that art has on us, like those of realism, are culture-bound, as we've seen. A better way of comparing arts and judging progress in art is by looking at art in cognitive science terms which correlate universal aspects of the composition of art with visual perception.

Just as visual processing can be naturally divided into levels, so can the composition of a painting. These levels or aspects of the composition of art each appeal to a different level in the viewer's visual processing by supplying information to different stages of the viewer's visual system. One aspect of the composition engages our attentive focus, another answers questions about space, shape, and volume, and another answers recognition questions. These are tasks that the visual system performs in normal perception and the painted surface of art delivers information for them. We will call the level of composition delivering information about space, shape, and volume, the *Third Dimension*, and the level answering recognition questions the *Characterizing Shapes*. Further, most compositions are constructed with an overarching pattern which directs our visual focus around the picture surface and unifies all the shapes into one composition. This task too yields a level of the composition to analyze which we will call the *Unifying Geometry*.

These three aspects of composition are very basic. Even when taking a picture with a camera these three levels are involved. Centering the camera in order to frame the subject to be photographed is using the Unifying Geometry. When focusing a camera, the photographer finds the center of interest and frames the picture around that center, thereby adding his or her own concept of what is important in the otherwise interest-neutral scene to be photographed. This gives the photographer the power of emphasis unifying the image around the center of interest he or she has chosen. In normal perception we ourselves choose what to focus on and where to look. Using the center as the hub around which the composition is balanced is universal, or near universal (Schufreider, 1985), in Western art (Arnheim, 1983). For example, the neoclassical artist used the center of the art as a pivotal point for the conceptual relationships in the art. This can be seen in paintings like David's *Death of Socrates* (see fig. 2.5 on p. 53), where the cup of hemlock is positioned in the center and is the pivotal point of the painting expressing the conflict between duty to state and to self. This center acts as a balancing fulcrum or hub for the composition as a whole.

Focusing the camera so that closer things look clear and crisp is adding a Third Dimensional geometry. The photographer focuses the camera so that the volumetric shapes and depth are clear. This helps both early vision and high-level vision find the information needed to form an idea of what the photograph depicts.

The Characterizing Shapes are involved in selecting a view that shows what is being photographed from such an angle as to make it recognizable to the viewer. The photographer generally looks for a view that clearly shows what the object is. If it is a photograph of a person, the photographer looks for a characterizing expression or pose.

Beyond these levels of control there is also color. Black and white photos can convey a complete illusionistic realism. We can perceive depth and recognize shapes without the use of color at all. Color acts as a counterpoint to shape, changing independently of it as the lighting changes and the surrounding colors change. Color is good at representing the time of day, the season of the year, and the atmosphere. Different colors produce different emergent mood effects: blue hues give a cold, distant look to things, and red and yellow hues seem hot. Color engages the viewer's emotion. Pink rooms are said to make people feel "weak"; green is said to be restful; red evokes a sensuous atmosphere. People have their favorite color, or have colors that they hate. People take colors personally.

Time is another important level of control in visual art. Cartoons in print media use the time dimension by showing events over a succession of panels. Movies and cartoons on film use the time dimension by projecting images in rapid succession. This allows us to see movement and changes over time and gives the images an even stronger illusion of perceptual realism. We view a film and then afterwards are not able to differentiate the film images from remembered images we've seen outside of art.

Once artists discovered how to add time to visual art with the invention of movies in the 1890s there have been many new levels of control discovered for art. Words and music are added to the image, for example, as well as many other sorts of control which affect the force of the image, including camera angle, juxtaposing images, zooming in on the figure, and so on. Exploitation of these further levels of control increases the power with which these media images can grab our attention and give us the visual experience of being personally present at the pictured events. These new levels of control also create the possibility of the projection of completely engrossing fantasies for the viewer to vicariously experience. They also allow us to have visual experiences of the impossible, from a talking duck wearing a sports jacket, to huge car crashes where the hero escapes without even getting his hair mussed. This has all given advertising and Popular Art power to grab our desires and shape our expectations about life. As we will discuss, these new film arts — movies and television — are expanding our capacities for visual thought.

Levels of Control and Progress

The Characterizing Shapes, Third Dimension, Unifying Geometry, color, and time are basic levels of control in art. Artists use these to make art that gives the effects desired by a particular culture. The effects on mentality which manipulating these levels of control can give are the powers of art. However, not all discoveries of levels of control in art give rise to new powers. For example, the impressionists discovered a great many things about the use of color. Because of the technology of color that these artists discovered, artists after them have been able to exploit color to greatly enhance the other effects in art. However, color has not been used to give the viewer a new sort of mind set, or new sort of experience. Not all discoveries of levels of control lead directly to new powers for art; some of them just add to the strength of existing powers.

It is, however, in the discovery of new levels of control that there is progress in art. Here, artists increase their tools. As more levels of control are discovered and used, visual art becomes a more functional tool for culture. Art can adapt and respond to cultural change more easily. In the technology of art we can see the evolution of visual art in general outside any particular cultural niche. Artists of all niches in the culture are educated in the technology of art. This is shared knowledge. Of course each niche uses only some of the knowledge, and each niche also has its specialized knowledge. However, they all learn from the same pool of mutually consistent, reinforcing knowledge about the levels of control in visual art, even though they use it for different effects. This technology is culture-wide and spans cultural niches. The whole of visual art, not just one cultural niche, evolves with each new discovery. This body of technology, shared between the cultural niches, is the art that all the art niches have in common. This communal technology of art is the art singularity that gets used and channeled into the various distinct cultural niches.

As artists learn more levels of control they can better do what they do. The levels of control are refined and expanded as art evolves. For example, in modern advertising art, written words are often added to the image to supersede the trade-offs between conceptual and perceptual reading of art. The advertisement with the photographic image of a sweaty man after a good workout, and a printed caption which reads, "Drink X brand Cola" uses words to add a conceptual level without sacrificing the viewer's real-world perceptual mind-set in relation to the art. The advertiser wants us to think of the image as a possible experience, but with their slogan attached. The use of words does not make the figures in the image take on symbolic value, but rather it adds an associated slogan to their perceptual interpretation. Adding a level of written words without compromising the rest of the image is possible because we *read* the words through different cognitive mechanisms than we use to disambiguate the other shapes in the art. Once we see that these shapes are letters we screen out the rest of the image, and just concentrate on spelling out the words. What the advertiser wants is for us to carry that association to our experiences. When we feel an after-the-workout-thirst, we should think of the slogan and X brand cola.

The discovery of this use of written words adds to the technology of art by adding another level of possible control on the effect of an image. Thus, this discovery counts as progress in art. As their knowledge of levels of control increases, artists can produce more sorts of effects with art and strengthen its powers. There are many levels of control which art has used in various cultures and cultural niches. Art can be compared across cultures and niches by which levels of control have been discovered and how they are used.

The Power of Characterizing Shapes and Third Dimension

Artists have discovered how to use levels of composition to control how viewers react to their art. By making the Characterizing Shapes strong the artist can make a picture that has a realism of recognition, engaging the viewer's concepts with the art. As we discussed, medieval artists found a way to use the harmonies and consistencies between the individual shapes in art to communicate symbolic content. All the geometry in their art was used to enhance the Characterizing Shapes. The images tended to be highly symmetrical with a strong center. This flattened the image, discouraging perception of any spatial depth and enhancing the meaning relationships between the shapes. The shapes were highly conventionalized, thus reading like words in a message. Color was used symbolically. For example, blue stood for purity, while gold stood for the luminosity of God. The overall effect was that each image had meaning, not because it represented what was seen, but because it evoked a series of concepts.

Exposure to medieval art maintained a yearning in its viewers to transcend the material world, and climb a ladder of abstractions, numbers, or light, to God. This was not just expressed in art, it was facilitated by art. With the help of the strong Characterizing Shapes, art was used as a tool to project individuals' spiritual selves closer to God and away from the material world. We read accounts of this in Abbot Suger

(c. 1148) who speaks of climbing the levels of meaning in art to the luminosity of God. Art allowed the medievals to practice and hold this mental posture of climbing to God. It also helped them see levels of meaning wherever they looked outside art in nature. This helped them practice their belief that nature was God's book wherein we can read God's thoughts. Thus, the art developed by the medievals had a strong spiritually enhancing power.

This was the posture towards art and life that Renaissance art as natural philosophy was trying to disrupt. The point of having the illusion of depth in the picture for the Renaissance was in part to prevent the viewer from engaging their concepts so fully with the Characterizing Shapes in art and thereby gaining the many levels of spiritual meaning evoked from medieval art. For the Renaissance artist to make "illusion" was to cause the viewer to take only the literal meaning and not see the symbolic meaning that medieval art projected. Renaissance art lacked the visual clues that gave paintings a spiritual meaning for the medieval person. For example, the medieval used a dove to show the influence of the holy spirit. The dove read as a symbol. In the Renaissance illusionistic realism, a dove would be set into a perspectival space and so would read as a real dove, not a symbol.

Using the conventions of perspectival naturalism, the Third Dimension, the artist gave the viewer the illusion of seeing a scene with depth in natural perception. Here the Unifying Geometry was used to reinforce seeing depth in art. The center of the Unifying Geometry was drawn as the point of convergence for the angles between the shapes to mimic their distances from the viewer in natural perception. Color was used to enhance this effect by using cool colors for the background and warm colors for the foreground.

By adding the Third Dimension and thus making the image coherent as the perception of objects in space, the artists caused the viewer to focus on literal appearances rather than the meanings of the objects depicted. Although many of the Renaissance artists still painted religious subjects, they painted them as they would appear to a viewer in real life. The Virgin and Child were pictured as a real woman holding a real child. Scenes from the Bible and various Christian stories were made literal by art, unlike those scenes in medieval art where their literal qualities were downplayed in order to lead the viewer to their moral and spiritual meanings. The mental posture practiced by seeing this sort of Renaissance art was seeing art as simulated perception. The main effect of this was to block the medieval spiritual approach to life and promote secularism.

The Power of the Unifying Geometry

The Unifying Geometry engages the viewer's focus of attention (Lind, 1985). The artist structures the image so as to engage our vision first with this, then that, across the picture surface. The artist builds consistencies and harmonies between individual shapes in the composition. The relationships between shapes either enhance the effect of the individual shapes, or allow a further level of pattern to emerge within which the individual shapes are just parts. Thus, the artist plays with the tendency for the eye to look at the picture as organized around the center of the physical picture space.

As we have already discussed, the Unifying Geometry can be used to enhance either the conceptual or perceptual interpretation of art. However, this is not the only way that it can be used. In Western art this level has also been used for aesthetic form. As we will discuss in chapter 2, artists use the center and the emergent harmonies between shapes in art to give the viewer aesthetic pleasure. Color can also be used to reinforce this aesthetic interpretation of art by creating an emergent pattern which visually dominates the individual shapes. Seeing the aesthetic form in art requires approaching art with a certain mental posture. The viewer must approach the art disinterestedly. To see the aesthetic form, the viewer needs to disregard what the shapes might represent and just see them as pure form. Repetition of this approach to art reinforces a certain mental posture, namely a *disinterestedness* and detachment from life. It is by reinforcing this detachment, which reinforces and resonates positively with rational thinking and theory making, that this becomes a power of art.

Non-Western artists have exploited the Unifying Geometry level of control for very different functions from Western aesthetic use. For example, the Navahos (Anderson, 1990) and others use this center to make mandalas which are then used for healing (fig. 1.14). Mandalas are highly symmetrical circular forms with poles radiating from the center, quartering the circle. Through the use of strong symmetries radiating from an explicitly drawn center, the self of the viewer or artist is drawn to and identified with the center of the art. The figures in mandalas are arranged as aspects of the self, nature, or life balanced against each other and united around the center like spokes around the hub of a wheel. Carl Jung said (1969) that making mandalas has a therapeutic effect on their makers, by helping them put together apparently irreconcilable opposites and splits in their natures or situations. Jung thought of the mandala as an archetypal form for helping people center themselves, heal and experience personal growth.

FIGURE 1.14 Like other mandalas, this Navaho sand painting mandala *Slayer-of-Alien-Gods* is used for healing. Through the use of strong symmetries radiating from an explicitly drawn center, the self is drawn to and identified with the center of the art. This is a use of the Unifying Geometry which goes beyond the Western aesthetic use. From *Mandala* © 1972, José and Miriam Argüelles and Shambhala Publications, Inc. Reprinted by arrangement with Shambhala Publications, Inc., Boston, MA 02117.

The Tantrics in Tibet use mandalas as meditation objects. They believe these objects help their enlightenment quest by aiding in the identification of their personal egos with the most universal self, and by helping untangle the overlay of thought from the fluid reality beneath (Blofeld, 1974). The primary power of all mandalas lies in their ability to organize and unite conceptual opposites around a center.

These images, from cultures as diverse as Tibetan and the Navaho, can be compared to Western images by how they use the Unifying Geometry of art. The difference between these uses is, in part, how the viewer approaches art. To see aesthetic form art must be approached disinterestedly. To use art for healing and for enlightenment, the viewer must associate themselves with the center of the art. These images can be compared across cultures because we have an objective standard, namely how compositional geometry is used. These cultures all use the same visual geometry to affect our mental posture when viewing the art, and we all process art through equivalent cognitive mechanisms.

The same basic levels of composition can be exploited for various powers. Which powers the artists in a particular niche choose to use is determined largely by which state of mind is most desired in the culture, not by something intrinsic to art. We cannot use the artists' choice of powers as our standard of comparison. For example, the Tibetans could have used their art to impart aesthetic form, since they had technology for using the Unifying Geometry; however, their culture had no use for that sort of art. Once the technology has been discovered there is a range of ways in which it can be used as powers of art.

Powers of Art

Each cultural niche is built around some small set of art powers. Powers are the abilities that art has to promote various mental orientations, and shape how we live and who we think we are. The ideologies and institutions of art set requirements that art must meet, and art technology is the engine that delivers satisfaction. Thus there is progress in the technology of art even though there is no progress measured by comparing art's powers. Art's powers replace each other, like the two realisms have, for reasons unrelated to the internal development of art. These powers are the use of art technology to deliver a certain effect. They are the way that a whole niche of art affects thought.

One way that the stream of art from a particular niche might affect our mentality is by reinforcing some particular mental orientation through repetition of a certain approach to art. This is the way that aesthetic form and the medieval art of spiritual enhancement work. Also the Renaissance use of illusionistic realism worked this way by blocking the medieval conceptual and spiritual posture to art and life. These powers all work by requiring a certain posture of the viewers when they approach art, which is then carried back into life.

Another way a stream of art from a particular niche might affect our mentality is by the kinds of experiences it makes possible. For example, as we will discuss in chapter 3, Popular Art promotes vicarious experiences and thinking by narration. This power of art does not work so much by reinforcing an approach, but by reinforcing a certain pattern of thought as we experience art. We approach art as illusionistic realism, but we then experience it as a facilitated daydream, where we project ourselves into the art.

Both of these sorts of powers come from art that is meant to be looked at and thought about, that is, from Fine Art, Popular Art, and advertising. Beyond these sorts of powers there are also those of the Design Arts. The levels of control in the Design Arts have to do with packaging and functional form. Although they have surfaces that can carry Fine Art, Popular Art, or advertising images, these objects also have presence and practical use. The powers in these design forms are powers of presence. That is, they tend to affect the space we live in, what we do, and our sense of personal identity. The Design Arts structure many of the details of daily life. The powers of Design Arts are over what we do and who we think we are, while the arts like Fine Art and Popular Art have powers that affect what and how we think. We will discuss the powers of design in chapter 4.

We can understand how art functions in a given culture by what sort of powers it has. By looking at what sort of mentality is being maintained through the use of art we can see where the culture is headed. Although we cannot see progress in art itself by comparing one power with another, we can see the evolving direction of a culture by which powers of art it chooses to use.

CHAPTER 2

∽❦∽─────────────────────────────

The Fine Art Cultural Niche

W HEN PEOPLE TALK ABOUT "art," most often they are referring to Fine Art. What we see when we look at Fine Art are ideologies and institutions that predate mass-media, mass-market culture. Fine Art now plays the role of art for art's sake, pure art, made in a context independent of mass culture. The role of the contemporary fine artist is analogous to the role of the researcher in science who does pure research without any immediate practical value.

In this chapter we will sketch out the historical evolution of Fine Art, showing how its institutions and ideologies have evolved from birth to maturity to its contemporary old age. Although most of the reasons that Fine Art is not as influential as it once was have to do with the growth of needs that it could not fill, there are also changes in Fine Art itself which have caused it to lose its controlling power in culture, as we will discuss.

1. THE BIRTH OF FINE ART

Imitative Craft

When we think of art in the twentieth century we think of paintings and sculptures specifically made to be admired for their aesthetic form. These art objects have no other function than to hang on the wall or sit in

FIGURE 2.1 An example of Greek sculpture: *Doryphoros* by Polykleitos, c. 450–440 B.C. The Greeks thought of sculpture and painting as imitative craft. Drawing after Roman copy, marble, height 6' 6". National Museum, Naples.

the garden of a museum and be aesthetically appealing. But there were no Fine Arts of this sort in European culture until after the Renaissance. Neither the ancient Greeks nor the medievals made a distinction between art and craft. Sculptors and painters were workers and hand laborers, and what they made was not differentiated from craft. The Greeks thought of sculpture (fig. 2.1) and painting as imitative craft (*mimetic technè*) and classed them with sophistry, the use of a mirror, magic tricks, and the imitation of animal voices.

People before the Renaissance did not conceptualize aesthetics as we do today. Either beauty was tied to functional good, where a practical item might be more beautiful than a painting, because it has a clearer function, or beauty was tied to moral good. Beauty was not tied to pleasing line and form in art, as in our contemporary concept of beauty as the aesthetic.

The theories of art up to the Renaissance were all imitation theories of art. Painting and sculpture were crafts which had as their end imitating reality. According to the imitation theories, the function of this imitative craft was to teach. It attempted to show the typical, or allow the viewer to look through the imitative appearances to the real beyond. Imitation theories focused on subject matter in art. Imitative craft was a mirror through which reality was reflected.

There were disputes in the medieval period about whether visual art should be allowed at all. Thinking of art as imitation, they felt that visual art caused people's attention to go to the sensuous, the physical world, and away from the spiritual. Although art could teach by showing Bible stories, and was used for spiritual enhancement, fundamentally the medievals were suspicious of visual art, and held it in low esteem.

Artists were educated as apprentices in workshops, where the art was made collectively for commissions. Much of this imitative craft was public art commissioned by the state in the classical Greek era, and by the church in the medieval period. The subject matter of art was determined by the buyer, not the artist. The customer might give the painter or sculptor an order for an altar piece, or for a devotional picture, but these were expressly commissioned for a particular place, to be placed in a particular room, and with a well-defined subject matter. Each piece of work had a definite purpose, and a concrete connection to practical life. There was a complete homogeneity between art and craft, and between art and decoration (fig. 2.2).

Plagiarism was permissible in the medieval period. Images were sold because they were the images that the patron wanted. If an image was good, it worked; other craftsmen were hired to copy it. Just as copying the shape of a hammer to make a new hammer is not considered a plagiarism or forgery today, so copying a useful item like a picture of the Virgin Enthroned was not considered a forgery or plagiarism for the medieval.

The Academies

During the Renaissance there was increased demand for works of art with the growth and enriching of towns. A class of collectors arose that didn't commission what they needed, but bought what was offered. These collectors were especially interested in rediscovered objects from the ancient civilizations of Greece and Rome. However, they also collected paintings and sculpture made by their contemporaries. Thus Fine Art began by filling the need of Renaissance aristocrats for collectable merchandise. Being made for a collection changed how paintings and sculpture were produced. Rather than being made from the buyer's

FIGURE 2.2 An example of medieval art: Drawing of *St. John the Evangelist* from Gospel Book of Abbot Wedricus circa 1147. Showing medieval realism of recognition, and the intertwinement of art with decoration. Société Archéologique, Avesnes, France.

description, these collectable items were made from the personal inspiration of the artist.

With the changes in the marketplace, the painters and sculptors emancipated themselves from the guilds. In sixteenth-century Italy, sculpture and painting separated from crafts in the movement of artists from workshops to academies. Medieval painters and sculptors had generally been members of the craftsmen's guilds. Painters were sometimes associated with druggists who prepared their paints, or with saddle makers whose saddles they painted. Sculptors were often classed with goldsmiths. Marsilio Ficino founded an academy in 1462, and by the time of Leonardo da Vinci (1452–1519) the right to practice art was no longer conditional on apprenticeship under a guild master. The term *Beaux Arts* (Fine Arts) is based on *Arti del disegno* which was coined by Vasari and used institutionally for the first time in 1563 at the Academy founded in Florence. Here the union of artist and craftsperson ceased and awareness of Fine Art as contrasted with mere crafts began. This was the beginning of the institutional underpinnings for the new cultural niche, Fine Art.

Membership in the academies, newly formed to educate artists, not only differentiated the artist from the craftsman, but also became a means for identifying the artists with the upper classes of the public. Artists were now educated alongside the upper classes, sharing their aspirations and ideologies. Thus, the artists came to identify themselves with the aristocratic class for whom they were producing. The cultured laymen who were educated alongside the artists were allowed to act as judges in matters of art starting in the 1550s. At this point, art theory began to be carried on mainly by non-artists, further untangling it from craft. It was the collector-layman who judged whether the items artists made were worth collecting. Thus, it was the laymen who now dictated what value was present in these new objects of art. The layman didn't have the knowledge to judge craftsmanship so he judged art for its form and subject matter rather than for its well-craftedness (Hauser, 1951).

Art objects began to be thought of as self-contained entities communicating an insight, or reminding the viewer of the ancient days of classical beauty. Otherwise the art object had no function except to be a collector's item decorating the buyer's house or garden. The ancient works of Greece and Rome, against which value was often measured, were also without function except as decoration and collector items. They had been taken out of their cultural contexts, and now had only the meanings which could be read off their surfaces.

The idea of the artistic genius, someone who works alone from personal inspiration, did not begin until the end of the fifteenth century. With Michelangelo Bounarroti (1475–1564) we see the first artistic genius in the modern sense. After his work on the Sistine Chapel, in 1512, he became regarded as the greatest living artist, and people called him *il divino Michelangelo*, thinking of him as super-human, set apart from other men. Unlike any previous sculptor or painter, there were two biographies written about Michelangelo in his lifetime. Michelangelo had managed to lift himself out of the category of workman to the new category of artist.

The Elite Ideology

In the medieval period, while poetry and music theory were ranked among the *liberal arts*, considered appropriate for the educated and noblemen to pursue, sculpture and painting belonged to the "mechanical" or "servile" arts. Sculpture and painting required using matter, and resulted in products that were made out of matter. The medieval had a very low opinion of making things from matter. Those who did the mechanical arts were classed among the manual workers and artisans.

Painting and sculpture were thought to need manual skill, but not the exercise of reason or the acquisition of scholarship, unlike the *theoretical arts* of poetry and music theory. Their crafted art was not autobiographical. It was not created from subjective expressive drives, but rather to perform representational tasks set by the buyer.

The Renaissance artists thought that painting should be considered one of the liberal arts, not one of the mechanical arts. As the Renaissance took hold, artists wanted the same prestige for visual art as there was for music and poetry. In this they succeeded. Painters and sculptors began to be considered on equal footing with poets and scholars.

This movement was helped by the artists' alliance with, and support from, the humanists. The humanists recognized the value of art as a means of propaganda for the ideas which, they felt, showed their supremacy over the old authorities of the churches. In sixteenth-century Italy, the humanistic *literati* became the authorities replacing the church and guilds, and were set up as the judges in matters of art. It was by way of the humanists and their academies that painting, music, and poetry became linked together into Fine or liberal arts. This is the origin of our current categories of Fine Art. They are not all linked together because they have aesthetic form and expressive power. Rather they all have aesthetic form and expressive power because they became linked together in the Renaissance under the same ideologies as Fine Art.

The academies taught the arts along with subjects such as geometry and anatomy. Art was thought to be a branch of natural philosophy. Artists did careful empirical investigations of foreshortening, animals, people, and so on. It was this conception of art that formed the basis of instruction in the academies. Artists investigated nature and worked out mathematical systems of proportion. Although the Greeks had drawn scenes with spatial depth, they did not use a systematic perspectival geometry. During the Renaissance a system of linear perspective was introduced. This was the technology that allowed artists to make the illusionistic realism we discussed in chapter 1 (fig. 2.3). This scientific conception of art began with Leon Battista Alberti (1404–1472). Although the science of linear perspective and its earliest demonstrations can be attributed to Filippo Brunelleschi of Florence in about 1425, Alberti was the first to express the idea that mathematics is the common ground of art and science, as both the theory of proportions and theory of perspective are mathematical disciplines. Alberti wanted only to represent what can be seen. He said that artists should use nature as a model, and make art a window.

FIGURE 2.3 An example of Renaissance art: Giorgione, *Adoration of the Shepherds*, c.1505. This shows realism as the illusion of natural perception. Oil on panel, 34¾-by-43½ inches. Samuel H. Kress Collection, © 1994, Board of Trustees, National Gallery of Art, Washington, D.C.

Neoplatonism

Along with humanism, the Academies taught the artists Neoplatonism. Neoplatonism is a mystical reinterpretation of Plato's doctrines, mostly focused on the *Symposium* doctrines of beauty, love, and the Forms. In the *Symposium*, Plato describes a way called the *ladder of Love* for coming to *see* the absolute form *Beauty*. This philosophy has inspired many as it was retold and reinterpreted by generations of Neoplatonists as a way for art to lead its viewers to the highest realms of spirituality. Love, Plato writes, is set in motion by the apprehension of the beautiful. The lover climbs a ladder of love from the particular individual body, to all bodies, to souls, to customs and laws, to learning and science, and finally to absolute beauty. Thus, through a process of universalization, the lover realizes ever greater and more universal beauty. Beauty that started with the particular body finally universalizes to the singular and unchanging *Form Beauty*.

During the Renaissance, Marsilio Ficino (1433–1499) gave the

West the first complete versions of Plato and the Neoplatonist Plotinus in Latin. He started the Platonic Academy in Florence, giving an institutional center to this revival of classicism. In Ficino's Neoplatonism, the ladder of love is thought of as a passage to God. Ficino's ladder of love starts with the love of a particular body which he describes as a homosexual love, as the ancient Greeks also did. In Renaissance Neoplatonism, the flesh was not a distraction away from our spiritual quest, rather its attractive force could be used to start us up the ladder of love.

For example, Michelangelo's Neoplatonic statue of *David*, made in 1501–1504, was taken to epitomize Renaissance civic veracity (fig. 2.4). It is almost seventeen feet tall and was made out of an eighteen foot block of flawless white marble named "the giant." Michelangelo believed the Neoplatonic doctrine which states that the ideas of the artist are an imitation of the ideas from which nature itself is derived. A look at his statue of a man was better for seeing the Form than was a look at a flesh man. The statue was a portrait of the ideal perfection of mind, body, and soul. Michelangelo did not show an individual man, but the Platonic soul of a perfect hero defending his city. The perfect nude body of *David* expressed a perfect inner soul. This facilitated the viewer's journey up the first step of Plato's ladder from the physical body to the perfect human soul. Michelangelo gave his *David* the body of a young Hercules, and the head of an Apollo, expressing a union of heroic qualities. *David* emanates righteous anger and intractable will. He is David, the giant killer, from the Bible. The next step on Plato's ladder is from the beautiful soul to customs and laws. The statue symbolizes the city of Florence, which thought of itself as a city, like David, willing to take on all comers in defense of its liberty. Thus, a viewer rises up Plato's ladder from love of an individual body to love of the virtuous soul, to love of the city of Florence.

In Neoplatonism, when an artist made something beautiful, he was making that object more akin to God's concepts, and was lifting the matter — stone or canvas — from mere corporeality to something that could be contemplated by the mind, and thus be infused more fully with the Divine. Through contemplating these Forms in art, which we are attracted to through their beauty, the viewer could also be lifted to understand a higher truth. For the Neoplatonist, beauty is an object of knowledge, and the artist is a truth seeker. Thus artists were people with a superior mission and superior knowledge. It is this concept of the artist and the beautiful that we see in the Renaissance Neoplatonists, like Botticelli and Michelangelo, who believed that by seeking beauty they were seeking the good and God. It is this concept of the artist that people were using when they called Michelangelo "the Divine."

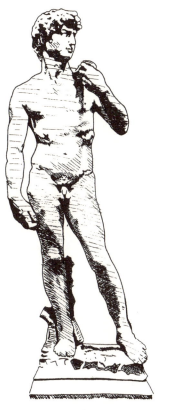

FIGURE 2.4 An example of Renaissance art: Michelangelo, *David. David* is the giant killer from the Bible, and symbolizes the city of Florence. With this statue we climb up a Platonic ladder of love from love of an individual body, to love of the virtuous soul, to love of the city of Florence. Marble, almost 17′ high. Academy, Florence.

Neoplatonism and the Cultural Niche Fine Art

Neoplatonism is important to this early forming of a new type of art. As we discussed in chapter 1, to have a successful cultural niche, the artists need to have a sense of who they are and a sense of their mission as artists. Ideologies dictating value in art are needed. These ideologies must cover all aspects of the artist's work. In the case of Fine Art these are: artistic mission, subject matter, stylistic conventions, and beauty. All of these ideologies must work together to make art that serves the general function of this particular niche of art. The general function of Fine Art was to make unique objects with no other function than to be appreciated for their artistic qualities, as defined by the Fine Art art world, and sold to collectors to be exhibited.

Fine Art also needed an ideology of craftsmanship to add to, or reinterpret, the ideology from the crafts niche they were evolving away from. In craft traditions there are doctrines about the proper kinds of shapes and decorations for each kind of material, and what respectful handling of the material entails (see chapter 4). To the craftsmanship doctrines of the medieval, Neoplatonism added the idea that the artist finds the Platonic Form in the matter being worked, and helps liberate it. However, by the twentieth century, Fine Art has drifted far enough from its craft-shop roots to no longer have ideologies that tell the artist how to relate to the matter of art. In twentieth century Fine Art, paint might be meant to be seen as paint, but there is no doctrine about what proper shapes are or about what respectful handling of the paint and canvas would be. There are art styles, like conceptual art and minimal art, within which artists do not even make the objects of art themselves at all. As Fine Art separated from craft, its doctrines stopped focusing on craftsmanship and the literal making of art. Fine Art became defined in part by its difference from craft. Craft was thought of as non-creative work where a pattern is repeated, while Fine Art was thought of as creative, where each object made is unique. In craft it is the work that is admired, in Fine Art it is the creative idea.

During the Renaissance and into the Enlightenment, imitation theories furnished the conceptualization of the mission of art. Art was conceived of as primarily representational with the goal of teaching. This conception of the mission of art was also a holdover from the crafts tradition. Since the classical Greek times, painting and sculpture had been thought of as having the mission of imitating nature and teaching.

Within this general concept of the mission of art, the artists also needed to know what to consider as appropriate subject matter for art, and what representational style to use. This is where theories like those of Alberti were useful as they gave stylistic standards and judgments of value for what should count as successful representation. Neoplatonism and humanism also helped dictate appropriate subject matter for art. Renaissance Neoplatonic philosophy gave the visual artist an intellectual task. However, subject matter and style were not as clearly prescribed here as they subsequently became during Enlightenment in the French Royal Academy.

Beyond artistic mission, subject matter, and stylistic conventions, this newly forming type of artist also needed a theory of beauty. That is, he or she needed a theory of what the overall visual harmonies of the art should do. In medieval times visual harmonies tended to communicate symbolic or mystical relationships between the represented figures in art; or else they were used for decorative harmonies picking up the rhythms and motifs of Folk Art (see fig. 2.2 on p. 44). Neoplatonism supplied a philosophy of beauty to substitute for these medieval ways of structuring the emergent harmonies of art.

Neoplatonism also helped the artists gain a sense of themselves as artists. It allowed an identification between the artist and the aristocrats in their rediscovery of Greek philosophy, and helped the artist see him- or herself as a sort of missionary for a Platonic rise to God through beauty. This philosophy directly counteracted the medieval negativity towards art's sensuous appeal. Helped along by Neoplatonism, Renaissance artists threw out the medieval disgust for the physical and the medieval consequent ambivalence to art. Here was a philosophy which could allow the artist to make the transition between medieval transcendence and Renaissance secularity. Neoplatonism gave artists a sense of themselves, of their mission, and a spiritual philosophy of beauty in art.

2. THE INSTITUTIONALIZATION OF FINE ART

Fine Art formed within its cultural niche during the Renaissance. The conditions for Fine Art arose, and slowly new art was made in response to those new conditions. An academy system for educating Fine Artists developed, and a new kind of art began to be made. By the beginning of the Enlightenment, there were Fine Art objects which were unique, made out of the personal inspiration of an individual artist, and then sold to someone for a collection. ·

The French Royal Academy

Fine Art was born in the Renaissance but did not become fully institutionalized until the Enlightenment. In 1648 as we move into the Enlightenment, the *Academie Royale de Peiture et de Sculpture* was founded in France. The original purpose of the French Royal Academy had been to free artists from the medieval restrictions of the old painters' guild, and thereby to elevate the artists' social and intellectual status. With the establishment of the French Royal Academy, Paris became the art capital of Europe taking over the role which Italy played in art during the Renaissance. Although Rome was still the place artists went to study classical art, Paris became the place they went to study "modern" art. In 1666 the French Academy in Rome was founded, and by the end of the century, French art had taken the pre-eminent position in Europe.

The academy had a monopoly on art education, supervising an

artist's education from its beginning to his eventual employment. Indeed after the reform of the academy by Colbert (1664), no artists outside the academy were allowed to give public instruction or let their students draw from life. The academy made state appointments, awarded prizes, bestowed public commissions, even conferred titles. It gave out pensions, permission to exhibit and take part in competitions.

Not only did the academy dominate the Fine Arts of this time period, but also the decorative arts and architecture. There were ornamental draughtsmen, tapestry-weavers, silk- and cloth-weavers, cabinet-makers, bronze-founders, goldsmiths, ceramists, and glassblowers involved in the academy productions. The early French artists were still associated with the craftsmen, although they were not thought of as being craftsmen. The paintings they produced were rated. They were evaluated by craftsman-like standards against a list of specifications concerning invention, expression, composition, drawing, and color. Artists were to use a uniform style, the style dictated by neoclassicism, to communicate their learning and culture. Also, artists were to have knowledge of history and literature so that their paintings would be accurate in detail and morally uplifting. The Fine Artist was an educated person with cultural messages to communicate.

The Ideology of the Academy

Neoclassicism became the dominating ideology in the art establishment in the seventeenth and eighteenth centuries. Besides the concern for beauty, it concentrated on moral values and revitalized the ideal forms of the great history painters of the late Renaissance such as Poussin. In neoclassicism, beauty became the special characteristic that art displayed. This ideology was formed in good part by the philosophy of J. J. Winckelmann (1717–68). In his writings, Winckelmann expressed the theory that the purpose of all good art is the attainment of "pure beauty." Pure beauty can only be achieved, he taught, by suppressing the individual features of the subject in favor of the general scheme. This was substituted for the Renaissance conception of illusionistic naturalism as imitating the true look of things in nature. To achieve these neoclassical idealizations, artists should imitate the Greek idealization of the figure (see fig. 2.1 on p. 42). This sort of pure beauty, he thought, was realized only by the Greeks, and moderns could only achieve it by approaching nature as he imagined the Greeks had done, that is, striving for the effects of "noble simplicity" and "quiet grandeur." Winckelmann saw Greek sculpture as being primarily an expression of beauty; he wrote (1764) that "a masterly contour" was the prime concern of the

FIGURE 2.5 An example of neoclassicism: David, *The Death of Socrates* (*1787*). By using the established conventions of neoclassicism as a language, artists could show how the characters in classical stories felt about the situations, and thus how one ought to feel.

Greek sculptor. Thus the academy artists were taught how to make art — collectibles — that imitated the paradigmatic collectibles, namely Greek statues. Only now they imitated the outer contours of Greek art, not the philosophy of the Greeks as Renaissance Neoplatonism did.

The neoclassical painters and sculptors idealized their figures for beauty, and to maintain a clear expressive form. The neoclassical artist could use Greco-Roman myths and historical events (fig. 2.5), or stories from the Bible, as "grandiose" subject matter, as Poussin had advised. These were stories shared with the viewer on which their art could comment. These shared stories made the narrative quality of art possible in that the artist could make references that the viewer would understand, and tell a single event from a story which the viewer could then use to think about the whole story. By using the established conventions of simplifications, uses of drapery, idealized body postures, and such things, as a language for expressing the human drama of the depicted scene, they could show how the characters in classical stories felt about the situations, and thus how one ought to feel. In this way the neoclassical style was very powerful in teaching about complex subject matter. Because it gave the artist a clear language of form, and there were shared stories between the artist and viewer, the artist could communicate intellectual content with the art. It could teach moral lessons, as well as speak allegorically about contemporary events. It also showed a naturalistic space, and detailed observations from nature, although these were played down when they conflicted with the demands of overall emergent beauty of the art.

As a theory of beauty, neoclassicism dictated what the overall visual rhythms and harmonies in a painting ought to be. With the doctrines of neoclassicism the artist could perform the task of cultural critic and advice giver. The artist gave images which helped give expression to the worldview of the aristocratic who bought art. The artist no longer had a spiritual quest. That holdover from the medieval attitude was dropped. However the cultural mission of art as teaching was heightened as the artists became more systematically educated, and used grandiose themes for their subject matter. Neoclassicism told artists that their cultural mission was to teach by pleasing, and please by teaching. Neoclassicism was substituted for Neoplatonism, changing the artists' relationship to the goal of representation and to the emergent geometry of art. The artist became a professional, a teacher, not a spiritual leader, but still worked within the imitation-theory conception of the mission of art.

In many ways the Enlightenment was the high point of the cultural niche Fine Art. Through the academy and salon there was a clear system for evaluating art and artists. There were clear and consistent ideologies about subject matter, beauty, stylistic conventions, and artistic mission. Although there were some tensions in ideology beginning to show in the split over the use of color between artists like Poussin and Rubins, there was an easy fit between cultural needs and artist. The ideology underlying art was complex enough to give artists a good idea of what their missions were, and the prescribed language of form was specific enough so that artists could use it to communicate clear messages that had cultural significance. There was an institutionalized system for judging value in art so that when people bought art from the salon they knew they were getting good quality. The institutions of art succeeded in educating artists, and maintaining value in art, and there was a good market for art. Thus, the artist could do what the culture required.

The Discipline of Art History

The discipline of art history arose with the market for art. Art history was needed to catalogue, label, and sanction the collectable Fine Art objects. There are very few cultures that have had a discipline of art history besides our own, perhaps only the Imperial Chinese culture, the

Japanese culture, and the Islamic culture; and they also had art collecting and an art market (Alsop, 1986). For the cultural niche of Fine Art to function it needs an accompanying discipline to keep track of the styles, and objects of art. Without this, people cannot judge the values of the objects in their collections.

The first history of art in the modern sense was written in 1764 by J. J. Winckelmann, *History of Art Among the Ancients*, providing a new methodical account of classical art. Winckelmann is considered the "father of modern archaeology." Winkelmann was the first to conceive of the history of art as part of the general evolution of culture. He began the idea of using the concept of style to characterize the manner of art of an entire period. He was the first to think of the style of art as reflecting the general philosophy and tone of a given period.

Art historians are responsible for building the context of art interpretation from the past against which contemporary examples are chosen as art. Thus art historians have a powerful role in shaping the Fine Art art world. A discipline such as art history is not needed for the Design Arts because their value stems from the functions they perform (fig. 2.6). Nor is such a discipline needed for Popular Art because the value of Popular Art is in the subject matter depicted. It was not needed for the crafted-art done before the Renaissance either, since that too took its value from its function or its subject matter. But because Fine Art is valued as individual collectable objects of art in relation to an art tradition, it needs an accompanying discipline to interpret, authenticate, and date its items. The discipline of art history is as important as art collectors are for creating art as collectable merchandise, which Fine Art is.

3. THE FORMATIVE IDEOLOGY: AESTHETIC FORMALISM

Philosophy of Taste

The ideology which is most formative of Fine Art as we know it today is the ideology of *Aesthetic Formalism*. This ideology began in the philosophies of taste during the Enlightenment. This ideology slowly replaced the imitation theory ideology held over from the crafted-art niche. For Aesthetic Formalism, aesthetics are a matter of taste. That is, as the philosopher of taste, David Hume (1757) said, beauty is in the eyes of the beholder. Aesthetics is a matter of sensation. Liking art is similar to liking food. We like those works of art that taste good, that is, that give us

FIGURE 2.6 An example of Design Art: Pepsi soft drink can. The best way to evaluate a soft drink can is in terms of Design Art criteria, that is, by how well it contains the soft drink while being easy to hold and drink from, and by how effectively and attractively its label projects the product image. Courtesy, PepsiCo, Inc. © 1993.

pleasure. Beauty is a matter of sensation, and therefore is subjective. Everyone has his or her own taste. There is no "real" beauty, so there is no dispute about taste. Which objects are beautiful is a matter of which objects give people pleasure. Beauty is not a quality inherent to objects, it exists merely in the mind which contemplates them, and each mind perceives a different beauty.

The problem with thinking of beauty as subjective, a mere matter of taste, is that there are no standards for judging some art as better than other art. It is inherent to this view that some of us have better taste and are more sensitive than others. These people serve as art critics, explaining to us what is good and bad in art. This view of beauty as a sensation in the beholder, along with the ideas of neoclassicism which put great emphasis on beauty in art, developed into modern Aesthetic Formalism.

This way of approaching art was also a way of approaching life during the Enlightenment. One needed to have "good breeding" to be able to have "good taste." Someone with good taste was able to approach art with disinterestedness. Disinterestedness means approaching from a distance without needs, and only the aristocratic classes could do that (Cotton, 1981). Thus this approach to art reinforced the aristocratic approach to life. This sort of art reinforces a distance from life, an objectivity and disengagement. This is a state conducive to the sort of thinking required for rationality. As the Enlightenment elite began making scientific theories of the world, they enjoyed practicing a mental posture through art where objective disinterested thinking would be reinforced. Art that is made to be approached primarily aesthetically, reinforces rational over spiritual, intuitive, or emotional reactions to art and to life.

Modern Aesthetic Formalism

Aesthetic Formalism in its modern form is the view that what is important about art is its aesthetic qualities, and these reside in the relationships between line and shape, that is, in the formal qualities of the art work. Subject matter is irrelevant to this. By the twentieth century the pre-Fine Art attitude or imitation theory, the idea that art should teach by presenting some subject matter, had completely disappeared. The main mission of Fine Art had become aesthetics. Indeed, in the most extreme form of this view, subject matter in art is considered a distraction. This extreme view is found in the Aesthetic Formalism of Clive Bell (1881–1964) and Roger Fry (1886–1934), who were especially influential on art done in the 1950s and 1960s. Subject matter in art, according to Bell and Fry, distracts us from appreciating art for its formal qualities which they call *aesthetic form* (fig. 2.7). As we discussed in chapter 1, one way of structuring the emergent geometry of art is to emphasize the formal patterns that make up significant form. Significant form, according to Bell and Fry, is the form in an art object that gives rise to aesthetic emotion in sensitive people. The point of art is to give us a rush of aesthetic emotion. The aesthetic emotion is an emotion about form only. It is a pleasurable emotion which we get from the recognition of order, and of the inevitability of certain relations.

To see aesthetic form, we must have the right mental posture. As Roger Fry explains this, in life, we have no time to contemplate the scene around us as an aesthetic experience. But in art we approach situations with a mind that is free from practical needs and issues of survival. Through the distancing of the aesthetic attitude in our imaginations, we can examine the patterns of life and contemplate them. This is the origin of the aesthetic.

For Aesthetic Formalism, subject matter is thought to be wholly outside art. Art no longer carries messages to be understood. With this attitude part of the motivating imperative with which Fine Art was born in the Renaissance drops away, namely, that art teaches and advocates the dogmas of the upper classes. The Aesthetic Formalists keep beauty but throw out classicism, and further, throw out the need for the artist to receive a classical education as had been provided for him in the Renaissance and Enlightenment academy structures. The

FIGURE 2.7 An example of aesthetic form without any subject matter. Subject matter in art, according to Bell and Fry, distracts us from appreciating art for its formal qualities.

narrative function of art completely drops away. Art does not comment on the world.

With Aesthetic Formalism, because we are comparing collectibles for their quality, the problem that arises is the problem of taste. For the sake of pure taste, artists make art which does not refer to life, nor get any of its meanings from life, since that would make the art less purely art. Motivated by the concern for the pure beauty of aesthetic form, artists make art that appeals to good taste. Since those with good taste approach art disinterestedly, subject matter becomes irrelevant to making beautiful art.

Aesthetic Formalism as an Ideological Stance

Although Aesthetic Formalism is not the only ideology that shapes how Fine Art is viewed and made, many approach art primarily from an Aesthetic Formalist perspective. The ideology of Aesthetic Formalism gets reinforced from many directions. Conventional art histories, besides looking at art as history and visual culture, compare and discuss art from an Aesthetic Formalist perspective. The ideology of Aesthetic Formalism sets the agenda for the discussions of art by most of the Fine Art critics and educated public. Philosophers who discuss problems of art, commonly call what they do *aesthetics* rather than *philosophy of art*, thus expressing this ideological orientation. One reason for this dominance of aesthetics in Fine Art is that it promotes a power in art. Aesthetic form promotes a mental attitude in the viewer which resonates with, and reinforces the rational mind-set that has been dominant in the West since the Enlightenment. As we will discuss in chapter 6, by supporting a certain mind-set, aesthetic art helped in the growth of science, technology, and the general secularization of society.

Aesthetic Formalism has been such an important ideological stance in good part because along with technical virtuosity, aesthetic form gives historians, and others, a standard to use for discussing and comparing art objects that is independent of any cultural context. Discussions of art objects in terms of technical virtuosity involve consideration of how the material of the art was handled by the artist for various effects. For example, they consider the quality of the brush stroke on a painting, or the care with which the relief was chiseled into stone. This is a Fine Art equivalent of a craftsmanship standard. Here art is compared and evaluated on the grounds of the physical handling of the material used. The advantage of technical virtuosity as a standard is that technical virtuosity combined with aesthetic form can be discussed without reference to the cultural context of the art.

As we have said, Aesthetic Formalism is the view that what is important about an art object is its aesthetic qualities, and these can be seen in the harmonies of its shapes and colors. These aesthetic qualities are independent of subject matter in art. For example, the highly respected art historian, Erwin Panofsky, writes that art history is a humanistic discipline and the art historian is a humanist who uses the records that have come down to us as works of art as his or her primary material. Panofsky (1955, p. 11) writes: "But a work of art always has aesthetic significance. . . , it demands to be experienced aesthetically. . . . It is possible to experience every object, natural or manmade, aesthetically. We do this, . . . when we just look at it (or listen to it) without relating it, intellectually or emotionally, to anything outside itself." Panofsky continues to say that unlike mere vehicles of communication, or mere apparatuses, a work of art's interest is not primarily in meaning or the function, but in the form.

Panofsky advocates an ideology of Aesthetic Formalism through which to view works of art, and through which works of art are defined in contrast to other sorts of things. When he says that all art objects have "aesthetic significance" and demand to be experienced aesthetically, he is advocating a particular mental posture we should maintain. In order to experience the aesthetic qualities we should be disinterested toward the art. We should not relate the art to anything outside itself. In doing this we will be uninvolved in either the subject matter or function of the art. From this perspective, we don't look through art at what it represents, as we did with classical imitation theory, but look at the art object itself in isolation. When we do this we can compare art objects outside their cultural contexts. With this posture we are able to pick out and appreciate objects of art as objects that are functionless except to be aesthetic. This standard reinforces the identity of Fine Art objects as objects that have no other function than to be collected and exhibited as art.

Given the standards of Aesthetic Formalism, art historians extend Fine Art all the way back to ancient people, Africa, and Asia. With the standards of Aesthetic Formalism and technical virtuosity, all shaped objects and painted surfaces can be discussed and compared. Such culturally independent standards are needed because art historians need some standard through which to compare and understand objects from diverse cultures and eras (see Podro, 1982). What does a primitive cave drawing have in common with a Manet, a Minoan vase, or an African sculpture? As art historians have said, you cannot always compare subject matter or function, since art works from different cultures are often in some sense incommensurable as far as their meanings and functions in their original cultural contexts are concerned. Further these standards are enough to ground a history of whatever art is discovered in terms of style change. By looking at objects outside their cultural functions and interpretations as such standards allow, a coherent sense of what art is emerges. From this perspective, art objects with aesthetic form and/or showing technical virtuosity are worth collecting. From this point of view all good art is Fine Art.

Problems with This Stance Toward Art

The problem with this way of evaluating art is that it gives the illusion that there is only one type of art, namely Fine Art. When people take the objects described in conventional art history books as art, they do not see the diversity of powers and different cultural niches of art. Consequently when they try to understand the nature of art, they look at isolated individual objects outside their cultural setting seeking what is common to all, rather than being guided by the history of art in its cultural settings to understand the functions of art.

Art viewed through this Fine Art ideology means that we apply that ideology to non-Fine Art cultural niches, and to works of other cultures that have no Fine Art cultural niche. Consequently we end up looking at all these objects as Fine Art merchandise, evaluating them for their excellence of conception and execution, and not for whatever makes them what they are in their native context. We blind ourselves to the powers of art outside Aesthetic Form and virtuosity. For example, while the aesthetic values we look for in Fine Art give disinterested pleasure, non-Fine Art objects like soft drink cans are not structured to elicit disinterested pleasure. They are structured to elicit our desire for soft drinks, and to project a product image. Thus, evaluating such objects by Fine Art standards misdirects our attention away from this art's power (see fig. 2.6 on p. 56). Seeing art in terms of its own cultural niche displays the function and power of that kind of art, and expands our understanding of what art can do. Evaluating all art by Fine Art criteria blinds us to the powers of other types of art.

If we want to understand art in general rather than just Fine Art, we need to look beyond Fine Art to the powers and functions of art within other art niches. To compare art across cultural niches we must use standards that are outside the ideology of any particular cultural niche of art. Only with such standards can we compare arts without simultaneously blinding ourselves to the powers of various diverse cultural niches.

4. DEFINING WHO THE ARTIST IS: EXPRESSION THEORY

While Aesthetic Formalism shapes how we relate to an art object, the ideology of *Expression Theory* shapes how we view the relationship between art and the artist. In the first theories of art, the imitation theories, art was thought of as an objective picture of reality. There was no need for a theory about art as the expression of an individual. For the imitation theories, art was a mirror or window on some subject matter, it was not an emotional expression of a genius artist. During the Enlightenment the artist was someone who was educated in the academy in geometry, history, and the classics. Art was to teach, and please by teaching. The artist was a professional, educated in the classics, and sanctioned as Fine

Artist by the academy and salon institutional structure. Art was not about artists, or their subjective experiences, but about grand subjects in history or mythology.

With romanticism, however, the concept of the Fine Artist and the artist's mission changed. Expression theories of art emerged. The romantics moved away from the Enlightenment attitudes about life and art. Where the Enlightenment looked for equality among people, the romantic looked for unique individual geniuses. While the Enlightenment emphasized reason, the romantics rejected reason in favor of emotion and intuition. Expression Theory is born out of romanticism.

For Expression Theories, the art object is of much less importance than the artist behind it. For them, art expresses, it does not represent. In Expression Theory art, the subject matter is reflected through the temperament of the artist. We cannot look at Van Gogh's *The Night Café*, for example (fig. 2.8), and see an objective idealized view of some grand subject as was considered the ideal for neoclassicism. Here we see something in ordinary life which is intentionally colored by the emotional perspective of the artist. As Van Gogh wrote to his brother, he used the color in this work to express humanity's terrible passions. The café did not really look the way that Van Gogh pictured it, with the intense halos of light around the lamps, and the distortions. Van Gogh was trying to express a mood. For Expression Theories, communicating the flavor of some particular place or person constitutes the value in art.

Expression Theory brings with it the idea that the artist should be sincere. As Tolstoy (1898) said in his theory of art, art is the communication of emotion, and successful art infects the viewer with the same emotion that the artist felt. The intensity of this infection depends upon the uniqueness of the situation described in the art, the clarity of the expression, but most importantly, the sincerity of the artist. Thus, the best expressive art is the most sincere art.

Within the ideology of Expression Theories, artists paint what they feel, using whatever conventions come naturally to their hands as they express themselves in paint. They tend not to be professional painters, but people who have a compulsion to paint. From this orientation, creativity and emotional sensitivity replace having a sense for beautiful form as the virtue that makes an artist great. Artists are thought of as highly creative people who take their inspiration from their personal lives. They take personal risks for their art, including drinking excessive alcohol, and taking drugs, like Coleridge did, to see exotic images and have more intense experiences. The artists live the extremes of life.

Figure 2.8 An example of Expression Theory art: Van Gogh, *The Night Café*. The subject matter is intentionally colored by the emotional perspective of the artist, thus projecting the emotional flavor of the scene without regard for aesthetic form or photographic realism. Yale University Art Gallery, bequest of Stephen Carlton Clark, B.A. 1903.

Indeed, since the romantic era, artists have been popularly conceived of as unstable people. The father of psychoanalysis, Sigmund Freud (1908), claimed that artists are oversexed, overly emotional, and in love with themselves. Referring to artists' compulsion to paint and their need to express their innermost feelings and fantasies, Freud called them "obsessive daydreamers," who make art out of their maladjustment to life. This sort of a description would never fit a neoclassical artist, since they did not paint their inner feelings and fantasies. This sort of description could only fit artists of the Expression Theory type, who paint because they are driven.

Given the crazy misfit popular image of the artist, unstable personalities tend to be attracted to doing art. Van Gogh is taken as a paradigm case of this sort of artist, as he went from one failure to another, recording his intense, and finally insane emotionalism. Even though Van Gogh was not successful as an artist in his lifetime, he has been enormously successful after his death. All unsuccessful artists

FIGURE 2.9 An example of strange and disturbing art: Willem de Kooning, *Woman and Bicycle*, 1952–53. Oil on canvas, 76½ × 49 in. (Collection of Whitney Museum of American Art, Purchase 55.35.)

can dream that they too are Van Goghs. Even if no one likes their art now, they might be vindicated by history. Someone emulating this personality is not the type of person who could make the disciplined neoclassical art, filled with meaning, and done according to strict rules. Someone of this sort would also not make art like the highly impersonal and beautifully crafted art of the ancients. This is the sort of person who would make strange and disturbing art like the art of the avantgarde (fig. 2.9).

Beside the ideology of Aesthetic Formalism there is also a conflicting ideology, Expression Theory, which shapes our concepts of art in the twentieth century. Aesthetic Formalism is thought of as a constituent of what makes an object Fine Art. Expression Theories, on the other hand, have added to Fine Art a conflicting sense of what makes someone an artist. Aesthetic Formalism slowly replaced artists' concerns for subject matter in art, and the Expression Theory sense of who the artist is, replaced the neoclassical. Expression Theory, which revolves around the art made by a genius, coexists uncomfortably with Aesthetic Formalism, where art is about giving the viewer an aesthetic emotion. That is, where Aesthetic Formalism focuses on the art object in isolation, Expression Theory looks through the art at the artist who created it. Also, where the appreciation of aesthetic form requires approaching the art with a disinterestedness, the appreciation of expressive art does not. Indeed, this contributes to the success of artists like Van Gogh. One does not need an attitude of disinterestedness to perceive the emotion projected in his art, and so anyone can appreciate it, even people who are uneducated in art.

The Expression Theory approach clashes with the Aesthetic Formalist concern for beauty. For the Aesthetic Formalists, the bottom line on art is its aesthetic qualities. Whatever beauty of aesthetic form we find in Van Gogh's art, for example, or in other expressive art, is only there to enhance the emotional effect. *The Night Café* does not show beautiful shapes and harmonies. The beauty of line and form have been sacrificed for expressive intensity. We look at the art and do not find aesthetics or objective subject matter, we find emotional intensity. Artists of this sort were willing to make ugly art if it truly expressed their mood. Thus, where the power of Aesthetic Formalism is to support a disinterested objectivity in the viewer conducive to rational thinking, Expression Theory art causes the viewer to feel emotion.

Expression Theory artists are not supported by an academy structure. It takes no education to make expressive art. Artists create without the help of an academy to dictate subject matter and style. Further, the ideology of the artist as someone who is expressive, but not educated into accepting an objective set of art rules, undermines the academy structure for art. If the artist needs no art education, then who dubs the artist as artist? If expressiveness on its own makes an artist, then anyone can be an artist, and this erodes the institutional structure supporting the cultural niche of Fine Art.

Expression Theory also gives rise to the attitude that all that matters about art is that it is personally satisfying or expressive for the individual artist making it. This is a combination of the idea that one cannot dispute taste and that art is about personal expression. From this perspective, no critical judgments are appropriate for art, except those made by the artist themselves, and if the artist is satisfied then the art is considered successful. In sum, from this orientation, not only is there no academy structure to tell us who is and who is not an artist, but there is also no objective standard for judging value in objects of art.

5. MODERNISM AND BEYOND

The Split Between Fine Art and Popular Art

By the 1800s, a split emerged between Popular and Fine Art. The academy system changed from producing art for the aristocratic classes to producing art for the middle classes. This change occurred as the aristocratic class in France died off in the French Revolution, and as a middle-class lifestyle spread with the beginning of the Industrial Revolution. This was the beginning of art for popular taste. Thousands of paintings were exhibited in each salon and sold to the middle class.

Popular Art continued the neoclassical tradition while Fine Art evolved from art made in rebellion to neoclassicism. We can see the first stirrings of this rebellion in Romanticism. The rebellion was completed with the impressionist painters following Manet (1832–83). These new Fine Artists produced art outside the academy structure. They invented new stylistic conventions and philosophies of form. With neoclassicism and the styles for popular taste that evolved from it, viewers were to forget that they were looking at a painting, and just think about the story depicted. But after the impressionists, and most especially the revolutionary art of Cezanne (1839–1906) (fig. 2.10), Fine Art began to show that it was paint on canvas. Fine Art became more and more art for art's sake. Fine Art was no longer clear glass through which some subject matter was seen, but rather one looked at the painted surface of the canvas itself. Cezanne is often called "the father of modern art" because through his influence the emphasis in art was so profoundly changed. When this new Fine Art depicted subject matter; it did not illustrate a story. If it showed life, it was not idealized. Fine Art became stylistically difficult to read, often irritating art that did not tell a story or even relate to life.

This split between Fine Art and Popular Art did not happen all at once. The artists we now admire as revolutionaries, like Cezanne, and Van Gogh, were not at all popular in their own time. The turn of the Fine Art art world towards modernism over neoclassicism came slowly. Afterwards historians retold the history, seeing greatness in artists who were not great in their own time but who prefigured modernism.

After the split, Fine Art continued to be one-of-a-kind items showing the unique perspective of an individual artist, while Popular Art was made to please the mass of people with themes that were sure to sell. In the twentieth century, Popular Art has become commercial mass-

FIGURE 2.10 Paul Cezanne, *Still Life with Peppermint Bottle,* c. 1894. With the Cezanne revolution, Fine Art started to look like paint on canvas rather then like a scene through a window. Chester Dale Collection, © 1994 Board of Trustees, National Gallery of Art, Washington, D.C. Oil on canvas, 26 × 32⅜ inches.

media art. The art objects are produced in quantity and reflect the viewer's taste rather than the artist's taste (see chapter 3). Fine Art tends to be hand-crafted individual items sold from galleries, displayed at shows where they compete with one another for prizes, and hung up in museums and compared to other items by Fine Art standards against the tradition of Fine Art. Fine Art objects are one of a kind, or limited edition, whereas mass-media art is produced in hundreds or thousands of copies. This is because the producers of mass-media art make more money as they appeal to more people and hence sell more copies of their art. The producers of Fine Art make more money if they appeal to a rich patron who will pay more for a single unique art object. Thus Popular Art and Fine Art share in the function of making objects with no other purpose than to be appreciated; however, economic forces mold Fine Art into unusual, unique art appealing to the classes with the most money, and mold mass-market art into objects that appeal to the broadest possible taste. Popular Art continued the neoclassical tradition of imitation, making it easy to understand narrative art. In this way it stayed closer to craft than Fine Art did, which turned away from imitation to expression and aesthetics.

Fine Art continued the cultural niche created during the Renaissance by having individual creators making unique objects for collections that are distributed through a gallery structure; while Popular Art is often made like old workshop arts as a collective effort making many copies which are distributed through the same economic circuits other goods and services are.

Thus, Fine Art is defined against craft on one side, and Popular Art on the other. As we will discuss in chapter 3, there continue to be turf wars between Fine Art and Popular Art over which sort of art should be displayed in public places and receive public funds.

Modernism

During the Renaissance and the Enlightenment, there were academies and clients who told the artists what to do. There were controversies about what should or should not be represented, and about some elements of style, but there was no ambiguity about art's mission, or what made value in art. However, with the revolutions against neoclassicism, artists themselves began to theorize about the mission of art, and value in art. Without the tight control of the academy and salon structure a whole range of art movements developed. As we move into the twentieth century, art has become increasingly splintered into various art movements. First there was impressionism, then expressionism and Fauve art, then cubism, dada, surrealism, avant-garde art, purism, Orphism, futurism, vorticism, suprematism, De Stijl, constructivism, kinetic art, pop art, op art, minimal art, to name just a few. This proliferation of art movements is often referred to as *modernism*. Modernism became institutionalized in the United States in the form of the Museum of Modern Art in 1929.

In modernism, the concern for subject matter was gradually replaced by a concern for aesthetics, subjective expression, or shock value and newness. Even in art movements, like photo-realism, which have a representational content, the point of the art was often not the subject represented. In fact, the subject tended to be something highly mundane like a still life or a storefront. The point of the art was aesthetics (fig. 2.11).

Of course sometimes this type of realist art expressed its non-artness by being extreme realism where aesthetics, meaning, and personal expression were not relevant. The only point of the art was to look

FIGURE 2.11 An example of photo-realism: Paul Wiesenfeld, *Interior with Apples* 1975. In photo-realism the point of art is not the mundane subject represented itself but the aesthetics. Oil on canvas, 43½-by-38 inches. Delaware Art Museum, purchased with funds from the National Endowment for the Arts, a Federal agency, and the Chicester Foundation, 1976.

as exactly as possible like some piece of ordinary unidealized real life. A good example of this type of art is that of Duane Hanson. Duane Hanson makes very realistic plastic sculptures dressed in real clothes, that are true to life down to the pores in the skin and the little hairs on the arms. As we will discuss in chapter 6, these statues are so realistic that they often fool people into believing that they are real humans and not art (fig. 2.12).

It is controversial just what ties all these art movements together, and what the true essential nature of modernism was, but certainly we can say that in modernism there was a concern for style and a desire to make pure art without a political or social message, or meaning. Also many of the artists within modernism were motivated by a concern for what art is. They made art that commented on the nature of art. Art was about art, either as an aesthetic experience, or some new experience created to shock the viewers awake. The questions that fascinated people were about what makes something art, and what the differences between artworks and real things are.

Many of these modern artists were motivated by the desire to make art that did not refer to life. They made abstract art to show pure harmonies, like the De Stijl movement (see chapter 4), or to show pure aesthetic form. Many made art spontaneously without interference of

FIGURE 2.12 An example of extreme realism: Duane Hanson, *Couple with shopping bags*, 1976. Cast vinyl, polychromed in oil, life-sized. In this type of realism, the point of art is to look as exactly as possible like some piece of ordinary life, not aesthetics, meaning, or personal expression. Duane Hanson's sculptures are so realistic they are often mistaken for living people. Photograph from *Contemporary American Realism Since 1960* by Frank Goodyear. Copyright © 1981 by Frank H. Goodyear, Jr. By permission of Little, Brown and Co.

the artist, through accidents like dripping or throwing paint on canvas, or by putting metal plates under the trees in fall, so that they become etched in intricate patterns by the decay of fallen leaves and the weather. Some gave up making objects altogether, in favor of performance art, conceptual art, and happenings.

Dada, the Avant-Garde, and Minimalist Art

Of all the philosophies that have impacted art, existentialism spawned the most disturbing art movements. Although people had been shocked at the first appearance of various art movements there was nothing similar to the shock value of the art coming out of existentialism. Fine Art had become associated with rebellion; it had rebelled against neo-classicism and its embrace of Expression Theory, an outgrowth of romanticism. This made existentialism attractive as the ultimate philosophy of rebellion. Indeed, shock value replaced beauty as a standard of taste for many of the existentialist art movements, while original-ity replaced virtuosity as the artistic virtue displayed in the work. Dada, surrealism, the avant-garde, and minimalism have all been intentionally disturbing and disruptive art movements inspired by existentialism. It is these movements that have chiefly caused people to declare Fine Art dead. Existentialism focuses on the purposelessness and meaninglessness of existence. Unlike Neoplatonism, which had inspired Renaissance art by giving artists a spiritual quest, a sense for light, spiritual beauty, and the Forms, existentialism gave artists despair, anguish, self-doubt, and nausea.

The first existentialist-inspired art movement was dada, beginning around 1914. Of all the modernistic art movements, dada contributed the most to the death of modernism by cleaning the slate of art. Dada allowed art to be free of its past. Dada was against art. Certainly the sense that dadaists had of art was an Expression Theory sense. As we saw, the Expression Theory attitude was that the art object is most fundamentally the expression of an individual artist. It is *that* which gives significance to the art object. It is the mysterious touch of the artist that causes ordinary objects to become art. Dada artists found ways to make things that were art in the Expression Theory sense, yet also not really art at all. For example, Picabia made a painting, *L'aeil Cacodylate*, which consisted totally of the signatures of his friends. This was in response to the idea that it is the artistic signature that makes value in art. Picabia wrote that works of art are not made by artists, but quite simply by men (Ades, 1974). The dadaists were preoccupied with pointing out the non-superiority of the artist as creator. They felt that poetry and painting could be produced by anyone. Here the Expression Theory idea that the value of art is how it expresses the genius artist finally turns into dada art, with an existentialist trick. Dada art is both only an expression of the artist — having no subject matter, nor aesthetic form — and also not an expression of an artist, as the artist's part in its creation is also rejected.

Marcel Duchamp (1887–1968) was one of the original dadaists and the inspiration for much of the avant-garde. After creating a few cubist works, he more or less gave up painting, and made *ready-mades*, which were machine-made objects merely chosen by the artist, and not chosen for any aesthetic purposes. Duchamp claimed to be indifferent to aesthetics. He (quoted by Tomkins, 1968, p. 40) said about his ready-mades: "The ready-mades were a way of getting out of the exchangeability, the monetarization of the work of art. The original work is sold, and it acquires a sort of aura that way. But with my ready-mades a replica will do just as well." Avant-garde artists following Duchamp concluded that in order to qualify as art, a work needed only to be chosen by an artist, as Duchamp had done with his ready-mades. This has given rise to a whole mini-genre of art "appropriation" where something is taken from ordinary reality, or from the work of another artist and signed. Artists with this idea have signed everything, including buildings, and the sky. One avant-garde artist, for example, takes prints of the works of famous artists, signs them with her own name, and frames them as her own appropriated work (Crimp, 1985).

Duchamp's most infamous ready-made was *La Fontaine*. This was submitted for display in an exhibition in New York City in 1917 sponsored by the Society of Independent Artists, which Duchamp helped found. This society was open to any artist who paid the six-dollar fee, and the show was open to all members with no restrictions on the art that could be shown. To test this artistic freedom, Duchamp bought a porcelain urinal (fig. 2.13), which he called *La Fontaine* and sent it to the show, signing it *R. Mutt*. The hanging committee refused to exhibit his urinal as sculpture, and art critics have been arguing about whether or not it should be classed as art ever since.

Avant-garde artists thought that the art game demanded an extreme form of creativity from them; they were to make art like none that had ever been made before. Unless it was new, and different, it was not considered good art. Doing something really new was to do something shocking, something that violated people's expectations somehow. For example, Piero Mangoni sent cans of his own excrement to his Milan gallery labeled "Mierda d'Artista" (McEvilley, 1983). Another artist put excrement all over himself and then rubbed it off on his viewers. One artist put up an ordinary pile of bricks. Robert Barry closed an Amsterdam Gallery for two weeks. Two artists, a male and a female, lived together for a year tied to each other with a rope. Cris Burden had himself crucified on a Volkswagen. One artist wrapped himself in a blanket studded with razor blades and filmed himself writhing around on the floor. Another artist photographed himself masturbating in a bed with hamburger. Another masturbated on stage with the head of a goose. Another masturbated under the floorboards of the gallery so that the viewers came and observed him, looking down at him through a hole in the floor.

These Avant-garde artists used their art to give people a new experience, much like the dadaists. When the artist turned the commonplace into art, they were displaying it *as* art. These artists invited spectators to participate actively in the creative process — by interpreting the work of art however they pleased, or, even better, by simply experiencing it without interpretation.

Minimalist art continued the Duchamp idea that to be art, a thing

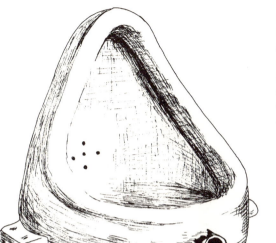

FIGURE 2.13 A urinal just like the one Duchamp signed for his infamous ready-made *La Fontaine*. Duchamp's urinal is art only because it was picked out and signed by an artist.

requires merely to be chosen by the artist; however the minimalists take art seriously, which Duchamp never did. Minimalist art objects are generally three-dimensional single unitary objects, or a series of identical unitary objects. For example, Don Judd made a row of galvanized boxes, Sol LeWitt made a regular three-dimensional grid (fig. 2.14), Larry Bell made a glass box bound by chromium strips. Most minimalist artists do not actually make their art objects, but have them made to order by professional industrial fabricators (Lucie-Smith, 1974). For example, Tony Smith's *The Black Box* was an imitation of a wooden file card box that he ordered made up five times bigger by a local welding company and then painted black. Thus, the art object becomes less and less important, it is merely an end product, and the emphasis becomes increasingly conceptual.

The minimalist Sol LeWitt wrote that his aim in making art is to make something where neither chance, taste, nor unconsciously remembered form can play in the outcome. He wrote that he does not attempt to produce a beautiful or mysterious object, but ". . . functions merely as a clerk cataloguing the results of his premise" (Lippard 1985, p. 211). This is art without the intervention of the artist, and whose other meanings are also reduced. This art movement continues the tradition of pointless, meaningless art that began with dada.

Minimalist works are deliberately anti-sculptural since they reject ordering and balancing areas (Lippard, 1985). The works are absolutely symmetrical and repetitive. As the minimalist LeWitt maintains, mini-

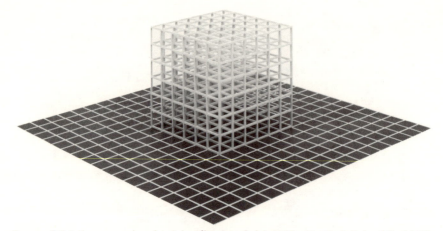

FIGURE 2.14 An example of minimalist art: Sol LeWitt, *Untitled Cube (6)*, 1968, painted metal, 15¼ by 15¼ by 15¼ inches. According to Sol LeWitt, his aim in making art is not to make something beautiful or mysterious, but to make something where neither chance, taste, nor unconsciously remembered form can play in the creative process. Collection of Whitney Museum of American Art, gift of the Howard and Jean Lipman Foundation, Inc. Purchase 68.45.

malism is disassociated from sentimentality, sensitivity, and good taste. Minimalists are ideologically against all set standards of taste. In other words, their art is intentionally tasteless, uninteresting, ugly, and meaningless without any special virtuosity displayed and no touch of the artist. The emphasis is conceptual, by default.

Some of these minimalist artists make immense earth mounds, trenches, and walls which are meant to be experienced as landscape-artificial landscape. For example, in 1968 Claes Oldenburg made a minimalist conceptual landscape called *Placid City Monument* which consisted of a trench extending between the Metropolitan Museum of Art and Cleopatra's Needle (an obelisk) in New York City, dug and then filled again by union grave diggers.

In popular culture doubt emerged about the sincerity of the modern artist. Were the artists just trying to fool the public? People were saying "art is dead." People did not understand modernism, did not like it, and made fun of it. They saw the artist as motivated in part by the desire to shock. The public was afraid that artists were really laughing at the poor fools who took their art seriously. Modernism seemed to carry a death wish. It was intentionally making fun of the seriousness of art. Artists made art that was intentionally tasteless, ugly, and meaningless, and thus rejected all those things that had made art attractive in the past.

The Death of Modernism

Unlike the art movements during the Renaissance and Enlightenment where art was stimulated to become more complex, meaningful, and powerful, here art was stimulated to become less meaningful, and more simplified. One power after another was shut down. Art no longer had subject matter, easily read stylistic conventions, similarity to the Greco-Roman paradigms, educated genius artists, nor technical constraints in which to show virtuosity. Even the Aesthetic Formalists participated in this trend since, as they sought artistic purity, they produced art which had only aesthetic form and nothing else. The art of the cubists and non-figurative artists like Mondrian contributed to this as well by using stylistic conventions which no longer communicated to any but the most sophisticated viewers. All ideologies dictating value in art except those of aesthetic form and subjective emotional expressiveness had been erased. Fine Art was left without a complete ideological structure. Thus, the one motivating idea for much of modern art was to make art about art because there was no clear ideology telling them what art was.

The general function of Fine Art continued to be objects bought for collection with no other function than to be art. However, ideologies needed to define artistic work in the niche Fine Art: subject matter, stylistic conventions, beauty, artistic mission, were now given by the mutually inconsistent philosophies of Aesthetic Formalism, Expression Theory, and Existentialism.

Subject matter was rejected by the more extreme Aesthetic Formalists, and others, on the grounds that art was not to refer to life. With dada and the avant-garde, sometimes artists did not even make art objects at all. There was no fixed ideology about stylistic conventions either; each artist and art movement made up their own. The Aesthetic Formalists tried to make art with beauty of form, but others rejected beauty in favor of expressive intensity, making ugly and shocking art.

There was no real unified sense of artistic mission, either. Each movement had its own mission. Cubists wanted to show real unconceptualized shapes of things in four dimensions. Abstract expressionists wanted to make abstract shapes that appealed to the viewers' archetypes, often through spontaneous accidents. Some artists wanted to give the viewer a rush of beauty, some wanted to express their feelings, and some wanted to do something new and shocking to awaken the viewer to the artistic qualities in the everyday world. Each artist had to decide what sort of art to make and which ideology of art to believe. Thus, for many, the mission of art was to discover art's mission. This also meant that although the disinterested posture of Aesthetic Formalism dominated, there were now other postures as well, and so art no longer reinforced a singular mental posture in the viewer. Besides giving an aesthetic emotion, some art was made to shock, some was made just to be experienced, and some was made to express emotion. Thus this plurality of missions worked against the power of art. Neither art that shocks, nor art that is expressive, nor ugly art requires a particular mind-set to experience its effects. These types of art do not necessitate the viewer to practice a particular mental posture or approach to life. Instead they merely dilute Fine Arts power to reinforce disinterested disengagement and objectivity.

Further, there was the problem of judging the quality of modern art. Whereas with representational art one can judge whether it is "good" or not by how much it creates an illusion, or by how profoundly it illustrates some point about life, most modern art was neither illusionistic, nor obviously making some point about life. Since there was no fixed canon of stylistic conventions, art could not be judged on how skillfully the artist used those conventions. Since there was no agreement on artistic mission, art could not be judged on how successfully it fulfilled its mission. People saw paintings to which their uneducated response was that their five-year-old child could make better art. Since there were so many theories, one had to know a different theory for almost every work. The viewer had to turn to the critics to "understand" the significance of the art and let the critics judge its quality. Not only did the artists have to create the work of art, they also had to create the ideological framework used to understand it. Indeed, it was often claimed that modern art had become completely literary; that is, it only illustrated the going theory of art (Wolf, 1975) (Danto, 1973).

Art had a greatly reduced capacity to communicate in modernism because in the frenzy for reductive purity in Aesthetic Formalism, and art about art, and in existentialist inspired art movements, it had sacrificed so many of its meaningful levels that the artist could no longer communicate complex messages. Nor did the artists have enough background culture and historical knowledge in common with their patrons to have any complex messages to communicate. Most artists no longer had an academic education in the classics and history, and neither did their patrons. The flattened intellectual space of Fine Art had left the artists without the ability to really intellectually engage the viewer — they had sacrificed that for aesthetic purity, expressiveness, shock value, or newness.

Today, everyone can be an artist with respect to Fine Art. The skills of the Fine Artist are taught to grade-school children. The computer and camera allow people to make art without needing the technical skills of the Fine Artist. Expression Theory ideology says that an artist need not be a professional. The profession of Fine Artist depends less on an academy structure. Since anyone can be an artist, people feel less need for a professional class of Fine Artists. Thus, although there still are Fine Artists, and they are still making art for a certain class of people with "good taste," most professional Fine Artists must get grants, teach, make commercial art, or have a part-time non-art related job to make enough money to live. The museum-gallery structure still markets Fine Art for collections, and art historians and critics still relate contemporary art to the long tradition of Fine Art. However, more and more artists study the technology of art as taught by Fine Artists and Fine Art history, but make commercial art, either Design Art, Popular Art, or advertising.

Post-Modernism and the True Vanguard of Culture

In the 1970s many people declared the death of Fine Art. But then in the 1980s it was seen that Fine Art had not died, rather, modernism had come to an end. The art that continued beyond modernism was called *postmodern*. This art was not held together by any ideological orientation, but rather, it was held together by its rejection of some of the main orientations of modernism. For one thing, modernism had put a great deal of emphasis on style and originality. But in postmodernism that is no longer important, since style is what you use to do whatever job you want done, rather than being itself the point of doing art. In the movements that made up modernism, art was to do art, and have no other function or message. This too does not continue into postmodernism. Art need not be pure. Within postmodernism, art can be ideological again, projecting social messages. Postmodernism comments on life.

Ultimately though, the ideological void and confusion that caused the "death" of modernism were not fixed. In postmodernism there is still a lack of full ideology so that the Fine Artist still does not quite know what he or she is to do. Artists still make up their own standards for value and artistic mission, and since a single mental posture is not reinforced in the viewer, Fine Art has lost most of its power to affect the development of culture. After about five hundred years from its beginning during the Renaissance, what is left of the cultural niche, Fine Art, is the backbone distribution system, critics, galleries, museums, art shows and art history. But Fine Art is still in a state of collapse without an adequate ideological structure, or sense of who is and is not an artist, or sense of what is and is not art.

Fine Artists act as researchers and teachers. The Fine Artist is a specialist in art. The Fine Artists investigate the capacities of the pure art instrument, and project their own expressions, messages, or sensitivities for aesthetics through the art. The experiments of Fine Art are the objects of art that are then sold to the patrons of the art world. Fine Art lives outside the mass market. It is consumed only by those who know something about art. It is individualistic and experimental. In general, it is isolated from mainstream contemporary life.

Often when people study visual art their objective is to achieve a sense of cultural direction. In the modernist culture, for example, when Fine Art was obsessed with issues of style and a reductionistic sense of artistic purity, similar trends could be found in other aspects of culture. Likewise, it is thought, if we look at the trends in Fine Art now, like postmodernism, we should get a sense of where culture is headed. Because Fine Art played the role of cultural vanguard before, people assume that it is still playing that role.

However, when we look closely at contemporary culture we see, at least with respect to visual art, that Fine Art is no longer the vanguard of culture. Although Fine Art still has a function in society, the money and energy of this culture are going into Design, advertising, and mass-media art. These are the commercial arts distributed on the mass market or through the mass media, and consequently reaching everyone. Fine Art objects tend to be sold as hand-crafted, one of a kind (or numbered limited edition) items outside the mass-market distribution system. Also, because most contemporary Fine Art is confined to the museum and art gallery, most people have limited exposure to it.

Furthermore, the insights displayed in Fine Art are those of unique individual Fine Artists or of some historical period other than our own. Whereas the insights shown in Popular Art, Design Art, and advertising are those of the contemporary culture at large and those of the moneyed elite. These new arts are directly yoked to the economic and technological engines of change. Thus, Fine Art objects reflect individual perspectives and the past in a culture completely dominated by the perspectives of groups — special interest groups, business groups, government — and the present. The mass-market and mass-media art objects are group products projecting the group values to stereotyped consumers.

Further, what we see in one Popular Art image, or on one Design Art product we see in many other Popular or Design Art images and products, and so the images impact us not as individual images, but by repetition of themes. These arts, as we will discuss, are eliciting mutually reinforcing mental orientations that are moving the culture forward.

Fine Art images do not have this sort of impact as singular objects projecting the insights of a singular artist. As we've said, Fine Art currently does not support a consistent mental orientation in its viewers. People continue to approach Fine Art disinterestedly, but this approach is not always successful, since Fine Art is also made for other approaches as well. Thus, although Fine Artists are making "pure" art like research science, and what they produce has impact on the technology of art which all the visual artists have in common, beyond that, outside the art world community, the messages and mental posture their art carries have very limited impact. There are cases where their art makes a stir by shocking conventional morality, provoking censorship, and dispute, but Fine Art is not pushing modern culture. At most it acts as an outside critic or opposing force to contemporary changes and preserves a long cultural tradition. If we want to discover what postmodern culture is really going to be like, we should look at advertising, the Design Arts, and Popular Art. Here we will find the contemporary powers of art. It is through these arts in the mass media and mass market that our contemporary reality is being shaped.

CHAPTER 3

The Popular Art Cultural Niche

CONTEMPORARY POPULAR ART INCLUDES paintings and ceramic figures made for popular taste, as well as illustrations for magazines, newspapers, books, and also movies, and television. Popular Art is positive, affirming, and not revolutionary. Its value is in its subject matter and its emotional appeal. It projects conventional values and emotions. It reinforces the current world view of its viewers. Some of Popular Art is highly sentimental. Children especially relate to this sentimental Popular Art. The illustrations of Sesame Street, and pictures of the three little pigs and the big bad wolf in children's books are sentimental Popular Art. The cute puppy illustrations on calendars (fig. 3.1), and the greeting cards with snow scenes and children on them are sentimental Popular Art. The ceramic figurines of children (see fig. 1.2 on p. 5), and Walt Disney cartoons are also sentimental Popular Art. Some of Popular Art is designed to be emotionally stimulating and sensationalist rather than sentimental. Action adventure movies, crime shows, and soap operas are emotionally stimulating Popular Art. Science fiction illustrations in magazines and books, and girlie pictures on calendars and posters are emotionally stimulating Popular Art. This art is meant to give the viewer an emotionally stimulating fantasy away from the everyday world.

From the perspective of the contemporary art world, Popular Art is thought of as a kind of Fine Art; that is, bad Fine Art or Fine Art in bad taste. It seems hackneyed and banal to the Fine Art art world. From their

FIGURE 3.1 An example of sentimental Popular Art showing an often repeated subject matter: cute puppies.

perspective, popular taste is bad taste. For example, the Fine Art critic Clement Greenberg (1961) thought of art made for popular taste as watered down, substitute culture. He said that present civilization is in a process of decay, and it is only in the avant-garde that culture is kept moving at all. Where we find an avant-garde, he said, we also find a rear guard, and that is Popular Art, all of which he calls *kitsch*. Kitsch, he writes, is designed for people who are hungry for diversion, but are insensitive to genuine culture. The precondition for kitsch, he writes, is the availability of a mature cultural tradition from which kitsch borrows its devices and images. Because it is turned out mechanically, it is an integral part of our industrial system. He writes that kitsch is "mechanical and operates by formulas. Kitsch is vicarious experience and faked sensations" (Greenberg, 1961, p. 10). This attitude toward art for popular taste is common in the Fine Art art world.

What Greenberg says about Popular Art is true in many ways. It does give us vicarious experiences, sentimentality, and diversion. It is an integral part of our industrial system and it is turned out mechanically. It is unoriginal and it does use the same technical insights used in Fine Art. People who consume Popular Art are insensitive to "genuine culture" if that is taken to mean Fine Art. The main thing wrong with this idea of Popular Art is that it judges Popular Art as though it were Fine Art. After all, Fine Art does not give us vicarious experiences. Fine Art is not mechanically produced, part of our industrial system, or unoriginal. When judged as Fine Art, Popular Art looks like bad art.

Although there are some commonalties between Fine Art and Popular Art, they are actually different and distinct types of art. Their conditions for production are different. Their distribution systems are different. They appeal to different audiences. They have different ideologies. They have different powers. Popular art is not bad Fine Art because it is not Fine Art at all, but art of a distinct and separate cultural niche. Popular Art has value and power in contemporary culture. As we discussed in the last chapter, Fine Art is not the true vanguard of culture at the present time. That vanguard is now in mass-media and mass-market art. Popular Art, Design Art, and advertising are pushing into new mental spaces and Fine Art is maintaining the old traditional ones like reason, objectivity, and critical thought. As we will discuss, the power of Popular Art is expanding our mental abilities in directions away from rationality and pushing culture forward.

1. THE FORMATION OF POPULAR TASTE

Popular Taste in Europe

Popular Art first became a real force when the court and aristocracy ceased to be the regular purchasers of art in the eighteenth century. In France, the aristocracy fell with the French Revolution in 1789 and the French Royal Academy and art-buying public changed. The market for paintings was shifted from a small aristocratic public who knew something about art, to a large and aesthetically uneducated public. The academy system changed from producing art that was meant mainly for the aristocratic classes, to producing art for popular taste. Thousands of paintings were exhibited in each salon. This art was sold to the middle class, who accepted the academy stamp of approval as a guarantee of good art, and was eager to buy art to acquire culture (Canaday, 1981).

As the art produced by the academy structure changed to suit the tastes of its new patrons in the middle class, it still continued to use the clear narrative style of neoclassicism. The viewers could look through the neoclassical works and think about some myth or story. There were no stylistic ambiguities to decipher. The style was meant to be so clear that the viewers could forget that they were looking at a painting, and just think about the story depicted there. They could see the story depicted as through a transparent glass. It is this transparent glass that continues into art for popular taste.

While the concept of style as clear glass continued, the subject matter itself changed. Rather than depicting grandiose subject matter, classical stories, or historical events, European academic art began to depict idealized domestic life, and sentimentalized or sensationalized fantasies. The taste of this new French art-buying public ran to art that was easy to understand, told a story, and showed off the artist's virtuosity, with every detail carefully painted. We can see paintings made for this popular taste in, for example, the pictures of Greuze at the end of the eighteenth century. In one of his paintings, for example, *The Village Bride* (1761) we see people gathered around a wedding couple. There is even a mother hen with her chicks pecking for grain on the floor. This is a painting of sentimental everyday life. We see this same taste continue a hundred years later in academic paintings sold at the French salon by artists like Adolph Bouguereau. In one of Bouguereau's paintings, *Youth and Cupid*, 1877, we see a nude woman smiling up at a cupid sitting on her shoulders. The folds of cloth in the background and the posture of the woman signal that it is done in a neoclassical tradition, but it is appealing to popular taste, rather than to Fine Art taste by using a formula guaranteed to please.

Popular Taste in Early America

In the early days of the United States the split between popular and Fine Art taste tended to lay along the line between indigenous taste and European taste. That is, the Fine Art art world in the United States imported art styles from Europe, while popular taste was formed by the conditions in the new land. Those patrons in the United States that thought of themselves as having good taste continued to purchase European pictures, and American painters painting for the American art world were encouraged to ape European styles, and receive art education in Europe. In this period the American art world was attracted to neoclassicism, even while neoclassicism began changing to fit the European middle class.

Americans outside art world circles were not attracted to neo-

FIGURE 3.2 An example of Fine Art in the neoclassical style that was rejected by popular taste: Horatio Greenough: *George Washington*, 1832–41. In this sculpture, Washington, the father of the country, was portrayed as Zeus, the father of the gods. Although people in the art world liked the statue, the general public did not, since, they said, Washington the man would never have appeared in public with his chest bare, wrapped in a sheet. National Collection of Fine Arts, Smithsonian Institution, Washington, D.C.

classicism because they thought it was not realistic enough. For example, in 1832, Horatio Greenough, an American sculptor who was educated in Rome (and one of the first American functionalists, as we will discuss in the next chapter) was commissioned by Congress to make a statue of George Washington for the Rotunda (fig. 3.2). In this sculpture, Greenough portrayed Washington as Zeus, modeling it after the fifth-century B.C. *Olympian Zeus of Philias.* He showed Washington with a classical body and posture, although he did not give him the beard of the Greek god. Greenough's Washington had a naked muscular chest and was wrapped in a toga to the waist, with his hand raised in a gesture of proclamation. On top of this idealized classical body, Greenough gave his Washington a "realistic" head modeled after a famous portrait of Washington. Greenough's statue was meant to be taken allegorically: Washington was father of the country, and Zeus was father of the gods. For those with cultured taste, neoclassicism of this sort proved that they were not backward. They also built buildings in a classical style so as to make the buildings equal to the great buildings in Europe. Having a statue of George Washington in a monumental style harking back to the great statues of the Greeks, seemed more than appropriate to them (Canaday, 1981).

Although intellectuals and people in the art world liked the statue, the general public did not. The common people wanted more "realism," less quoting from the Greek past. A thing should look like what it is, according to the popular taste. If it is a statue of Washington, then it should look like Washington, not like a Greek god. Washington having a naked chest bothered the vernacular taste in America in that time period (Canaday, 1981). The people thought of Washington as a man, not a Greek god, and Washington would never have appeared in public wrapped in a sheet with his chest bare.

Popular taste in the United States went to realism. Americans liked literalism in their art. They liked landscapes where every detail was exact, and factually correct (Kouwenhoven, 1948). They liked anecdotal and photographic pictures with sentimental themes, such as Jozef Is-rael's (1824–1911) *Alone in the World*, or Thomas Hovenden's *Breaking Home Ties*, a painting that was voted the most popular in the 1893 World's Columbian Exposition. Indeed, such sentimental paintings as well as literal realism continue to be popular with those outside art world circles.

American popular taste was different from popular taste in Europe at that time. Whereas popular taste in Europe liked nude classical reference in their paintings and sculpture, popular taste in the United States thought nudity in art was indecent. For example, the American public had been shocked at the nudity of infant cherubs in another piece that Greenough had done called *The Chanting Cherubs* (1828–30, now lost). Where neoclassicism was already on its way to becoming a style for the middle classes in Europe, in the United States it was still the style preferred by the cultivated classes and the art world.

When the Armory show opened in New York in 1913, many Americans were exposed for the first time to the modernism that was being produced in Europe. This was the first exposure to the American public of modernism as a systematic movement with a tradition (Taylor, 1979). After this exposure many in the American Fine Art art world turned away from the European academic painting which was the de-scendant of neoclassicism, and away from the American academic art which imitated it. Many in the Fine Art art world began to see European and American academic art as too traditional, while modernism, as seen in such artists as Cezanne, Picasso, Matisse, and Gauguin, looked revo-lutionary and exciting. This revolutionary new art was primitive and childlike, in contrast to academic art, which appeared stale and over-done. Once the American Fine Art art world was exposed to modern art, it was imported to America and the ideologies of modernism began to take an increasing hold.

The acceptance of modernism by the art world caused an even greater distance between popular taste and Fine Art taste. As modern art became the orthodoxy in Fine Art, the Fine Art art world began to class European and American pre-modern academic art together with the realism enjoyed by popular taste as all equally backward and bad art. Classing all art made for popular taste together reinforces the illusion that all Popular Art is really just bad Fine Art. Something else that reinforces the identification between the two art niches is that the two of them serve the same basic function. Further, there are Fine Art objects made to appeal to popular taste as well as Popular Art objects made to mimic Fine Art.

2. CONFUSIONS BETWEEN FINE ART AND POPULAR ART

The Shared Function

Perhaps the main reason why Popular Art is generally thought of as bad Fine Art, rather than as a completely different sort of art, is that Popular Art has the same basic function as Fine Art. Like Fine Art objects, Popular Art objects also generally have no other function than to be looked at and appreciated. It is because of this shared function that Fine Art can be made for popular taste, and Popular Art can be made that mimics Fine Art. However, even here there are big differences between the two. Fine Art objects and Popular Art objects are not appreciated for the same qualities.

Fine Art objects are appreciated for their uniqueness and their artistic qualities in the context of the art world. It is these art world standards that made Popular Art seem to be bad art. It is against these standards that Popular Art looks like bad taste, banal and insipid. According to most art historians and critics, Popular Art shows nothing genuine, yet exhibits false sentiments and clichéd ideas. When compared to Fine Art objects using Fine Art standards of creative uniqueness, aesthetics, expressiveness, Popular Art comes up short. In Popular Art, aesthetics are sacrificed for sentimentality; creative uniqueness for con-ventionality. Its themes and subjects have been done many times before.

However, Popular Art is not meant to be appreciated as Fine Art. The way that Popular Art is appreciated is *for* its sentimentality, the way it makes vicarious experiences possible, stimulates emotion, and narrative thought. These are the powers of Popular Art. None of these effects are valued in the art world context. Popular Art objects are not put in shows and judged against each other. They are not judged as art, but as merchandise. They are judged by their popularity, by how well they sell. The things that people buy this art to do are quite different from the things that Fine Art does. However, because both art for popular taste and art for art world taste serve the same basic function, they can mimic each other, compete for public resources, and for viewers.

Fine Art for Popular Taste

Some art for popular taste comes from the cultural niche Popular Art, while some of it comes from the cultural niche Fine Art. For example, works like those of Bouguereau (1825–1905), although sentimental and generally appealing to the middle class rather than to the art world, nonetheless were made in a Fine Art institutional context. This art still has the institutional marks of Fine Art. Although these art objects were made to please the sentiments of the middle class, they were still made out of the personal inspiration of the artist. These objects were still single unique objects distributed through a gallery, the French salon, and evaluated in the art world context. These works are still made in the cultural niche Fine Art. Thus, they are not really Popular Art, they are Fine Art for popular taste.

There is also art made in the Popular Art cultural niche that mimics Fine Art. This art also confuses the distinction between Fine Art and Popular Art. An example of this sort of art is the art sometimes referred to as "starving-artist-sale" art. Starving-artist-sale art is produced in factory workshops in such places as Taiwan and Mexico. The paintings are made in an assembly line process, where typically several canvases are tacked up on the wall, and first all their backgrounds are painted, then, say, the grass on each canvas or the trees on each canvas are painted, and then the center image on each canvas is painted. Sometimes each part of the painting is done by a different artist, and sometimes one artist does it all. In any case, it takes only a short time to do each painting, and the paintings look quite a bit alike. The subject matter tends to be landscapes, seascapes, cityscapes, clowns, and horses done in realistic styles. These paintings are then sold in hotel ballrooms in the winter for very low prices.

These paintings mimic Fine Art. They are intended to look like Fine Art — original unique paintings done from the inspiration of a genius artist. But they are really workshop art, unoriginal paintings done by teams of artists, distributed in a setting that mimics a gallery show but is not, and sold to people who have no experience of "real" Fine Art. Buyers of these art objects tend to be buying them to match the decor and color of their living rooms. Starving-artist-sale art is Popular Art dressed up as Fine Art. By mimicking Fine Art, this art also confuses the distinction between Popular and Fine Art, reinforcing the impression that these two are the same kind of art.

What this shows is that both the Fine Art cultural niche and the Popular Art cultural niche can make art for popular taste. The European academic art, like that of Bouguereau, is Fine Art for popular taste made from the Fine Art niche. The starving-artist-sale art is Fine Art for popular taste made from the Popular Art niche. Popular taste represents a market to exploit, and both cultural niches can deliver to that market. However, the distribution system of the gallery and the number of paintings a single Fine Artist can deliver limit the ability of the Fine Artist to exploit this market. Thus, the Popular Art institutions are better at delivering these powers of art than the Fine Art institutions are.

3. THE INSTITUTIONS OF POPULAR ART

In the contemporary context, there is very little overlap in institutional structures between the cultural niches Popular Art and Fine Art. They differ in production, distribution, and intended audience.

Production

Popular Art continues the tradition of imitation, and thus stays closer to craft than Fine Art, since Fine Art has turned away from imitation and hence has turned further away from craft. Not only does this mean that the Fine Artist and Popular Artist have different relationships to the technology of art, but also their literal working arrangements tend to be different.

A Fine Artist tends to have an inspiration which he or she makes into art, and then tries to sell the finished product. Popular Artists tend to be seen as art technicians rather than as creative original artists.

Popular Artists tend to work like craftsmen for commissions. Someone hires them to do a particular illustration, or work as part of a team.

The exceptions to this are movies and television shows. Although the media have all the other marks of Popular Art, they tend not to be made for a commission, but rather from the personal inspirations of the producers and directors, after which the finished product is sold. Because of this, the movie and television media can also be used to make Fine Art by being personally expressive or aesthetic. These shows then appeal to an art world audience and are distributed through Fine Art institutions, by being shown in art world galleries, art movie houses, or on educational television. They are also judged by Fine Art standards. However, most commonly the movie and television media are used to make Popular Art, appealing to a mass audience, distributed through Popular Art institutions, and judged by how well they appeal to popular taste.

Popular Art is often done in a workshop setting produced by teams of artists, not by an individual creative artist in his or her own studio. For example, the cartoons in newspapers, magazines, and comic books are typically produced by a team of artists, where the tasks of drawing the figures, coloring them, doing the lettering, and planning out the story are done by different artists. The cartoons are then distributed by still another group of people to the mass market. Illustrators often work in an art department under an art director who gives them assignments and critiques their work. The movies and television are also produced by groups of artists. Many sorts of artists work together in the production of movies and television shows: set designers, costume designers, camera men, editors, actors, directors, scriptwriters, makeup artists, musicians, and more.

Of course this distinction between Popular Art as workshop art and Fine Art as art produced by a single individual in their own studio is not an absolute and clean distinction. There will always be exceptions to such divisions between these cultural niches of art. Occasionally there are individual Popular Artists, who are professional illustrators, and produce illustrations in their private studios which they then sell to a publisher, or cartoonists who do all the work in their cartoons themselves. Even in these cases, however, turning the illustration or cartoon into the final mass-media product takes a team. There are also occasional workshop Fine Artists like Judy Chicago, whose work is produced by a team of artists. However, in the Fine Art context, an individual artist, like Judy Chicago, is generally given credit for being the singular Fine Art creator.

The same artist can produce both Fine Art and Popular Art, and artists overlap in where they are educated. Popular Artists tend to be educated as illustrators. Illustrators and Fine Artists often attend the same art schools, and learn the same technology of art. Fine artists more often get master's degrees than Popular Artists do (of course there is still the tradition of completely uneducated Fine Artists, too), since they are educated not just to produce Fine Art, but often also to teach.

Whereas the Popular Artist tends to make all his or her money from the art he or she produces, all but the extremely successful Fine Artist tends to require additional money to live over what can be made selling art. The Fine Artist tends to get this money from grants, art competitions, or more commonly from teaching art, or from a job not related to art. This accounts for the charge against the Popular Artist from the Fine Art art world that the Popular Artist is just doing it for money. The Popular Artist often is, whereas the Fine Artist is not. The Fine Artist is often sacrificing monetary rewards to make their art. This difference comes from the distinctive ways in which the two sorts of art are distributed.

Distribution and Audience

Popular Art tends not to be distributed in museums and galleries. As we discussed, it tends to be mass-media art, where there is not one unique piece of art produced but many identical copies are produced and distributed either on the mass market as paintings, ceramic figures, posters, and calendars, or over print media as book, magazine, or newspaper illustrations. Movies are distributed through theaters, and through videotape that people rent or buy to watch on television. Although both Fine Art and Popular Art are exhibited, Fine Art tends to be exhibited in museums, art shows, and galleries, or homes of the well-to-do, while Popular Art tends to be exhibited in the kitchens and living rooms of the middle and lower classes.

For popular taste, the distinction between an original and a copy is made differently than it is made for Fine Art. For the viewers an exact copy of a cute puppies picture is just one more cute puppies picture (see fig. 3.1 on p. 81). It is not considered a forgery, fake, or mere reprint. It is the image in the art, the subject matter, not the uniqueness of the art object itself that is important. Because of this, many copies of the same image can be distributed all of equal value. Because Popular Art is produced not as one of a kind items, but in quantity, economic pressures push it to please the largest group of people it can so that it can sell the largest number of copies. Popular Art is very cheap compared to Fine Art, and is marketed in stores where the greatest number of people have access to it.

For Popular Art, a drawing of the art is still considered property of the original artist. For example, the image of a telephone in the shape of Garfield is owned by Paws, Inc., a company that distributes merchandise with Garfield images. A drawing of a Garfield phone is not considered a derivative image, but is classed as another case of the primary image. If it looks like Garfield, then it counts as a Garfield no matter how it is produced and can only be used by someone if permitted by the owners of Garfield. There is no original for much of Popular Art in the sense that a Fine Art image like the *Mona Lisa* is an original, and all copies are treated equally.

With Fine Art, there tends to be an original, and then any copies are either sanctioned "reprints" or they are considered forgeries. Although often the original art object is considered in the public domain because it is displayed in a national museum and/or the artist is long dead, the museums themselves own rights to the photographs of the images. To use such an image one needs to get permission of the museum. However, a drawing of an image tends to be considered derivative and hence not owned, unlike drawings of popular art images like Garfield. Thus, for Fine Art objects, there are originals and copies that are treated differently. The one-of-a-kind item hanging in the museum or gallery is considered the true art object. Photographs, reprints, or other copies are not considered as good as the original. This limits the ability of the artist to distribute many copies of the same image. People tend not to collect reprints as they would originals. They collect unique items or "limited edition" items. The Fine Artist, generally limited to selling a single copy of an image at a time, must be able to sell that work for the highest price possible. Thus the economic pressures at work on Fine Art cause it to appeal to those who can pay the most for a single image.

Popular Art appeals to those sentiments and values that the majority of people have in common. Indeed the culture promoted by art for popular taste in television, movies, and magazine illustrations, has become an international culture, overshadowing the art of local folk cultures. This began in the years between the World Wars, when American movies dominated the world movie market. American movies dominated not because they were better, but because of the way financing and marketing was structured (Sklar, 1975). Americans were producing more films and had access to more theaters worldwide than film producers of other nations had. Like the movies, American television is exported to places as diverse as Latin America, Asia, and Europe. American television shows have become popular in places as far away as Israel and Japan.

As we discussed, in order for Fine Art to function as it does, institutions of art history and art critics must exist. They interpret the art in the context of the Fine Art historical traditions and the contemporary art world context. Popular Art needs no art history because it is not interpreted in terms of art traditions, or art world context. However, for some Popular Art, specifically the film arts of movies and television, there are people who function as art critics. The primary job of these people is to tell us whether we would enjoy seeing the art. The art is rated on its mass appeal, its degree of sex and violence, and the quality of the acting. Sometimes it is evaluated on the grounds of its message as well. Although there are comparisons made between movies, or between television shows, they are not rated by their art world qualities, but by their entertainment value for the consumer. Thus, critics perform a different function for Popular Art than for Fine Art. We do not turn to the movie critic to help us understand a movie's meaning in terms of art world ideology, or understand what a movie tells us about life, as we might do if it were Fine Art. We turn to the movie critic to hear whether the movie would be the sort of thing we would like to see, whether it would be entertaining.

Fine Art and Popular Art overlap in where the artists are educated, and in that both Fine Artists and Popular Artists have access to the same art technology. Also, their art serves the same broad function, as we said. However, in all other institutional structures that support them, Fine Art and Popular Art are different. Whereas Fine Art tends to be made by a single individual from his or her own studio, Popular Art tends to be made for a commission, in a workshop setting, often by a team of artists. Fine Artists tend not to be able to live on the money they make from selling art, whereas Popular Artists can and hence are professionals in that sense. Fine Art tends to be distributed through a gallery, museum structure, whereas Popular Art is distributed on the mass market, or through the mass media. Popular Art appeals to the lowest common denominator; whereas Fine Art appeals to those things that distinguish the Fine Arts patron from everyone else. Thus, the conditions out of which these two art types are produced are different: the distribution systems are different; the economic pressures are different; and the audiences they are trying to reach are different.

Although Popular Art has different institutions from those of Fine Art, it has the same ideological slots as Fine Art. That is, because they share basic functions, they have the same sorts of ideological needs.

Within the Popular Art cultural niche like the Fine Art niche, artists must have ideologies telling them what their artistic mission is, how to structure the Unifying Geometry of art, what appropriate subject matter is, and what sort of stylistic conventions to use. The ideologies in these slots dictate how to approach making Popular Art, just as the ideologies in these slots dictate how to approach making Fine Art. But, these slots have different ideologies in them in Popular Art and in Fine Art.

4. ARTISTIC MISSION

Popular Art and Expression Theory

Because Popular Art tends to be workshop art done for a particular purpose, like a greeting card, or illustration, there is less need for a sense of artistic mission than there is for Fine Art. Popular Art is not personally expressive. It tends to be professional art, done for money. So Expression Theory is not part of Popular Art ideology as it is for Fine Art. Popular Art has no use for an ideology that ties art to the personal biography of the artist. It is workshop art. Thus, in personal orientation to art, the Popular Artist and Fine Artist differ. Sometimes the same person can be making both Popular Art and Fine Art, and the difference between the arts they create is in part whether the art is personally expressive. When they are being personally expressive and making something original from their own inspiration they tend to be producing Fine Art, and when they are working on an assignment they tend to be producing Popular Art.

In general, Popular Art reflects the viewers' taste and values back to them. It does not express the personal taste or feeling of the artist. This means that often this sort of art is criticized by the Fine Art art world for being insincere since the artist is not projecting their own views but producing art that is calculated to affect the viewers in a certain way, and pander to the viewers' taste. For example, a horse is painted with big eyes to look cute; but the artist does not necessarily really feel the emotion projected; rather the cuteness is a constructed emotion calculated to be appealing (fig. 3.3). The Popular Artist is a technician skillfully manipulating the medium to make art that appeals to popular taste.

For Fine Art, true art is sincere. Sincerity for the Fine Art art world means that the artist expresses his or her own true ideas and emotions.

FIGURE **3.3** An example of highly calculated sentimental art: illustration of *Flutterby* by Robin James. The flying horse is painted to look cute, by having big eyes and eyelashes and so on. Because the artist is a technician, and most likely did not personally feel the emotion projected by the art, this sort of art is often thought of as insincere. Copyright © 1976 by Serendipity Communications. By permission of Price/Stern/Sloan, Inc. from *Flutterby* by Steven Cosgrove.

Because Fine Art tends to be made by individual artists expressing their personal orientation, this is a meaningful standard. But since Popular Art tends to be done by a group as an assignment to please popular taste, this standard is not appropriate.

Indeed, Popular Art completely misses the ideological problems caused by Expression Theory. Popular Artists don't think of themselves as wild and crazy. They tend to be technicians. There is no tradition of amateur artists or artists working out of a compulsion to paint. From the Freudian perspective, Popular Artists would not be neurotic since they are not painting personal fantasies. Popular Artists have not rejected the academic art skills the way that modernist Fine Artists did. Popular Artists work within the limitations of style and their success is not measured by their creativity. Thus, their art tends to be unoriginal because it is judged on how well it works. The images that have proven successful in the past are used again. There is no value in originality for the Popular Artist, since originality as such has no mass appeal.

Because Popular Art does not have a tradition of Expression Theory, sincere art is art that clearly communicates. It may be that the artist does not really feel what he or she is drawing, and the idea projected may be banal, trite, and generally unoriginal — like cute puppies in a basket (fig. 3.1), but if it communicates then it is sincere enough for popular taste. Thus, sincerity for popular taste means well-crafted professional-looking representational art. For popular taste, modern art looks insincere because it looks like it lacks skill. If the paint looks like paint, or the art is not representational, the response of popular taste is that the artist is probably cheating the viewer. The art is being made just for money and has no true value.

Popular Art and Imitation Theory

As workshop-crafted art, Popular Art continues the imitation tradition of the imitative-craft niche. Within imitation-theory ideology, the artistic mission for neoclassicism was to teach by pleasing and to please by teaching. This teaching was done through the representation of historical events and mythological themes. This was a modification of the imitation-theory goals of the imitative-craft niche before Fine Art, where the picturing function of craft was done with the mission of imitating reality, either through the realism of recognition of the medieval, or before that, the illusionistic realism of the classical Greeks.

Contemporary Popular Art has dropped all the intellectual pretensions of neoclassical imitation-theory. It is not trying to teach, but only to please. It continues the representational goals of crafted-art, but has given up appealing to the mind, and reason. Generally, Popular Art is meant to entertain, to stimulate emotion, or project sentimentality. All these things are really antithetical to intellectual goals. Whereas the Renaissance and then the Enlightenment artists needed to have a reason to make art, a way to see art as uplifting and worthy of the attention of the intellectual classes, there are no motives like that behind Popular Art. The Popular Artist wants to appeal to everyone, and so needs to make art that needs no education or intelligence to decipher. The mission of the Popular Artist is to make art that has mass appeal. Thus, the Popular Artist makes representational art because that art is most easily understood. Also, representational art is easier for an artist-technician to produce. It does not require inspiration or stylistic experimentation or excessive creativity. The art director can say: "Draw a rabbit eating a carrot in a cartoon style" and the artist knows what to do. The Popular Artist makes money by being good at making art that pleases a large audience. This tends to mean making clearly representational art which is entertaining, sentimental, or emotionally stimulating.

Stylistic Conventions

Popular Art has access to a wide range of techniques due to the progress in the West in the technology of art. Popular artists learn to use realism of recognition, and illusionistic realism. They can use images as symbols, like Christmas trees, and Easter bunnies, and they can make clear illusionistic realism. This range is open to them because they have access to the technology to do both from the pool of technology they share with Fine Art and the other visual arts in this culture. Also, most of the art broadcast over television and movies is this mass-audience entertainment Popular Art, and Popular Artists are using and expanding these most recent technologies for producing images. There are no tight stylistic restrictions for Popular Art as there have been in the various Fine Art movements. The only restrictions are that the art be clearly readable representational art that performs the mission of pleasing a mass audience. It should be entertaining, sentimental, or emotionally stimulating art. Within that limitation, the limitation provided by the containing institutions, distribution system, and workshops for production, the Popular Artists use whatever style works to perform the mission of Popular Art. The art objects tend to be judged by their mass appeal and the quantity sold.

Popular taste likes art that looks professionally done. The art that appeals to the popular taste gives the indication of being made by a professional displaying skills the viewers do not have. They don't want to see the artist or the art in the work, but only the depicted subject. Fine Art, on the other hand, is judged on its aesthetic form, creative uniqueness, meaning, or shockingness. All these criteria are irrelevant to judging Popular Art. Popular Art is not judged as art, but according to how well it works to do its intended job. Popular Art uses clichéd ideas and conventional style because they are what work. Popular art is clichéd art on purpose. The clichéd images are the images shared by the largest number of people. These are the images that people recognize without education in art or high culture. Sentimentality and vicarious experience works best in compositions that have no surprises, as we will discuss. The viewer is not supposed to notice the style of the art except as it reinforces the effect projected. Thus the mission of Popular Art is to produce art with mass appeal. The stylistic conventions used generally deliver clear representation which is narrative and sentimental, or emotionally stimulating.

5. APPROPRIATE SUBJECT MATTER

Popular Art continues the imitative-craft concerns for subject matter, but not all subject matter is considered appropriate. The sorts of things that are considered appropriate subject matter for Fine Art are not all considered appropriate for Popular Art. However, because there is generally no distinction made between these two arts, attempts are made to conform all subject matter to one standard of appropriateness.

Sexual Explicitness

For example, there was a controversy in Buffalo, New York, in 1984 about a sculpture called *Green Lightening* by Billy Lawless. The art was a parody of a carnival midway, or the streets of New York City, containing various figures from popular culture. It had an open steel framework which supported four Plexiglas boxes illuminated with neon, a circus-like arch, and decorated twirling stars. Surrounding all this were five earthbound lightning bolts which pointed skyward. The neon images that were superimposed upon the rest of the carnival structure were cartoonish renditions of male sex organs sporting top hats and canes. These figures were supposedly derived from the Mr. Peanut commercial logo (fig. 3.4). When the lighting system was turned on, these figures danced and did a hat-doffing bow across the front of the Plexiglas panels.

The mayor decided that the dancing neon figures in the sculpture were too pornographic to be put on display in front of the city. Within fifteen minutes of its having been turned on, he had wrecking crews come out and take it down (fig. 3.5). The city claimed that the artist misled them with his model which they claimed did not show the pornographic parts of the work; and they took the artist to court to have his statue removed from public land. The court ruled that the artist could go on exhibiting the piece on public land, but he had to keep it unlit, since when the sculpture was lit it became a "public menace." Finally in 1985 the work was moved to Chicago where people did not find it offensive.

FIGURE 3.4 The MR.
PEANUT logo that
inspired part of
Green Lightning by
Billy Lawless.
Copyright and
Trademark of
Nabisco, Inc.

Billy Lawless responded to critics who said that the work was too pornographic by retorting that it was less pornographic than the copy of Michelangelo's *David* (see fig. 2.4 on p. 49) which was in the Buffalo Delaware Park. In the Fine Art tradition, nudity in sculpture is quite common. The nudity of Michelangelo's *David* is an imitation of the nudity in classical Greek art. The nudity in classical statues reflected the Greek's love of male beauty and the commonness of nudity in their society. In the nearly two and a half millennia since classical Greece, nudity in public society has become not only uncommon but generally forbidden. This accounts for the difference in attitude between the Fine Artist and popular taste about nudity in art. The Fine Artist is making art that reflects and imitates the values of traditional Fine Art within which nudity has been common ever since the Greeks. Sometimes the nudes in Western Fine Art have been intended to shock their viewers for whom nudity is taboo, but again this was done in the context of a long tradition which has had statues of nudes. However, Popular Art reflects contemporary taste and is not made or valued in terms of the traditions of Fine Art. Popular Art is evaluated by contemporary standards of decency, and in contemporary society full frontal nudity is generally taboo in public, and so it is also considered taboo in art. Thus, the attitude toward nudity in art is very different for Popular Art and Fine Art, because Fine Art is evaluated as art in terms of a long historical tradition, whereas Popular Art is not evaluated as art, but instead in terms of the subject matter projected and contemporary standards.

Another example of art which was disturbing for its sexual explicit-

DANCING DOGBONES — For a brief and shining moment this autumn, sculptor Billie Lawless's "Green Lightning" made a singular contribution to Buffalo art history. Officials at the unveiling — struck by their own lightning bolts of recognition — quickly pulled the plug. The sculptor suggested the dancing neon figures must be dogbones, or, hey, anything else you might want to see in them, but Mayor Griffin saw red, and two of the panels were cut down before the courts intervened.

FIGURE 3.5 Tom Toles cartoon appearing in *Buffalo News*, 1984, about the mayor's decision to order wrecking crews to take down *Green Lightning* by Billy Lawless on the grounds that it was too pornographic to display. (Toles copyright 1984 The Buffalo News. Reprinted with permission of *Universal Press Syndicate*. All rights reserved.)

ness was the photographs of Robert Mapplethorpe in 1989. Mapplethorpe, who died of AIDS, made a series of homoerotic and sadomasochistic photos, and also photographs of nude children. These photographs, along with a photograph by Andres Serrano which depicted a crucifix partially submerged in urine, were shocking enough to popular taste that an amendment was proposed to the National Endowment for the Arts, which had funded Mapplethorpe and Serrano, to ban all federal funding for obscene art, or art that denigrates people or beliefs.

This amendment, proposed by a Republican from North Carolina, Senator Jesse Helms, expressed the popular taste sentiment about what sort of art ought not to be produced, or at least should not receive federal funding. It read that the federal government ought not to fund any art that depicts sado-masochism, homoeroticism, the exploitation of children, or individuals engaged in sexual acts. Further, the Helms amendment banned any funding for art that denigrates the objects or beliefs of any "religion or non-religion," or that debases people on the basis of race, creed, sex, handicap, age, or national origin. Although this amendment did not pass, the NEA grants were consequently restricted to art which was not obscene or offensive, and funding was tightened. Some artists were even required to sign a pledge not to use the funding for art that might be judged obscene. In the Fine Art context, the art of Mapplethorpe and Serrano was not really that controversial. It fit into the mainstream of expressive art, and in the case of Serrano, of avant-garde art. However, for popular taste, federal money should not go to art that insults Christianity, or to obscene art — and homoerotic art is *de facto* judged obscene.

The Helms amendment was an attempt by consumers of Popular Art to ban the display of Fine Art. People are unaware that there are really two kinds of art here, and they use Popular Art standards to judge quality in Fine Art. People with popular taste do not see why they should pay for art that they themselves do not consume. As can be seen by the list of items banned, popular taste is looking through art at subject matter. It wishes to ban anything in art that would be inappropriate in polite society. In polite society people do not display their sex acts, and so according to popular taste they should not be displayed in art either. For popular taste pictures like Mapplethorpe's homoerotic photographs are not art objects to be contemplated for their aesthetic form and cultural value; rather they are reacted to first and foremost as photographs of naked homosexuals. Art is not approached as a comment on life, or as something outside life, but as something within life.

On similar grounds, people objected to three bronze figures put up in the South Bronx, in September 1991, because they were thought to project unfavorable stereotypes of African Americans (fig. 3.6). One statue, they said, looked like a drug pusher, while another looked fat and lazy, and another they thought looked zombie-like and on crack (Collins, 1992). They found these statues objectionable enough to have them removed within a week of their being erected, even though they were in a clear representational style, and had been cast from people in the neighborhood. This shows again that people with popular taste judge art by standards having nothing to do with art, but only with the subject matter portrayed.

FIGURE 3.6 Three bronze figures by John Ahearn put up in the South Bronx in September 1991. They were removed within a week of being erected because people thought they projected unfavorable stereotypes of African Americans.

Non-representational Art

Generally there is competition between the Fine Art art world and popular taste over public art. Although the mass media are dominated by Popular Art, people complain that public art, sculpture mainly, but also murals, ought to reflect popular taste. People outside the art world have generally not liked modern art since its introduction into the United States in 1913. They do not like non-representational art and generally complain about Fine Art being shown outside the museum context. An example of the conflict between the Fine Art art world and popular taste over non-representational art is the case in 1979 where Richard Serra received a federal commission for $175,000 from a program called "Art-in-Architecture" to create a sculpture for a circular plaza in front of the Jacob K. Javits Federal Building in Manhattan. He completed the project in 1981. He made a minimalist seventy-three ton curved steel wall, twelve feet high, and one hundred twenty feet long entitled *Tilted Arc*. This wall bisected the plaza and over time it acquired rust, and graffiti. The federal workers who had to look at it day after day thought it looked like industrial debris (Malcolm, 1986).

Thirteen hundred federal workers who worked in and around the plaza signed a petition to have the Serra work removed. The Washington agency that ran "Art-in-Architecture" held a hearing, and after three days of testimony, recommended that the piece be removed. Rosalind Krauss defended the sculpture by explaining the artistic intention behind it. She said (Malcolm, 1986, p. 66) : ". . . this sculpture is constantly mapping a kind of projectile of the gaze that starts at one end of Federal Plaza, and, like the embodiment of the concept of visual perspective, maps the path across the plaza that the spectator will take." Many people from the modern art world came to the hearing to testify in defense of the sculpture, saying that it brought the opportunity to the working people there to be confronted with, and challenged by, minimalist art. Minimalist art is intentionally tasteless and meaningless. So, from the perspective of the art world, the art was a success.

The main objection to the sculpture was that it so radically changed the space of the plaza. The plaza became an extension of the sculpture, and so it became an issue of whether the people would have this huge piece of minimalist sculpture or whether they would have a plaza where they could just sit outside around picnic tables and eat lunch.

The museum is a different sort of context for art. There people go to see art and be challenged to think about the big issues outside of daily life. They are not working, they are leaving life to go see these works. There, as Fine Art, a large intentionally tasteless metal wall might be interesting. Museum viewers would be curious about it, and use their minds to investigate. Disturbing minimalist art is appropriate for the museum. However when people look out their office window, they don't want to be challenged. They are more likely to want something which makes them feel light, something easy to look at as they gaze upon it, thinking about work. Surely the workers would have had no problem with a fountain or decorative sculpture; it was the aggressiveness with which the *Tilted Arc* completely dominated their space and its lack of any relation to life that disturbed them: it looked like a piece of industrial debris to them.

Thus, popular taste objects to Fine Art outside the museum context. The masses want to see public art that does the same sorts of things for them that Popular Art does. Art should be representational. Subject matter in Popular Art is judged by the same standards it would be judged by outside art. Although movies and television show intimate moments that would be counted inappropriate in public, public sculpture and murals should not. Public art, according to popular taste should not be disturbing but soothing.

6. THE POWERS OF POPULAR ART

Incompatibility of Sentimentality and Aesthetic Attitude

The division between popular taste and the taste of the art world and its patrons is not arbitrary. The mutual exclusivity of Fine Art and Popular Art has to do with the incompatibility of sentimentality and the aesthetic attitude. This incompatibility is both a difference in the mental posture of the viewer to each kind of art, as well as a difference in how the geometry of the art is read.

There are three different and often mutually exclusive ways to read the visual geometry of art. Art can be read as projecting an illusory realism, or a realism of recognition, or aesthetic form. For example, a drawing of a big man and two little men can be interpreted in three different and mutually exclusive ways (fig. 3.7). The relative sizes of these "people" can be interpreted as indicating 3-D perspective — the big man is closer in space to the front of the picture and the little men are farther away. Alternatively, the relative sizes can be interpreted as depicting a conceptual relationship between depicted people — the big man is more important than the little men and so is drawn to look bigger. A third way in which the relative sizes can be interpreted is aesthetically. Under this interpretation, the relative sizes have nothing to do with the relationships between depicted people, but have to do with the relationships between the shapes themselves — the big shape as shape is being contrasted with the small shapes around it.

While it is possible once you realize that there are these various interpretations to see them all, one after another, usually people only see art in one way and suppress other possible interpretations. Also, artists select one of these interpretations to reinforce with the other aspects of the geometry of the picture space, effectively inhibiting other interpretations than the one that they intend.

Fine Art since the Cezanne revolution has emphasized the aesthetic interpretation of art. As discussed in the last chapter, aesthetic interpretation of art reinforces a disinterestedness in the viewer, and is the primary power of Fine Art. Fine Art gives its viewers disinterested pleasure and intellectual challenges.

Popular taste does not see the aesthetic form in art. As a midwestern art editor, Richard Campbell (1984), wrote to complain about a minimalist sculpture that was put up in the Columbus, Ohio, Airport:

FIGURE 3.7 The relative difference in size between these three men could be read as indicating different locations in space, difference in relative importance, or as difference for aesthetic purpose.

"The one called *Crossings,* by Athena Tacha, . . . consists of multi-colored pipes meandering around a nicely planted area. You may think a plumber made some kind of mistake. But the lady sculptor got $25,000 for it."

Another artwork called *Observation* he describes as "concrete circles with some free-form pieces of concrete on top of each circle" for which the sculptor was paid $25,000. The editor continues to say that there should be signs put up around such artworks saying that "This is art" so that people know the art is not just "construction goofs."

Those with popular taste don't see the aesthetic form in art at all. The writer is not "disinterested." He does not approach the art with an aesthetic attitude. He cannot see the art because he sees "multicolored pipes" in the plants, not horizontal streaks of red and blue and yellow against vertical patterns of green. He does not see "art" since he looks with a "what-is-it?" frame of mind.

To see aesthetic form the viewer needs to contemplate the work of art without functional real life involvement with its subject matter. One must be disinterested to see the beauty in art. If we care what the picture is a picture of, then we are looking at it in a judgmental and purposeful way. If it is supposed to be a tiger, we look to see if it really looks like a tiger, and our pleasure in its beauty is muted by the need to make that judgment. We look for features in the picture that tell if it is indeed what it is supposed to be, rather than looking for pleasing rhythms or balanced forms. When we look at art, we can actively engage our minds with the art object in ways that we are not free to do with things in real life. We are free to look for aesthetic patterns, where in real life we are tied to looking for things like tooth and claw. Maintaining the sort of objectivity required for this perspective on art means maintaining a mind-set that is rational and detached. As we said in chapter 2, the role of aesthetic form for the culture is to help maintain a mind-set conducive to reason and theory making.

Those with popular taste look at the subject matter in art as though it were life. They approach art with a "what-is-it?" real life engagement. This means that they cannot see aesthetic form and cannot understand non-representational art. As the Columbus, Ohio, art editor remarks (Campbell, 1981): "Representational art, you understand, means that the viewer has some idea of what, if anything, the artist had in mind. There are many examples of paintings and sculptures around which make it obvious the artist had nothing in mind but the price tag." Notice that the writer does not consider aesthetic form as what the artist might have had in mind. Unless the artist makes the art representational, the assumption is that the artist did not have anything in mind at all. Popular taste does not stand back from the subject matter, but takes art literally. A picture of cute puppies is not art for those with popular taste, it is just "cute puppies." One can feel, "Aah, how cute!" whenever one wants to in relation to the image. The picture acts as a stimulant for emotion, or for narrative thinking. Those with popular taste do not look at the art, but through it. Thus, popular taste is completely blind to aesthetic form.

The values that Popular Art gives its viewers instead of aesthetic form are sentimentality and vicarious experience. Of these, sentimentality is closer to an aesthetic value. For example, the art of professional illustrator Norman Rockwell is a great favorite with popular taste because of its sentimental tone (fig. 3.8). One of his paintings shows a family around the Thanksgiving dinner table with the father about to carve the turkey. Another painting shows a scene at a doctor's office, with the boy holding his arm out bravely but with his head turned away and flinching as the doctor gives him a routine back-to-school shot. Generally Rockwell's work shows patriotism, like the picture of a Boy Scout saluting with the unfurled American flag flying at his back. These images are shown on calendars and postcards, and even on things like serving trays and placemats.

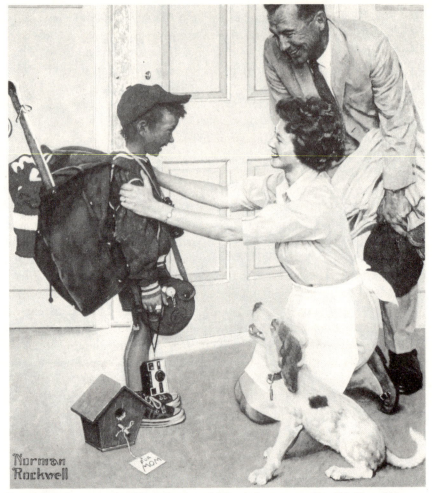

FIGURE 3.8 An example of Popular Art which reinforces narrative thinking: Norman Rockwell, *Home from Camp* ©1968 Top Value Stamps. The viewer is given all the clues needed to vicariously experience a complete story. Details like the Bandaid on one of the little boy's fingers, the dog, and the present for Mom make the experience a sentimental one.

This sort of art sentimentalizes our world. It makes things look human. It reminds us of the small things of domestic life. It puts the world on the right scale. Television news shows us great terrible events — wars, famines, natural disasters — but when we look at the wall and see a picture of a Thanksgiving meal, or of cute puppies, or see a ceramic Dutch girl on the kitchen windowsill, we feel connected with the emotions of small-scale domesticity. These feelings are from everyday life, and they are enhanced and exaggerated in the art.

To appreciate sentimentality we must look through the art at the subject depicted. Sentimentality is an emotion about a subject. To appreciate aesthetic form we must look at the surface of art, not at the subject matter. This is why people in the Fine Art art world cannot see sentimentality. The values in sentimental art come from the feelings we have about the depicted subject matter, not from the formal qualities of the art object.

In this way, Popular Art has taken the opposite direction from that taken by Fine Art in the revolution against neoclassicism. After Cezanne, Fine Art became increasingly seen as art about art. The distinction between art and life broke down with Duchamp and his ready-mades in that life began to look more and more like art. In art for popular taste, the distinction between art and life also breaks down but for the opposite reason. For popular taste, art is not seen as art, but as life.

The Fine Art art world is blind to the sentimentality of Popular Art, and those with popular taste are blind to the aesthetic form of art, because they take different perceptual postures to art, and read meaning off of different levels of the visual geometry. Fine Art gives the viewer disinterested pleasure, Popular Art gives the viewer interested pleasure. Consumers of Fine Art have an aesthetic attitude, they are disinterested. The person with popular taste is engaged in the subject matter and hence not disinterested. This is the essential difference between them. It is the disinterested posture that makes challenging art unthreatening to the elite, and allows them to get satisfaction from art. For example, it is because they can stand back from subject matter that the Fine Art art world was not shocked at Mapplethorpe's sado-masochistic and homo-erotic art; and it was because they only see subject matter that popular taste was so shocked by it. Where the art world saw photographic line and form, popular taste saw kinky sex. This difference in perceptual posture lies at the heart of their inability to enjoy each other's art.

The difference in perceptual posture means that these arts are supporting different mental states in their viewers. The consumers of the different arts approach life with different attitudes. Popular Art explores the viewer's ability to merge art and life, while Fine Art encourages the viewer's ability to stand away from life and view things objectively.

Using Art for Vicarious Experience

Since the romantic era the boundary between life and art has broken down, and so now the viewers can see themselves in the hero's shoes and see themselves as hero (Hauser, 1985). The modern viewers of soap operas on television, or romance movies, for example, see in the heroes a fulfillment of their own lives. By identifying with fictional characters, the viewers find the realization of experiences that they have missed. This is unlike the way in which people related to Renaissance art, for example. In Renaissance art, we are looking through a window at a scene as though it was in real space. Popular Art is not something seen distantly through a window; you see yourself in the art, or vicariously experience the art's emotional tone.

For example, one of the buyers at a "starving-artist-sale" in Buffalo, New York, said that she wanted a placid seascape where she could imagine that she is walking along the beach, or standing in the depicted water. Another buyer said that she wanted a summer mountain scene and winter mountain scene so that in the winter she can look at the summer scene, and in the summer at the winter scene. Another buyer wanted to imagine herself standing in a scene with mist-shrouded mountains and pretend that her feet are on the bank of the water in the foreground, or that she is bathing in the pictured water (Huntington, 1986).

Those with popular taste allow themselves to make fully formed images in response to art. They let their concepts construct a complete scene of whatever the artist depicted. The conventionality of these images plays a role for them. Since they have seen what is depicted in the art before, it is easy for them to imagine themselves relating to it as if it were a scene in real life. This art is conventionalized and stylized so that individuality is completely lacking. The fact that this art is not new or creative doesn't bother popular taste at all. In fact, people like the comfortable familiarity of the conventional image, and its complete conventionality facilitates their engagement with the subject matter so as to have a vicarious experience. Doing this with an unconventional image would be more difficult.

Those with popular taste imagine themselves in the art work and vicariously experience the associated emotions. With Popular Art people undergo a vicarious experience which takes them away from the world, or they feel a vicarious experience that reinforces their domestic sentiments and sense of themselves in their own lives. In both cases, it lets them feel a desired emotion, and vicariously experience either another world or their own world sweetened. They undertake a form of visual thought. This way of using art reinforces narrative thinking.

For example, on a Norman Rockwell calendar, distributed by Mary Jane Carr Realtors in Columbus, Ohio, the picture for June is of a little boy just home from camp (fig. 3.8). A few sentences, placed to the side of the art describe the sentiment in the art. Under the art are the slogan and logo of the Realtor. Below that is the calendar itself.

The picture shows a boy, mother, father, and dog in front of a front door. The figures in the art make a circle. The center of the picture space is between the mother and boy. This focuses our attention on that relationship, the mother and her child. As we think our way around the circle of figures, a story unfolds. The boy is balanced against the parents and dog. His backpack and birdhouse form a visual line with the open door. We surmise that he is either coming in or going out. The father wears his coat and hat, he must have been outside with the boy — the father brought him home. The mother has her apron on. She must have been home, perhaps in the kitchen, and has come to the door with the dog. The note on the birdhouse reads "For Mom," so the boy must have just come home from camp where he made a birdhouse which he is giving to his mother. Rockwell gives the viewer all the clues needed to see a complete story, and just in case the viewer didn't catch it, Rockwell writes it beside the art. "Home from camp," begin the words that propagandize the sentiment in this particular painting. The Unifying Geometry of the art is used to reinforce the story relationships in the art.

The art is sentimental. Everyone feels good, even the dog. They are a happy family. The image includes all sorts of small significant details that make the space sentimental: the camera, the Bandaid on one of the little boy's fingers, the present for mom, the dog, and the smiles. There is nothing disturbing in the art. A complete story emerges from the art. The art communicates by relating directly and predictably to all our expectations. We read the art without allegory, the art is not a comment on anything, it doesn't mean anything.

Looking at the art when we look at the calendar in June, we think about summer vacation for the children. Maybe we think about sending the children to camp. Maybe we think about how the dog loves the boy in the picture, and maybe we should get our boy a dog. The pictured experience is so specific that we can find our own experiences there. The art acts as a stimulant to thoughts about domestic issues, and we smile when we see it.

Paintings of idealized family life and outdoor scenes could help in narrative thinking about domestic life. A Norman Rockwell print of the little boy at the doctor's office might help narrate the viewer's own trip with the children to the doctor. The viewer can think through what happened, and what they should feel, as they narrate the story with themselves in it but with the Norman Rockwell sentimentalized tone. This is not catharsis because the emotions aroused are not purged. It is a walk through a simulated experience. The emotions of the viewer are guided by the emotional tone of the art. As the viewer leaves the art he or she can carry its emotions into life. It is an emotional stimulant. This ability to use art to have a vicarious experience is the main power of this art. Popular art allows the viewer to have an assisted daydream in response to art.

Art made for popular taste is made for people who think dominantly through narration. That is, they think through a situation by imagining themselves as the central player and in that way they can understand it. They think by imagining themselves walking through a scene. They rehearse their actions. Popular art is made to make such narration easy. The art helps give spatial illusion to inner narration. People project themselves into the art and then allow it to guide and focus a waking dream. The viewers imagine themselves as the hero of the romance; they imagine themselves walking in the water pictured in the landscape; they look at Norman Rockwell's art and think about their children's summer vacation. The art is used to focus and visualize the viewer's private thoughts of themselves in the situation projected in the art. This way of relating to art is inhibited by theoretical and logical thinking. To relate to art in this way means an acceptance of the depicted scene not as a painting, but as the scene depicted. To relate to art in this way, people do not think about the scene, they feel themselves part of the scene. The thinking stimulated by art made for popular taste is not about ideas, history, aesthetics, or art. It is not rational, objective, or deductive thought. It stimulates thoughts about the self, or it gives people the opportunity to escape from themselves and their lives through a completely engaging art experience. Movies and television allow viewers to watch dangerous, fantastic, and grotesque events at a safe distance. They further allow viewers entrance to intimate space, to see someone else at close range in their living room and bedroom. Viewers can escape their own physical reality by mentally projecting themselves into the art.

This way of relating to art has been greatly enhanced by the technology of the mass media and is exploited by advertising, as we will discuss. Indeed, there is a growing computer technology to enhance this effect, namely the technology of *virtual reality*. With video games, people can interact with images on the screen. They can cause movement and change in the image by pushing a button or moving a joystick. Virtual reality takes that interaction one step further; one can interact with objects in a three-dimensional space — one can be inside a projected world. Currently, this is done by having the viewer wear gloves, earphones, and glasses which are wired into computers so as to change the image when the viewer moves. This gives the illusion of a deep space, in which one can move around and can manipulate objects. These capacities are being used to search through computer data visually, and to train the military with elaborate battle simulations (Peterson, 1992). These technical developments enhance the power of Popular Art to give vicarious experiences and focus narrative thought. It enhances our ability to imagine ourselves inside the art and personally identify with moving art images as though they were our own selves. This is the power of video games, virtual reality and simulations. Through these technologies the user experiences art as life as realistically as possible, but leaving out the physical consequences of things in life. We can have virtual reality battles where no one is really killed, and virtual reality romantic encounters without physical contact. The video image does not leave its machine. A mental world is created, and we dream.

The mental response to television, movies, and other Popular Art is passive. It is like absorbing daydreams produced by someone else. The images it projects are then in our memory store of images, undifferentiated from images of things we have personally experienced. Thus, the movie or television image enters our minds as an experience in the world outside art. Much advertising is built on that idea. Advertisers want you to remember their product as though you already use it. It is familiar, so when you shop you will recognize it and buy it. Television images are inherently believable as real life experiences even though they are really carefully constructed art images. We have to educate ourselves to be skeptical about them. There are many who use the information they get from television to help them handle things in their own lives. They imitate the things they see in television drama; behavior is affected. We imitate the behavior we have seen and vicariously experienced. We make no distinction between vicarious experience on television and personal experience outside art. Popular Art affects our actions outside art through this power of vicarious experience.

7. POPULAR ART AS THE VANGUARD OF CULTURE

Popular Art as Cultural Niche

Both Fine Art and Popular Art serve the same broad function, as we have discussed. In that sense they are similar. They are both appreciated just for their effect on our mind. Because of this they can potentially be substituted for each other, except that their institutional structures and ideologies make each type of art best suited to serve the needs and markets of its own niche. The ideological categories which Popular Art has in common with Fine Art are filled in with different ideologies. The artistic mission of Popular Art is filled with an imitation theory ideology to please a mass audience with representational art. Stylistically, Popular Art should be representational and narrative. It should look professionally done, and conform to viewer expectations. Unifying Geometry is used to enhance sentimentality or other emotion, and narrative meanings. This requires a posture in the viewer just the opposite of that required to see aesthetic form. The appropriateness of subject matter for Popular Art is judged by contemporary standards of decency. If people are not seen nude in public society, then public statues of them should also not be nude. For popular taste, public art should be soothing, not disturbing.

The powers of Popular Art and Fine Art represent a pole with the aesthetic on one end and sentimentality on the other. This polarity is based in the compositional geometry of art and how it can be made to affect the visual processes of the viewer. If we concentrate on seeing Fine Art aesthetics, we reinforce rational, objective, detached thinking. If we concentrate on having a Popular Art vicarious experience, or feeling sentimental, then we reinforce emotional engagement, and narrative thought. It is possible for there to be two art niches where objects have no other function than to present an image to be appreciated not because there are different classes so much as because there are two mutually exclusive postures to hold when appreciating art.

Combining these ideologies allows Popular Art institutions to deliver art for the mass audience. Popular Art with these ideologies has developed the powers of giving its viewers vicarious experience and enhanced emotion. Whereas Fine Art is in old age and decline, Popular Art is at its peak of maturity. Popular Art is where Fine Art was during the Enlightenment. It has firm ideologies that are well adapted for delivering its kind of art. There are no ambiguities about its mission. When people look at it they know what sort of effect to expect and are not disappointed.

Beyond the function of being appreciated, Popular Art also serves a Design Art function by being decorative. People use Popular Art for decoration as well as for its Popular Art effect. Norman Rockwell paintings adorn placemats and serving trays. Disney cartoon figures are put onto children's clothing, and there are Mickey Mouse watches. Starving-artist-sale art hangs on people's walls and matches the colors in the furniture. Not only can we look through the surface of the art at some subject matter, but the surface of the art itself becomes part of the Design Art products, as we will discuss in the next chapter.

Advertising uses Popular Art to sell products. Advertising uses a sentimental or sensationalized narrative of Popular Art to convey a story about the use of a product. We see sentimental pictures of a grandmother serving brand-name lemonade to grandpa who is sitting in a rocking chair on the front porch of a traditional house looking out on a small town front yard. On television an advertisement shows a woman arguing with her husband, a dog stealing the dinner she just cooked, and her children shouting and fighting, and then she takes a brand-name head-ache pill to relieve her tension headache. Where Popular Art just pro-jects viewers back at themselves, advertising inserts a message. Thus, both Design Art and advertising use Popular Art to enhance their own effects and fulfill their own artistic missions.

The Vanguard of Culture

We have discussed that Fine Art is not at the vanguard of current culture. It is Popular Art, Design Art, and advertising that are. These three arts receive the most cultural energy and economic support, and are intimately involved in the shaping of our everyday lives. We sit in Design Art chairs, eating popcorn in Design Art dishes, to watch Popu-lar Art television shows interrupted every few minutes with advertising art. These arts reinforce each other and shape our world physically and mentally.

Popular Art plays an important part of that shaping, by facilitating the viewers' projection of themselves into art. Popular Art makes a group-mind possible. It facilitates us taking the images we see on televi-sion as our very own thoughts. These images are the very own thoughts of thousands of other people simultaneously. We all think together. Then we use those shared thoughts as the metaphorical structure through which to discuss events with others. These thoughts are vicarious experi-ences that we carry with us in memory as though they were something we had experienced outside art.

In this way the power of Popular Art to give us vicarious experi-ences expands our mental capacities in an important way. It gives us a mind-set which opens a new external mental space for us to use through television and computers. It allows us to use our artifacts to expand our minds. The television has fantasies for us, the computer does our income tax. We use these artifacts to do some of our thinking for us. Popular Art helps this by facilitating our projection of ourselves into the mass-media images so that they become our own thoughts. The narrative thinking which Popular Art promotes is not more advanced than the rational thought promoted by Fine Art aesthetics. Indeed, just the opposite is true. Narrative thought is more primitive than rational thought in the sense that it is like the thought ways of non-literate and pre-scientific cultures, as we will discuss in chapter 6.

Popular Art is part of the vanguard of culture even though it is unoriginal and merely reflects the viewers' attitudes back at them. It is not because of its subject matter or the values it projects that Popular Art is in the vanguard of culture. It is part of the vanguard because it helps us invest our artifacts with mind. It lets us expand our minds into television and computers.

CHAPTER 4

The Design Art Cultural Niche

THE INDUSTRIAL REVOLUTION AND the growth of technology have brought great changes in art. Along with technology came the development of movies, television, the print media, and the mass market. Popular Art developed with these new media, and Design Art developed with the mass market. Design Art tends to be art made by machines for the mass market. It is the art of the manufactured items that we buy. It is the fashion of our clothes, the houses we live in, the furniture we sit on, the dishes we eat off of, and the design of the television set on which we watch Popular Art. Sometimes designers only make the look of the product, other times they play the role of engineers or of advertisers. Design Art is the design of the products and machines that comprise much of the material culture of modern life.

The distribution system of Design Art is the mass market. The production of Design Art is institutionalized by the systems of manufacturing, machines, and factories. The Design Artist tends to be an anonymous team member working in a workshop setting, and tends to be educated in schools of art and design with popular and Fine Artists. The ideologies of design must evolve within the constraints of these institutions. The ideologies and institutions must be able to educate artists who can make art of this sort.

Design is relatively new. It is still forming its ideologies and institutions. As we will discuss, in many ways design is at the point equivalent to where Fine Art was during the Renaissance. When we look at design as a cultural niche we see that it is just forming. We do not see a mature cultural niche with ideologies all in place, like Popular Art has. Certainly we do not see a niche in old age and decline the way that Fine Art is. What we see are influences and tendencies. Some of the ideology is fixed for now, but some of it is unformed. We can still see birth forces shaping what Design Art will become.

The birth ideologies of design come first of all from craft. Design Art replaced craft, and carries some of the same concerns as craft since it is also making useful objects. However, the needs it satisfies are broader than those that had been satisfied by craft. Just as Fine and Popular Art continued some of the orientation of imitative craft, Design Art also carries some of the concerns and ideological orientations of non-imitative craft.

1. THE NEED FOR DESIGN ART

The ancestor of the Design Arts is craft. During the Greek period, art was not separated from other types of creating from a plan. Art and craft were united. But during the Renaissance, as we discussed, the arts and crafts were separated. Crafts continued to be made in workshops and in village homes in traditional ways, passed down through an oral tradition.

With the advent of the Industrial Revolution, however, the crafts tradition changed. The objects and tools that people used in everyday life now were produced by manufacturers. By the middle of the nineteenth century, Europeans could afford to have manufactured items in their homes. There was a dramatic drop in the cost of ceramics and textiles. This meant that many items which had been made by craftsmen, like crockery and cloth goods, were now cheaper to buy from a mass manufacturer than they were to hand make (Garvan, 1967). With the progress of the Industrial Revolution, isolated rural communities which had been the market for crafts, slowly disappeared. People's tastes changed with exposure to manufactured items so that they wanted things that were modeled in a style after those manufactured goods. This also had a negative impact on handicraft. Not only could items be bought that before had been made, but also items could be bought that had previously not been available at all to the lower levels of society. The lower class could enjoy many of the comforts of middle-class life. Before the Industrial Revolution, people's homes consisted of all-purpose rooms with very little furniture. After the Industrial Revolution, there was great availability of discarded high-style furniture. People's homes changed to cluttered single function rooms with well-stuffed furniture, richly colored walls, and elaborately carpeted floors. These rooms were often filled with paintings and elaborate curtains, all of which had now become cheap and available due to mass manufacturing, rapid transportation, and mass communication (Garvan, 1967).

Thus, with the impact of the Industrial Revolution, the craft traditions for making things for domestic use were overcome by the values and products of the manufacturers. The products of the Industrial Revolution dominated crafts products. This was the beginning of Design Art. Design became the art involved in making manufactured products. Although there continued to be small pockets of crafts and folk arts done here and there, they mostly died out. At the end of the nineteenth century, the urban artist and manufacturers took over some of the folk patterns so as to introduce them to the elite as purity of design, thus making manufactured items that looked just like the hand-crafted ones. These items even more directly competed with the handicrafts.

Further, manufacturers began making machines for domestic use. Vacuum cleaners, washing machines, and sewing machines were invented and sold, with the thought of rationalizing labor at home the same way it had been rationalized in the factory. Such things saved labor for the housewife. Along with that, the invention of things like canning for food goods, and store-bought clothes, made earlier craft skills used for ordinary domestic life obsolete. No one needed to know how to can, sew, or hand wash, and so on, anymore; one could buy products that would do it all.

The need for Design Art was born. The Industrial Revolution created a need for consumer items. Mass-produced items made a middle-class lifestyle possible, and people forgot their craft skills. So people needed cheap products to substitute for the crafted things they used before. Also they needed domestic machines that now did their domestic work. These needs created a market, or a demand to be filled. Just as popular taste is the need for which Popular Art is made, these needs for products are the needs for which Design Art is made. These are the needs that support the niche Design Art. The general function of Design Art is to make useful objects fulfilling these needs. Because these needs are new, a result of changes brought on by the Industrial Revolution, Design Art is new. The institutions of Design Art support a niche to satisfy these needs. That is, institutions are created to educate artists to Design Art of this sort, and to make and distribute the final art products.

2. THE IDEOLOGIES OF CRAFT

Decorative Designs

In crafts the nature of the materials is very important. The nature of the material sets constraints on what forms can be used. Certain shapes are natural for stone, others for wood, and still others for metal, and so on. Decorative motifs arise in part as ways to bring out the beauty of the materials, the grain in the wood, or shine of metal. They also show off the virtuosity of the craftsman. They allow the craftsman to play with the materials and enjoy the process of working with them by skillfully embellishing the functional form. Craft motifs tend to be designed to be physically pleasurable to produce. The physical process of putting a spiral into a pot on a potter's wheel, or sculpting curls onto a wooden implement, for example, is pleasurable. The creativity is in the workmanship not in the invention of the decorative motifs, so craftsmen tend to use traditional patterns which are then skillfully worked into the material being used. Because the decorative design and functional form are traditional, it is easy to judge quality in such work. One can see if the motif has been skillfully rendered because one knows what would count as a mistake and what counts as virtuosity. Thus, the craftsmen can perfect their skill, since there are clear standards for what is good and what is not. The craftsman knows what the surfaces should look like and feel like, and further, other craftsmen know what is hard and easy, and the craftsman then creates within that range.

Preliterate people tend to ascribe definite meaning to the decorative designs on objects they use. The designs are not *just* decoration, with merely an aesthetic function. The designs are more like pictographs. Sometimes the designs mark ownership of property, or the identity of the user, denoting paternity, rank, or vocation. Some designs are good luck designs, or magical patterns like those on weapons or ships meant to protect the users or to enliven the item with the spiritual power of a totem animal or entity (Miles, 1963). For example, in the folk arts of the Indians of North America we find dug-out canoes which are painted with animal forms. The painted animal forms invoke spiritual protection. Often, the designs are symbolic renditions of stories, or are especially suited for being a part in some ritual. We have similar decorative patterns used in our own Western culture, for example: the evergreen tree pictures in December accompanying the Christmas rituals, or the rabbit and egg pictures on items in the spring accompanying Easter festivals.

FIGURE 4.1 An example of geometrical style on archaic Greek pottery: *Geometric Amphoria,* dipylon style, Athenian eighth century B.C. Its simple geometric patterns were mere echoes of the elaborate pictorial symbolism of the art of the great ancient civilizations behind it. Drawing after the piece in Metropolitan Museum of Art, New York, Rogers Fund, 1910.

Like these, the decorative motifs on items throughout history have also contained highly condensed symbolic motifs for ritual.

Highly formalized design work is often the result of a degenerated tradition, where a once meaningful pattern is repeated long after its meaning has been lost. Times in history which are dominated by these sorts of formalized patterns tend to coincide with cultural upheavals and social unrest (Christie, 1969). In such times, craftspeople imitate cultural patterns which are no longer clear and alive. The patterns continue to be imitated because they are part of remembered patterns long after their true meaning has been forgotten. Just as most of us no longer know why rabbits bring eggs at Easter, or why the evergreen tree is important at Christmas, we still decorate with those motifs in our celebrations. After a while, a decorative pattern is no longer constrained by living cultural meanings, and becomes an empty pleasing pattern with more of the meaningful extras of the pattern erased and only the geometrical bare bones left behind. This was the state of archaic Greek pottery, for example. It has a "geometric" style (fig. 4.1). Its simple geometric patterns merely echo the elaborate pictorial symbolism of the art of the great ancient civilizations behind it. Thus, from the perspective of craft, decoration is not just for beauty, it also adds to the use value of the crafted item, by adding meaning or spirituality to the other functions of the object.

FIGURE 4.2 Victorian decorated
machine, an ornamental turning
lathe, *Rose engine*, built c.1750. Here
we see the decorative motifs of craft
being imitated on the machine.
Drawing after piece in Science
Museum, London.

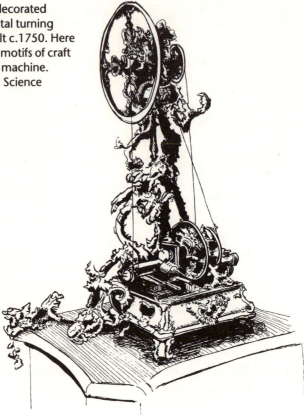

The Decorated Machine

The relationship between decoration and functional form is not a problem for the crafts tradition as it is for the designer. The biggest conflict
for the ideologies merging to make the design cultural niche was about
the role of decoration. There were no clear standards, or sense of what
sorts of designs fit the new materials and shapes of machines.

At first European manufacturers felt compelled by their own sense
of aesthetics and also by the aesthetics of the users of the goods, to
imitate the decorative motifs of craft in the manufactured goods and even
in the machines that did the manufacture (Mumford, 1962). For example, some Victorian designers embellished their machines with Doric
columns, or put floral decorations on them (fig. 4.2), or even put ornamental holes into the iron frameworks of their new structures. Workmen

transferred the patterns from one set of design solutions and technology to another different technology. This sort of transfer is common in decoration. Even the Bronze Age metalworkers were motivated by a similar desire for mimicry as they put lines on the sockets of their ax-heads which imitated the binding-thongs that Stone Age artisans had used to secure their tools to the hafts (Christie, 1969).

The Victorian designer divided the object to be designed into two parts; one designed for mechanical efficiency, and the other designed for looks that imitated the crafted looks of folk products. These were the patterns that were known and could be judged for quality. The decoration on the Victorian machine was not flat, nor was it integrated with the functional form. The Victorian designer made a machine and then put the decoration on top. The design of the decoration matched the style of current architecture and furniture.

The problem for the designers making these new machines and designing the new machine-made products was to find those decorative motifs which arose naturally from the functional forms of machines. What sort of decorative flourishes would show off the craftsman's skill on a sewing machine, for example? This was not just a question of taste, it was a question of good design. Because designers do not generally make final products, machines do, this radically changed their relationship to products from that of the craftsman. The crafts decorative motifs were in part there to display workmanship, but the machine products did not show workmanship, since no human worked them. So the role of decoration changed. From the perspective of craftsmanship, which lines and motifs would go with machine design? What decorative motifs would show off the material that the machine and its products are made of, and integrate well with the process of producing these machines and machine-made products? What is virtuosity in machine design? The Victorian machine designer was making decoration so as to humanize the product and make it resemble the crafted things with which people were familiar. The new designer needed an ideology that covered the issue of decorative forms in this new context.

Arts and Crafts Movement

The Victorian machine designer imitated the craft designs in the new industrial situation. However, this was not a comfortable or satisfying solution. Both in Europe and America there were reactions against it. The English arts and crafts movement reacted by trying to reestablish the folk crafts and decoration, and throwing out the machine.

The arts and crafts movement was started in 1848, sponsored by William Morris (1834–96). William Morris had a disgust for the machine-made objects that people had in their homes, and he also disliked the values of the Industrial Revolution. Morris felt that the separation between arts and crafts had led to the degeneration of both. He felt that this separation had led to Fine Art being amusement to only a few, and to craft disappearing altogether as it became overwhelmed by manufacture. These two, he felt, should be reunited into a close companionship between beauty and use.

Morris thought that architecture and furniture ought to be designed with an eye to the nature of the materials and working processes. He thought that the surface decoration on items should be flat and non-illusionistic. Morris thought that only handicraft could have aesthetic value. He felt that the decorative art on the machine should not be just stuck on like icing on a cake, as it was on a Victorian machine, but should live a life of its own as it had in the past folk crafts tradition. However, while the decorations he had in mind were there to humanize the product, and make it more beautiful, they did not add meaning or spiritual value the way that the decorations in craft traditions do.

The arts and crafts movement was a romantic rejection of the machine, and a retreat into the handicrafts tradition and folk values that were being destroyed by the Industrial Revolution. This movement tried to revive the purely handicraft techniques of weavers, printers, and cabinet makers by revitalizing these old craft technologies. These handicrafts were disappearing, only surviving in isolated and backward places.

Morris felt that before the Industrial Revolution, people had experienced the happiness of making useful objects which had given them the opportunity to express themselves in their work. He felt that people should again make useful objects, and that making useful objects is the highest and best artistic activity. He wanted to replace the shoddy products of the machine age with the handicrafts revived from the pre-industrial past. He wanted art that was made by the people, for the people, as a happiness to the maker and user both.

This movement is important in the development of design because the ideas it expressed about craft were integrated with the ideology of machine-style functionalism in the first academy of modern design, the Bauhaus. The arts and crafts movement preserved the craftsman concerns for an integration of beauty and use into a harmonious design, and gave people a sense of what decorative motifs could be like in the machine age.

3. IDEOLOGIES OF FUNCTIONAL FORM

From its beginning there have been ideological struggles in design between the principles of craft and decorative design on one side and machine-style functionalism on the other. Machine-style functionalism has its origins in the Industrial Revolution and in the American aesthetic assimilation of the machine.

Frontier American Tool Design

The folk craft of the American frontier is unique in that America is the only major world power to have taken form as a cultural unit in the period when technology from the Industrial Revolution was already spreading throughout the world. The frontier Americans put their energy into making tools. They put effort into the design of useful things. As a result, American tools of the time were far in advance of those of the Europeans of that day. This was because, first of all, European machines were less likely to be improvised than the American ones. Secondly, the European machines were rarely made for the personal use of the designer, or even of the buyer. Rather, machines were made for a workman employed by a buyer, and this required that they be made to operate as nearly as possible without the intelligence of the workman, even if the original cost of the machine was high (Kouwenhoven, 1948). The Europeans had a highly developed craft workshop tradition which had to be converted to the new machine technology. Whereas in the frontier, American workshops were just being set up, and new products were needed which could be manufactured with the new machines.

In the United States, machines were frequently made for the designer's own use, and were usually sold only to those who would use them and understand their use. Also, the American tools were lighter, since they were made of steel rather than iron. Because they were made outside a crafts tradition, and outside an old and stable culture with symbols and motifs that are traditionally associated with each activity, the Americans had no use for decoration. The items they made had only functional form, and not the surface decorations or entwined animal shapes of some hunter-and-gatherer craft. They were not made in the context of long oral tradition. There were no totem animals or mythological creatures that people felt the need to entwine with their tools. The craftsmen were increasingly outside the cultural European tradition as well, isolated in a new land, and were ethnically diverse, not having one culture to look back on to imitate its good luck charms and decorative motifs. The Americans started with a need and created a tool to fit that need. This meant that the things they made were new, innovative, and embodied a new sort of economy and simplicity of design.

Frontier American Building

Because Americans' needs, as well as the materials they found in abundance in their new land, were different from that of the European, the Americans were forced to innovate in the design of even their houses and bridges. Most construction in the United States was of wood, and in Europe it was of stone. The Europeans saw wood as an inferior material for building since it was not durable. In Europe the aim was to build strong, safe, durable structures, and the cost and speed of construction were of only secondary importance.

In the United States, however, speed of construction and cost of materials were of primary importance. In America, they built houses to last one generation only. Since people were not stationary and did not wish to spend much on their houses, and wood was a cheap available building material, they built with wood. At first Americans copied in wood the stone-made details of English houses. But soon decoration took on more and more of the essential features of wood. In the United States, even when they made iron bridges, they copied the wooden forms rather than copying stone techniques (Kouwenhoven, 1948). As they moved to using new materials they used even less of the decorative motifs that had gone with the old European forms. Wood construction helped undermine the cultivated tradition from Europe. It led to new and more flexible forms, and people had to rethink how an object they wished to build could be built using these new sorts of materials.

When they built a bridge, parts of the bridge were prefabricated. The main principles of design were economy of materials and standardization of design. Because bridges and canals had to be made in a hurry there was no thought to durability or to aesthetics; just crude function counted. Such structures were made to serve their purpose efficiently, be cheap, and quick to assemble, so that as traffic increased they could easily be enlarged and improved.

From the accumulation of such effects, a general aesthetic ideology developed which had no room in it for the workshop craft tradition of decorative form. The early Americans reacted to Victorian machine design by throwing out the workshop craft decoration and developing an ideology of functional form.

Functionalism

One of the first people to develop this functional ideology into a philosophy of functional form was the American sculptor Horatio Greenough (1805–52) (see fig. 3.2 on p. 84). Greenough (1853) writes that in nature, forms are adapted to functions. Even color in nature is an adaptation to function. What is beautiful about a lion or an eagle, he says, it is adaptation of form to function. When we admire the form of an eagle's beak, we are really admiring a functional form. After all, said Greenough, it was not made that way to be aesthetic but to be functional. In nature, all superfluous decoration is stripped away. There is no meaningless decoration. This is what the artist and craftsman should also do. For Greenough, decoration is just pleasing design added on as superfluous beauty.

The reason that people add decoration to the functional form, Greenough said, was because they sense a complex rhythm and harmony in the natural world, and try to imitate that harmony in their products by adding decorative elements to them. Humans, he writes, are not gifted with a sense for completeness, and our designs are therefore often incomplete. We add decoration to otherwise functional designs so as to make up for their incompleteness, and make them more beautiful by creating harmony with the complexity and completeness we see in natural design. But, said Greenough, the harmony and rhythms that give nature her complexity are not just ornamentation, they are many-sided functions. If we see something in nature which looks like decoration, it is really there for some function that we have as yet not discovered.

In shipbuilding the form is adapted to the function, Greenough said, so it should also be in architecture. He said that design should be adapted to site, that an architect should work outward from the heart of the building achieving external expression of the inward functions of the building. All meaningless decoration should be stripped away. Ornamental architecture is not good because it consumes labor disproportionate to its utility.

The slogan for the functionalist movement, "form follows function" was originated by architect Louis Sullivan in *Kindergarten Chats*,

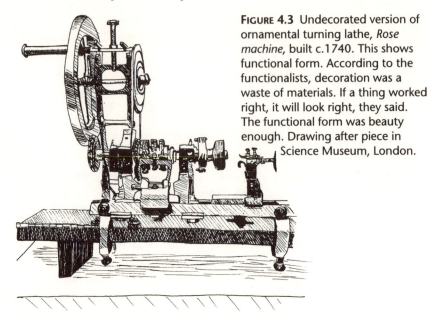

FIGURE 4.3 Undecorated version of ornamental turning lathe, *Rose machine*, built c.1740. This shows functional form. According to the functionalists, decoration was a waste of materials. If a thing worked right, it will look right, they said. The functional form was beauty enough. Drawing after piece in Science Museum, London.

in 1901. If a thing works right, the functionalists say, it will look right (fig. 4.3). Things should be built with economy of design, simplicity, and flexibility. The paper clip was praised as a work of art because in a paper clip there is a perfect integration of function and form (fig. 4.4). The paper clip is a completed form. The smooth rhythmic line of the paper clip are also the exact shape that works to hold the papers together. Those paper clips with detail rough texture at one place on the curve add that point of visual interest and complexity because then the papers don't slip out of the clip as easily. Thus, the paper clip exhibits a perfectly functional form.

According to this extreme early view, there should be no decorative elements. All elements of a design should serve the needs of function. The criteria for evaluation of a design should be efficiency, simplicity, and flexibility. These are all functional notions. Decoration was not seen as having any other function than aesthetic. Those who held these views felt that they could revise people's sense for the aesthetic so that the machine form would look aesthetic. This functionalism continues into the twentieth century both in industrial design and architecture.

These functionalist designers and thinkers thought that the design of an object should be only functional. This is a distinctly anti-romantic attitude. They wanted to make items which conformed completely to what they saw as the aesthetics of the new industrial age. They had no

FIGURE 4.4 Paper clip. The paper clip was considered a perfect functional form because its smooth rhythmic line is exactly the right shape for its function of holding papers together. Thus, there is a perfect integration of function and form in the paper clip, and it was praised as a work of art.

room for cultural, humanistic, and religious decorative patterns, or ideas attached to the slick smooth lines of action which were the functional form. They had no consideration for the craftsman way of relating to the materials being handcrafted. They thought of decoration as independent and external to the making of a functional form.

The mentality of crafts and the mentality of machine-made design are quite different. In crafts each product is considered an individual item to be skillfully produced, while for machines and machine-made items, a line of production is set up where many items are produced out of the same pattern. It is the original pattern that shows skill, not the craftsmanship in the production of the final product. The functionalists think of decoration as an extra to design, rather than as something displaying skill and virtuosity in the production of the item.

As the architectural critic Lewis Mumford (1962) points out, the machine devaluated rarity, or the single unique object. The machine devaluates age, it puts emphasis on the new and on slickness, smoothness, gloss and cleanness. The machine strips away all sentimental value. Sentimentally is not attached to the machine-made object, as it is with the hand-made one. When the machine-made object gets old and needs repair, we tend to throw it away and get a new one; whereas with hand-made things, older ones take on additional value, they become *antiques* and we tend to have them fixed. Thus machine-made items bring new values with them. We have a different relationship to them than we have to crafted items with the same function.

Ideological Incompleteness of Functionalism

Some ideas about the design of a machine follow clearly from functionalist principles. For example, a machine must be designed not just to work, but also to be operated. The controls on the machine must be made so as to facilitate the operator's interaction with the machine. Good design of the controls, say industrial designers, uses the figure/ground ideas of

Gestalt psychology (Mayall, 1968). Those things that are important for the operator to notice should be figure against the rest of the machine as ground. The important information should be presented in a way that can be easily understood. That means that the controls should be where they can be seen without distractions. The controls should be grouped by function, in a logical manner so that their uses and relationships are as obvious as possible. The controls must be well related to the work area. For example, the controls of a car that you need most to be able to drive the car without taking your eyes off the road, like gas, steering, brakes, and turn signals, are within easy and comfortable reach, while those things that are not used so often, like the heater, or radio controls are further away, although still within reach.

Further, products should appear to be an orderly whole, say the industrial designers. There should be orderly relations between the parts. The machine should show a common visual objective. The machine will only look right, if it not only works, but is also easy to maintain, and easy to control. The machine needs to be designed so that it clearly displays all the features that the operator is concerned with. The designer should try to optimize maximum operating efficiency, reliability, safety, minimum size, ease of maintenance, ease of control, good appearance, and low cost. The parts of the machine should relate to each other visually — rounded shapes with rounded shapes, squares with squares.

However, there are other aspects of machine design that do not clearly follow from functionalist principles. For example, color is a problem for the functionalist designer. Color can be used to define work and control displays, but color has emotional qualities which can often overcome its objective application (Mayall, 1968). The wrong use of color can often hinder rather then help the operator. For example, for large machines installed in a factory, a light color is desirable, but white can create a glare, cause cleaning problems and also look too clinical. Light gray, gray-green, gray-blue, all cool and slightly receding colors are suggested as having the advantages of white without the emotional tone. Brown-gray gives the impression of warmth, though a little more obtrusive then the receding colors, it feels more sympathetic. For mobile or dangerous machines full-hue bright colors are suggested, like yellow or orange. Thus, although function helps us some with color choices on a machine, there is still room for style and decorative effect, things excluded in functionalism in principle.

An even bigger problem for the functionalist machine designer is that in many modern machines the works are encased. This is not for decorative reasons, but to solve a design problem of either bringing forward the parts that the controller must watch, or so as to protect the workings of the machine from the dust, keep them lubricated, or to protect the user from danger. This casing creates a problem for the functionalist designer in that it prevents the user from seeing what the machine does. So, functionalist industrial designers say, when the machine is encased, the outer shell must somehow reflect the machine's functional qualities. Thus, though we cannot see the refrigerator's mechanism, we should be able to tell somewhat from its outer shape that it makes things cold. This is often a problem for the functionalist designer because, if a machine is right it will look right, but a casing is not the machine, and so its look is not given by the function of the machine. Also, there are machines like computers where it is hard to see what would signal its function in the outer design. This means that the functionalist principle, form follows function, does not tell what forms the casings should have. Functionalists need some other principle to dictate the design of the outer shell of the machine.

Even in normal design situations, the problem of designing the outer surface of the object and designing those parts of the object that are not directly involved in the machine's functioning like the casing, still arise for the functionalist designer. What should the colors do, what shape should the casing be, what should be the overall style of the machine? It turns out that all these things are not necessarily determined by the function of the machine. Even a paper clip could be green or yellow, elongated or more circular. Even a pure functionalist must make style choices and from these choices arise a decorative form. This is a problem for the functionalist because he or she wants to completely exclude decorative form from his or her design solutions. For this reason some functionalist designers have even preferred not to work with objects at all but just with disembodied functions, since any object requires non-functionalist decisions, decisions of style. For example, an industrial design textbook in the 1960s (Niece, 1968), states that the best design might be to eliminate the visual object altogether. Since it is the function of the items that is really important, the best design would be to have the functions performed invisibly and dispense with things as visible objects. All the emphasis of design should be fitting the best form to function, this textbook explains, and anything over and above that is unneeded, even ugly, as it interferes with the efficient, clean functional lines of the design.

What we see from this is that functional form and the machine style are not enough to give a complete design ideology. There are still decisions to be made that are outside of it. Beyond an ideology of functional form, designers also need an ideology of beauty or of decorative form. This sort of ideology was added to functionalism in the Bauhaus movement.

4. THE BIRTH OF DESIGN

Academies for Design: Bauhaus Movement

The first academies for design came from the Bauhaus movement. The Bauhaus movement stemmed originally from the attempt by the Deutsche Werkmund to synthesize the machine-style functionalism with the arts and crafts concept. This was a movement to combine art with the design of useful items.

The Bauhaus was formed out of the School of Arts and Crafts in Weimar Germany when Walter Gropius became director of the school in 1919. Walter Gropius (1888–1969) was an architect who had already proven that he could make architecturally appealing buildings using the new mass-produced materials. Because of political pressure, the school was moved to Dessau, then Gropius resigned and was replaced by Hannes Meyer (1889–1954) who emphasized industrial design. Finally it was closed in 1933 by the police for being politically subversive. After its closing, its instructors spread out to various countries in Europe, starting other schools that used the Bauhaus concept. Bauhaus instructors also came to the United States and started schools of art and design putting Bauhaus principles to work. The Bauhaus instructor Laszlo Moholy-Nagy established the Institute of Design in Chicago, and Gropius became chairman of the department of architecture at Harvard.

The Bauhaus evolved a methodology of design and design teaching. Almost every major design school in the United States still uses some version of the basic Bauhaus foundations design course. The Bauhaus thought of themselves as developing a new guild of craftsmen—the designers. By the 1930s the new art profession *design* had been launched.

In the Bauhaus curriculum, the first year was devoted to the principles of art, and then the next years were spent in workshop settings, learning the physical properties of various materials, and of functional form, by experimentation. Students were taught in large part by doing. One problem they tackled was reconciling the crafts' individuality with the uniformity promoted by the machine. Also there was a concern for how the mass-produced new materials — metal, plastic, glass — could be used artistically. More modern design schools, building on the educational philosophies of the Bauhaus, also stress educating designers in visual and verbal communication, cultural history, and sociology. Some Bauhaus-inspired schools now also include the study of non-art subjects like biology, physics, and philosophy. Others include courses on marketing and the psychology of the consumer.

The aims of the Bauhaus were to provide designs for objects which were needed in modern living. Gropius took some of his ideas from the theories of Morris (and Ruskin) about the production of artful domestic objects. He thought of the useful arts as united with Fine Art within an architectural synthesis. There should be no distinctions among the Fine Arts, decorative arts, and architecture. This synthesis should take place within the context of mass production. Thus, unlike Morris, Gropius was working with the modern industrial system to produce machine-made mass-market items which were, however, also aesthetic.

The instructors were both artists and craftsmen. Gropius believed that there was no difference between artist and craftsman (Hamilton, 1972). The Fine Artists taught the perceptual properties of artistic form and materials. Some of the Fine Artists who participated in the Bauhaus, like Lyonel Feininger, were German expressionists, teaching their students the expressionists' discoveries about the use of color. Instructors Paul Klee and Vasily Kandinsky were former members of the Blue Reiter group, artists experimenting with primitive expression and abstract images of inner life. Instructor Laszlo Moholy-Nagy was interested in the structural properties of new materials. He experimented with translucent and transparent plastics and encouraged his students to develop designs for lighting fixtures. Students investigated both the theoretical principles of space and form as well as designing objects for mass production. Bauhaus student Marcel Breuer created the tubular steel chair, which has become a common article of furniture worldwide (fig. 4.5). His design showed how a chair can be made focusing on lightness and space rather than weight and mass. Bauhaus student Josef Albers invented new designs for furniture, windows, ceramics, and typography.

The Bauhaus taught their students a sensitivity to functional form (machine style), materials (crafts tradition), and aesthetic form (Fine Art tradition). The Bauhaus sought to educate the designer in the visual language of mass production as well. This prepared them to design machine-made objects. Thus their teaching dialectically preserved the three traditions; craft, new machine-style functionalism, and Fine Art aesthetic form. This continued the arts and crafts idea of making

FIGURE 4.5 A Bauhaus designed piece of furniture: Chrome-plated steel tubing chair with cane and wood back and seat, 1928, Marcel Breuer. This tubular steel chair design has become a common article of furniture worldwide. By focusing on lightness and space rather than weight and mass, it gives the chair a simple stripped-down functional form like that of the paper clip.

domestic items that were pleasing to use, and the craft sensitivity to materials. The designer learned the strengths and weakness and what was natural to a certain sort of material, and then worked with that material to find the form that emerged naturally from it. This craft sensitivity also expressed itself in many early designs constructed to be enjoyable for the user to assemble. The designs used non-traditional mass-production materials unlike the crafts, and gave thought to the functional form and machine aesthetics beneath. Bauhaus designers considered the use of objects, thus finding the form that was best suited to that use — form follows function — and the abstract qualities of the design which would give that design a maximum character also as a work of art.

One of the original issues in design had been how to unite craft decoration and functional form. Designers needed something to tell them how to handle those parts of the design that were not constrained by function, like the color or casing. The Bauhaus solved this problem by integrating aesthetic form of contemporary Fine Art with machine functionalism. They did not take the tradition of decoration from craft. They taught an ideology of aesthetic form and the integration of that with functional form as an integrated whole. This was a modernistic movement in design. This movement echoed the formal orientation of the Fine Arts of the time, where design, like art, would show the universal harmonies of the machine age.

The Bauhaus movement was very important as the beginning of an academy structure for educating all the various specialties of designers alongside the Fine Artist. This accomplished an alliance between the new machine-age craftsmen and Fine Art in an academy structure, analogous to the alliance between art and craft before the birth of Fine Art in the Renaissance. These new artists, the designers, benefited both from the functionalism of the machine style and also from the aesthetic traditions and accumulated technology of Fine Art. The Bauhaus idea had such a large impact because it educated designers with a vision of technological society and mass production, along with a sensitivity to the humanistic crafts and Fine Art traditions. It prepared them to be a blend of engineer, Fine Artist, and craftsman. It prepared designers to design things in the new situation of mass production for the mass market. Further, by combining these three traditions it produced a complex enough set of ideologies to evolve as art within its own niche.

These schools of art and design serve a similar function to that served by the Renaissance and Enlightenment academies. They ally the artists with the power elite who can then educate artists to promote their values. Now, however, the elite are the business and manufacturing elite; and the artists are not taught to make art for collections but to make art of manufactured products.

However, design education has not reached the level of institutionalization that Fine Art had reached with the French Royal Academy during the Enlightenment. Although the Bauhaus idea underlies most education for designers, there are still a wide range of approaches to design education swinging between the more utopian and humanistic approaches of Bauhaus-inspired schools, to approaches that are more like vocational education, where designers are educated wholly as technicians. This is consistent with the polarity in the function of the designer. At one end the designer acts as an artist, designing an object with sales in mind and with aesthetics and product symbolism. On the other end, the designer acts as an engineer, working to improve the functional form of the product, that is, such things as its safety, ease of use, and cost of manufacture. Often the designer works as a mediator between the marketing department and the production engineers. Thus there is a broad spectrum of things for the designer to do. No single educational structure has emerged that spans the whole range and that all designers attend. Also there is no certification structure fixed for designers. Thus, the education of designers has not stabilized.

The International Style

The Bauhaus taught what came to be known as the international style. This style became the orthodoxy in architecture just as modernism was the orthodoxy in Fine Art. It became a common style in product and machine design from the early 1950s through the 1970s. This international style has also been called the *black box aesthetics* (Dormer, 1990). Here the works of such things as radios and televisions and electric shears were put into smooth plastic, white, black, or gray geometric cases. This was a functionalist and severely geometrical style avoiding decoration, but with an aesthetic sensibility like that of the abstract art of the constructivists and De Stijl. This aesthetic style was well suited to reinforce the simplicity of functional form. It was not a decorative style, but a highly formal and geometrical Fine Art style. It invites you to stand back and taste its harmony. Thus, even a machine-style functionalist could use this aesthetic to make design decisions on such things as color, casing, and general style of the outer shape of a machine or other product.

The De Stijl art movement was an art movement contemporary with the Bauhaus that was also experimenting with, and formulating, the international style. This movement lasted from approximately 1917 to 1931. Both Bauhaus and De Stijl were investigating the interface between the objective machine and aesthetic form. Members of De Stijl also believed in mechanization and new technology. Both the Bauhaus and De Stijl held the conviction that what they were looking for would best express itself in a synthesis between the applied and Fine Arts. Like the Bauhaus, the members of the De Stijl movement also believed in bringing together Fine Art, architecture, crafts, and the applied arts like interior decorating. The most prominent Fine Artist involved in De Stijl was Piet Mondrian (fig. 4.6). Another primary member was Gerrit Rietveld who primarily made furniture and designed interiors but also designed buildings (fig. 4.7). Like the Bauhaus, the De Stijl movement included painters and sculptors, interior designers, furniture makers, and architects. Theo van Doesburg edited the magazine *De Stijl* which broadcast the ideology of the movement, and displayed some of its art. Van Doesburg gave lectures at the Bauhaus, although he was not a faculty member, and there were other overlaps between members of De Stijl and the Bauhaus.

De Stijl had a distinct aesthetic doctrine which was a doctrine describing what they took to be the international style. The De Stijl artist believed in using only flat smooth primary colors, black, white, and gray, straight lines, and rectangles in abstract designs. The Bauhaus designers also preferred designs using these colors and smooth clean geometric shapes. This was a modernist Fine Art aesthetic of pure international aesthetic form. This pure form they advocated resonated well with the formal compromises needed to put aesthetic form together with machine functionalism.

FIGURE 4.6 An example of De Stijl art: Piet Mondrian, *Composition with yellow*, 1936. Oil on canvas, 38¾-by-26 inches. The artists of De Stijl felt that with straight lines and primary colors they could express spiritual meanings. The opposites of vertical and horizontal lines making squares and rectangles imagistically reconciled the opposites of universal/ individual, nature/spirit, masculine/feminine, abstract/ real, determinate/ indeterminate. Courtesy Philadelphia Museum of Art: Louise and Walter Arensberg Collection.

International style was thought to be a styleless style in the sense of not carrying the flavor of any particular culture's style. That is, what makes a style particular to one culture or another is the way it is used to represent something. The international style is pure without any representational content and hence is without taint of this or that culture, and truly international. So, just as machines are international, and functional form is international, this new aesthetic is also international. The new art is like typewriting is to handwriting, said Mondrian (1937), lacking the mark of individual personality and without traces of human weakness. Thus the international style unites technology and art.

The artists of De Stijl felt that with straight lines and primary colors they could express spiritual meanings, thus uniting the spiritual with the design of domestic items. As Mondrian believed, following Rudolf Steiner, the opposites of vertical and horizontal imagistically reconciled the opposites of universal/individual, nature/spirit, masculine/feminine, abstract/real, determinate/indeterminate. These opposites are laid out as horizontal and vertical lines making squares and rectangles (Overy, 1991). These opposites would then be used in the color schemes and designs of interiors, furniture, and buildings. We would be surrounded by the harmonies, colors, and forms of art. Then the forms and activities

Figure 4.7 Housing designed with De Stijl principles: Gerrit Rietveld, Schröder House, Utrecht, 1924. The opposites of vertical and horizontal lines make squares and rectangles which expressed the spiritual for De Stijl. Artists could use the color schemes and designs of buildings and rooms so that one could live within art's spiritual harmonies and conform life to them.

of life would be controlled by this universal spiritual visual harmony, and the environment would be pure and complete in its beauty, and hence would redeem mankind.

The De Stijl idea of living in realized art was the idea of not having an isolated painting on the wall as the only art in the room, but making your whole surroundings into art. The idea was to live in the art — sit in your sculpture, and have your walls, ceilings, and floor be the painting. As Theo van Doesburg wrote, by making an interior like a painting it would be possible to enable the viewer to be inside the painting and participate in it rather then just standing in front of it (Overy, 1991, p. 89). Van Doesburg called this sort of art *monumental art*. This idea of living in art resonates with the Popular Art idea of vicarious experience. People step into Popular Art; they bathe in the pictured waterfall. Design also lets you step into art by making your house into monumental art.

5. DESIGNING FOR SALES

Design ideologies that were collected together in the Bauhaus were all there to make designs for use. These were designs that had the best functional forms and were also aesthetically pleasing to have in the home. They united functionalism, aesthetic formalism, and the craft sensitivity to materials. But all of this just developed one approach to design, that is, designing things to be harmonious and useful. However, in business and industry, designers were not just designing objects for use, but also objects for sale.

Promoting Aesthetics

By the 1920s business and advertising agencies had realized that putting style and color choices into the products they made increased consumption. For example, in 1926 Henry Ford decided that the way to sell cars was through stylistic innovation rather than by standardizing the design and style. The success of this decision showed that style rather than function had the most impact on sales. This has been part of the conception of car design ever since. Further, from 1930 to 1945, the styling idea of streamlining from car design was used as a style for other domestic items as well. This streamlining style gave items a smooth slippery form. Streamlining really did not improve the performance of cars, and certainly was not an improvement in function of other items where it was used, like writing tables and radios (fig. 4.8). It was used as an expression of progress, and since the car expressed this progress most dramatically, the styling of the car was imitated in people's homes. The styling allowed people to feel their participation in the modern sense of speed and spirit of the age through the styling of products. It expressed their optimistic desire to shoot forward into space with the car, the train, and the plane.

Through the use of advertising and by designing stylistic variety into their products, manufacturers elevated things into the category of fashion goods that had before just been utility goods, like towels, bedding, and bathroom fixtures (Marchand, 1985). Previously these items did not have any style component, but now designers added decoration to their functional design. This meant that now consumers could choose products not just for function, but also for style. People could now have pink sheets, green toilets, and blue phones. The designers and

Figure 4.8 An example of the streamlining from car design being used as a style for other domestic items as well: *Fada Baby Radio*, 1934. From 1930 to 1945, this streamlining style was used as an expression of speed and progress.

advertisers were promoting the idea that all these various items ought to be considered not just for their practical uses, but also for their use as fashion and decoration. The items should be coordinated to go with the rest of the consumer's environment in the home; the towels should go with the toilet, the phone with the room decor.

Along with these fashion choices the designers and advertisers showed consumers how to put beauty in their lives through making these choices "tasteful." The manufacturers thought of themselves as uplifting the taste of the masses by promoting aesthetics. They were transferring Fine Art taste to the masses. Designers and advertisers were putting style into items and then teaching consumers that they had to show good taste when they put these style items together by coordinating them into a "look." The room can be made to look sensuous or dramatic or wider, or higher through the manipulation of shapes and colors. The body can be made to look thinner or taller, younger or older, through such things as cloth patterns, color, and shape. The advertisers were telling people that with these fashion goods people could make themselves and their houses aesthetic masterpieces (fig. 4.9). They were teaching consumers how to make monumental art.

The principles of "taste" are explained in advertisements, by the clerks in the stores where the items were sold, and in magazines like *Better Homes and Gardens*, and women's fashion magazines. There are also experts, fashion consultants, and interior decorators to consult. Consumers are told that they should not just accumulate things without concern for the overall impression they make, just because they liked the individual items, as people did with crafted items, but should make them harmonize with one another into a pleasing overall design. Thus when a new product is bought, the old ones need to be replaced or recolored to "go" with the new fashion choice. The consumer's bags, shoes, dresses, and watches all should match — that is, fit into a unified style. By selling style in consumer products, consumption of goods was increased. Now

FIGURE 4.9 Designed interior. To increase the sale of domestic items, designers and advertisers put style into the items and taught the consumer how to put these style items together to make their houses into "aesthetic masterpieces."

people needed not just utilitarian bag and shoes, but a different bag and shoes to match each outfit design and color. Consumers needed not just a lamp, but a lamp that fits in with the color harmonies of their new sofa. Thus, although aesthetic form like that in the international style can be used to complete the design decisions left open by stark functionalism, aesthetic form can be used not only to complement the functional form of the item, but also to make the object attractive as part of the general look of a room. The style of a product could be used as part of a room decoration and have nothing much to do with the object's functional form.

Thus the artistic mission of making people's surroundings into art, promoted by Bauhaus, was taught to the general population as a means to get them to buy more goods. This became a way of designing things for obsolescence. People threw things away for style reasons. Indeed, in the 1950s designers began to see the throwaway aspect of products as the fundamental principle of mass-market goods. They designed products like paper handkerchiefs, and paper towels, and paper cups that are used once and then thrown away. Also, products are often death rated, that is, designed to break once the warranty runs out. Sometimes they are designed to be lost, like the potato peeler that is colored brown so that it will be thrown away with the potato peels (Papanek, 1971). Here we can see a tension between design for use and design for sales. The international style was designed for use but Fine Art aesthetics and the idea of making your surroundings into monumental art could also be used to design for sales.

Postmodern Design

There is a tension in design style between aesthetic formalist styles like the international style, and design styles that are figurative. Those wanting abstract design tend to look for a single design aesthetic for the world, based on design principles that fit well with the new materials and industrial processes. They look for a style that fits well with the functional form of the product, and design for use. However, this sort of style made items lack individuality; that is, objects with the same basic function are styled in the same basic way.

Those favoring figurative design tend to think of products as coming in a great variety and designed to appeal to the various tastes of consumers. Here the style of the products are not dictated by function, but by market pressures. This is a further development of design for sales. This gave rise to what is known as *niche marketing*, where the styling is targeted to a smaller, more specific group than mass marketing is. Thus, they shun the idea of a unified worldwide machine aesthetic.

In niche marketing designs, while the functional form of the products are uniform, the styling reflects the values of the consumer. The same functional item could come in a great variety of shapes and colors. That is, the same functional form can be packaged in a great variety of outer forms. For example, a razor can be pink with flowers on it to target it to female users, and black with blue accent lines to target it to male users. The razor is the same, but the razor is packaged with different styling to sell the product to different markets. In designing for niche markets, the styling reflects the class, age group, profession, and aspirations of the target group. This goes hand in hand with advertising, and requires a great deal of research to discover what these values are and what styling motifs succeed in communicating them. For example, cigarettes are marketed to young male smokers by showing a cartoonish camel who smokes cigarettes with his friends and to young female smokers by showing romance with an upscale version of themselves. Through the design of its package and its advertising image the product is targeted to different consumer markets. Thus designers look for appropriate symbols to use for styling their products, and consumers are given symbolic content with their products which is what identifies them as a group. This plays off the power of Design Art which is, as we will discuss, to reinforce people's identities. These identities are often international, since people of the same class, age, profession, and aspiration might have more in common with one another in different countries than with people of other market niches in their own countries.

Along with niche marketing, another trend in design away from modernist aesthetics, is narrative design. Some have called this movement *Postmodern Design* as it rejects the ideas of pure design based on function and modernistic abstract form. In postmodern design, form is dictated by the consumer's psychology and market pressures. Postmodern design expresses meaning and uses metaphor. The marketer tries to discover what people want and what their hopes, fears, loves, desires, and ambitions are, so as to reflect these values back to them in the product (Dormer, 1990). The style of a product is not just dictated by aesthetics but by symbolism that appeals to the consumer. This might mean that the product is styled to radiate luxury and extravagance in a period of economic depression, or environmental consciousness in an era when that is in the consumer's mind. Style communicates values, not just aesthetics. In postmodern design, the outer design, the art package, of the object is figurative — TV lamps in the forms of animals, and clocks in the form of teapots, or lunch boxes designed to look like loaves of bread. Some of the motifs are references to television or film characters, some of the narrations fit into a bigger narrative package provided by the advertisements. There is a great range of possible art packages here. For example, the beautiful naked lady with a clock in her stomach, or the lamp shade that looks like a football helmet, or the lunch box that has a superhero on it all have art packages that add value to the product, but are not related to the function of the product. Each of these art packages adds a different sort of value to the product. Like in the previous three examples, the art package can add sexual attraction, or sports fan identity, or vicarious experience to the product. These art packages don't just fill holes in the functional form, as the international style did, they sit on top of the functional form and are valued for themselves.

Although this design is called *postmodern* it is not really Fine Art stimulated design at all, but rather the incorporation into design of principles of Popular Art. Designers discovered that Popular Art sentimentality and narrative sells. This competes with the designs that promote modernistic aesthetics, since the appeal of these figurative items is not formal but narrative. These items do not go together to make a unified aesthetic form, but appeal more the way that craft did, where each item is enjoyed separately.

Rather than designing objects to look impersonal and international without individuality so as to fit with the clean impersonal lines of every other designed object in the artistic harmony of monumental art, postmodern designers give their objects personality. We see in the product's art package reflections of ourselves, or at least reflections of what marketers think we believe to be ourselves. This is another way in which this sort of design is like Popular Art. Popular Art also reflects the viewers' values back at them. Unlike modernism which advocated pure forms unrelated to life, this postmodernism advocates forms reflecting life and subject matter. Postmodern designers, like the British architect Charles Jencks, want to give their designs purpose for existing through their symbolic meanings. Thus, in redesigning his house, Jencks gave everything a meaning. Each room has a theme; winter, summer, and so on. He celebrates the positive aspects of human civilization (Dormer, 1990). This postmodern design is a reaction against meaningless objects that don't refer to anything beyond themselves as we have in the international style. Where these postmodern designers find meanings and use meanings to coordinate products, the international style used unity of style and aesthetics, unity of color and line to coordinate products. Here again the narrative values from Popular Art are replacing the Fine Art values. People are moving from rational detached aesthetic harmonies to narrative themes, and to art that reflects their values.

Many countries are aware of design styling as a way to sell more of their country's goods. In several countries, like Britain, Sweden, and Japan, agencies have been set up to promote design consciousness through exhibitions and the mass media. These agencies aim at establishing national design criteria and increasing their country's share of world markets. They create an "image" for their country's designed goods, promoting aesthetic reform and "good design" in products as a way of gaining a bigger share of the world market (Sparke, 1986). An international style makes this sort of thing impossible. There would be no difference between countries in style. Each product no matter where it was produced would have the same basic styling. From the perspective of design, Fine Art aesthetic formalism is an international and unifying style which leaves no room for competition between countries. Thus economic pressures cause design to develop niche marketing and postmodern design since that opens more possible markets and makes more variations in style possible. The phone can be styled to look like Mickey Mouse or the cartoon cat Garfield; it doesn't need to have only the slick functional line of the international style.

In this progress of development we can see the slow reemergence of design with meanings. That is, crafted items made in the traditional cultures had good luck charms, animals, or other religious decorations, because that made them more enjoyable to produce and gave the object specialness. Using the decorated item enhanced the user's participation in spiritual life. Modern designed products with decorative motifs again give the objects meaning and specialness, but this is not meaning by way of participating in the spirit world, but participation in the world of the mass media and Popular Art. A Garfield telephone brings Garfield off the comic page and into the room so that the user has a piece of Garfield in his or her own life. Designers use Popular Art images on their products that reinforce the user's vicarious experience with that Popular Art situation. For example, *Star Wars* lunch boxes that boys take to school provide fantasies about zooming through space like the movie's hero while they eat their lunch. As we will discuss in the next chapter, advertising narratives also provide a myth-like context in which we participate when we use the advertised product.

6. THE POWER OF DESIGN

Design as the Spirit of Our Age

Just as Fine Art formed in the Renaissance atmosphere of humanism and Greek revival, Design Art is forming in an atmosphere of design. The new cultural niche design comes from the needs and conditions produced by the mass market. Additionally, there is a general move in culture away from "pure" art and science, toward engineering art and science.

Most of modern science is guided by the pursuit of results which can be put to use in industry. More and more science is done in an industrial setting for industrial goals rather than in academic settings for the pure pursuit of truth (Ravetz, 1971). In the new industrial setting the goal is control of environment and usefulness for industry.

The newest sort of science might be called design science, or engineering science. This new science is science of the artifactual or the artificial. As Simon writes (Simon, 1982) sciences of the artificial are sciences about those things that are man-made rather than natural. Design science looks at nature from the perspective of function and goal orientation, so as to design artifacts. For example, from the perspective of design science, the heart has valves so as to facilitate its task of pumping the blood. Understanding the heart in this functional way helps us to design artificial hearts. If someone wants to make a heart, then he or she needs to know what the parts do. Sciences of this sort are concerned with the design of natural and artificial things, and characterize these things by the functions they perform and the goals they achieve.

This sort of science is very close to Design Art. Both design science and Design Art are close to engineering since they deal with making synthetic or artificial objects with desired properties. For example, David Marr (1982) as a design scientist analyzed the external constraints on vision so that he could design robot vision. Design scientists design machines to be intelligent, farm animals to be more efficient meat producers, and plants to be more resistant to disease. Scientists study the designs of nature so that they can imitate that design in man-made objects; Design Artists do the same. Design Artists are not just designing style in products. For example, the Design Artist Victor Papanek describes using the configuration of a pussy willow to design an implement to make seed planting in extremely hard soils easier (Papanek, 1971, p. 203), and the design of packaging that is derived from the study of the pea pod (Papanek, 1971, p. 201).

Some designers are thought of as artists, some as scientists, and some as engineers. Design Artists have an art background and tend to design not just function but also the look of products within the context of an art cultural niche; design scientists have a science education, and are interested in discovering general principles within a science cultural niche; and engineers are interested in applying scientific principles to the building and maintaining of useful artifacts within an engineering cultural niche. However, there is a great deal of overlap between them. There is an atmosphere of technology in contemporary culture which supports the ideologies of design. The ideologies of design span across the distinctions among art, science, and engineering, blurring the traditional separations between these disciplines. Both design science and Design Art intertwine the disciplines of engineering and technology. Design Artists are the engineers of art.

The Package

In modern products the design is broken into two parts. One is the design of the use aspect or functional form of the product, and the other is the outer look, or art package, of the product. The standards for a good functional form, namely, simplicity, economy, flexibility in the design are quite different from the principles governing its art package. The art package can be designed not just for aesthetic form, as we discussed, but also with Popular Art sentimentality and narrative form.

Art Designers use the package to reinforce the user's identity and to carry Popular or Fine Art. Design packages give viewers a way of surrounding themselves with style that reinforces their sense of themselves. The art packaging we choose to decorate our houses reflects who we are to others. This effect is even more obvious with clothing fashions. How we dress reflects how we want others to perceive us, and we identify with others who make the same fashion choices that we do. We want to be seen as art and the Design Art we choose to wear or put in our houses, projects who we are to others. People judge us by our choices. Also, people use Design Art as a creative outlet. Where once people could create crafted objects to express themselves, now people tend to go shopping and make color and fashion choices with Design Art as personal expression. People choose Design Art as a personal reflection of their taste and lifestyle. They use it to create their own monumental art.

Designers determine style for the manufacturer, in the decision of which styles to offer and advertise to which target group, and for the consumer by advocating through the media what the desired look is. Advertisements show us a product being used by a stereotyped consumer with whom we identify by wearing the same clothes or using the same products. As we will discuss in the next chapter, in this way designers and advertisers shape our self-image and our group identifications. Advertising goes hand in hand with Design Art, and intensifies Design Art's power to enhance our personal identify. It is in advertising that the power of packaging is most fully exploited.

As we have already discussed, design uses the power of Fine Art, to reinforce functional form or to make monumental art. The power of Design Art to reinforce the user's identity and the power of aesthetic form to create a distancing in the viewer can both be present in the same object. We can feel disinterested satisfaction in a painting which also reinforces our sense of ourselves as having good taste. We can make our surroundings rich with aesthetic harmonies through the use of design objects, and thereby feel a sense of personal fulfillment and expression. One's sense of self is heightened by the aesthetic harmonies created.

The power of design does not interfere with the power of Popular Art, but rather reinforces it. We can hang up a calendar with a picture of cute puppies and feel the sentimentality that comes from such images. While the calendar serves the Design Art function of decoration and telling us what month it is, the cute puppies image reinforces our identity as someone who enjoys sentimentality, and flavors our room with sentimentality as everyone who enters the room also feels the sentimentality of the image. When someone who has been in our house and seen our picture of cute puppies sees cute puppies somewhere else they might think of us. Also, our sense of personal identity is heightened by our vicarious experience as we mentally step into the Popular Art image displayed on our Design Art object.

Businesses sometimes use popular sentimental art with their products, like the Norman Rockwell calendar we discussed in the last chapter (see fig. 3.8 on p. 106), with the logo of a realtor reading "Deal with the realtor that goes the extra mile" in big red letters under the art on the calendar page. As your heart opens to think about boys coming home from camp, you feel warmth by association for the realtor who says she'll go that extra mile. Thus, we identify with the Popular Art image, but also associate the sentiment projected in the image with the company that put out the product. The Popular Art image thus acts as a bridge between us and the company.

Beyond packaging products in art images, designers also try to package some products with the prestige of a Fine Art object so as to acquire a Fine Art aura of good taste and high culture for that product. For this purpose design items are collected as examples of contemporary culture to be written about and eulogized. This gives the items more status, and can be used as a marketing tool. Anyone can own the very same object that is on display as a profound example of twentieth-century design. Examples of products packaged in this way are the Mont Blanc pen and the Copy Jack 96 pocket copier (Dormer, 1990). This is further cultural packaging that is added to design styling. By buying these objects one also buys a piece of official contemporary culture. Beyond its functional value, and the added art package value, the product also has a level of cultural meaning and so can also function as Fine Art, that is, something to be collected for its own sake.

Some manufacturers are taking advantage of this possibility for further cultural packaging by putting out catalogue booklets about the cultural values of their products. For example, a West German manufacturer, FSB, has put out such a catalogue on door handles (Dormer, 1990). This booklet attempts to elevate the door handles they design into fully idealized cultural objects by discussing them intellectually in terms of the philosophy of design. The catalogue was produced from a workshop FSB held on designing door handles. Thus design is "elevated" to Fine Art, and sold as Fine Art, that is, as something to collect for its cultural meaning.

7. DESIGN ART AS CULTURAL NICHE

Design was born with an ideology for functional form, for craftsmanship, and for decorative form. Later an ideology about marketing and packaging was added which facilitated design using Popular Art and selling its items on the mass market. From the background ideology of design and the forces of marketing, Design Art began developing the power of packaging and its use for reinforcing the user's identity. The contemporary designer is educated with a sense for functional form, materials, aesthetics, a sense of what will sell, and of the designed object as a vehicle for values and cultural symbolism.

Design Art has different ideological categories than either Popular Art or Fine Art. Within the Popular Art and Fine Art cultural niches, artists must have ideologies dictating their artistic mission, how to structure the Unifying Geometry of art, appropriate subject matter, and which stylistic conventions to use. The Design Art cultural niche has ideologies about craftsmanship, functional form, decorative form, artistic mission, and marketing. However, none of these ideologies is completely stable. They are in a formative state. We have already discussed the conflicts about design for use as opposed to design for sales, and conflicts about using pure aesthetic form as opposed to figurative decoration in the art packaging of designed items. What the designer's artistic mission should be, has also not been resolved.

Artistic Mission of the Designer

The mission of Fine Art as institutionalized in the French Royal Academy was to teach and distribute moralistic messages. The mission of design has nothing to do with morals or teaching. However, exactly what it does have to do with has not yet become clear. At first, design's mission was to make monumental art which would make domestic life more harmonious. The original social mission of design was to make an international style and to unite people across nations and religions. Designers wanted to unite the applied arts with Fine Artists, and to help workers by designing aesthetic as well as useful items for domestic life. However, there are contemporary designers that have other ideas about the artistic mission of designers.

For example, the professional designer, Victor Papanek, gives voice to a different conception of the designer's artistic mission when he writes (1971) that the designer can make our lives better by designing in an ecologically conscious way for people's real needs. Designers ought to be designing for the real world, writes Papanek. That is, they should use available materials to make products for real people (fig. 4.10). Not everyone is middle class, although many products tend to be designed for middle-class lifestyles. Designers should make designs that fit the lifestyles of the poor, as well as products that fit the many other non-mainstream life styles.

Papanek writes that Design Artists should use a systems approach to solving problems. He has an ecological philosophy of what counts as a good solution to a design problem. There should be no "trash" or garbage at the end. The whole process and the final product should be designed in such a way that there is no waste, and the design fits into a system. For example, such a good design would be low-cost dishes, which come with a container in which they can be washed, dried, and stored. Broken dishes could be returned and recycled as raw material. The dishes would stack, and if they break, their pieces could be remelted into new dishes. This is a good design idea, writes Papanek, because there is no waste, and there is attention to the ecological processes involved. Another example of good design, using a systems approach, would be to recycle our own body wastes through letting them mature in tanks then using them to fertilize our gardens and using the fumes from composting them to cook our food. Papanek's point is that waste cannot be thrown away. When the trash men take the garbage there is no real place to put it; it just gets moved. So, we should think in terms of designs with no waste.

Where the early American engineers compromised their designs towards speed of construction, Papanek compromises his designs according to the whole system of design. He is thinking of the whole use cycle of the product and designing not things, but solutions to problems. As Dormer (1990) points out, one way to cause people to choose items that have responsible design would be to increase awareness of how products are produced. For example, if people knew that producing their kitchen cleaning product involved producing toxic chemicals

FIGURE 4.10 An example of a product designed from low-status materials: cardboard chair designed by Janne Ahlin, Jan Dranger, Martin Eiserman, Johan Huldt. Drawn after illustration in *Nomadic Furniture* ©1973 by Victor J. Papanek and James Hennessey. Reprinted by permission of Pantheon Books, a division of Random House, Inc.

and that when it is washed down the drain it causes toxic pollution, they might think twice about using it. Thus, people would make better consumer choices if they know the ethical and environmental aspects of how the item was made, and of the whole cycle of production.

Where the Bauhaus designers were thinking in terms of which materials were appropriate for the functional form of the item, Papanek is thinking about which materials are ecologically responsible. Designers should use available materials for their products even if they are not status materials, says Papanek. For example, corrugated cardboard is strong and could be used for furniture. Also, the cans that food comes in could be used in many creative ways. Papanek has a design for a third world radio which uses a tin can, for example. The point is that these sorts of materials are generally not used because they are not status materials. Although a cardboard chair might be just as functional as one made out of conventional status materials, we don't use cardboard because of its low status.

Papanek wants designers to be aware of the real world and to design for it. The Design Artist, he feels, should see himself or herself as someone who has a function in society to help people live better. Papanek is against patents, and copyrights. He thinks that designs should be available to all. We should each design our own solutions to our life problems with economy and an eye to ecology. This is the functionalist part of his ideology. Papanek does not see the designer as primarily solving problems of selling products for his or her client company, but rather he sees the designer as a maker of products for the people's good. His emphasis is not on aesthetics or the decorative value of domestic items, but on social utility. He does not advocate designing monumental art, but designing items to solve social problems.

Thus, the artistic mission of the designer is still in flux. Some designers see their mission in Bauhaus terms of making attractive and useful items, while others, like Papanek, see their mission in terms of solving social problems and ecology. Some designers design for sales, designing items that increase consumption, while others design items for use. Presumably as Design Art matures in its cultural niche, a clear conception of artistic mission will emerge which designers will agree about.

A Potential Competitor of Design

Just as with Fine Art, which has a competitor, Popular Art which shares its basic function, but is distinct in its institutions and ideologies, Design Art also has a potential competitor, namely the studio-crafts. The studio-crafts are hand-crafted items made by semi-professional craftsmen working individually. These studio-craftsmen tend to be middle class, with a job, doing crafts as a hobby. People buy the studio-crafts in part out of an appreciation for their hand-crafted look and their display of virtuosity. Both of these are values not found in mass-market design or in much of Fine Art. In Fine Art many of the artists have given up on displays of virtuosity or craftsmanship, and in mass-market design such displays are not possible because the products are made by machines. Thus these studio-crafts display another aesthetic and set of values outside the dominant art cultural niches. These items appeal because they are not anonymous but made by an individual for another individual's enjoyment. Mass-produced items are deeply anonymous. Further, these new studio-crafts radiate an ideology of personal freedom, as they were made by someone on their own outside the vast industrial complexes. The studio-crafts offer alternative values and metaphors from the slick and professional flawless forms of mass-market design. Design carries mainstream culture, while these new studio-crafts can carry values outside that culture.

Craft shows and fairs, craft shops, and consignment shops give studio-crafts their own distribution system, and people's nostalgia for the past give them a market. Although the ideology for them is thin, there are recognized standards for judging the craftsmanship since studio-crafts imitate traditional forms, and look hand-made, thus maintaining a contrast between them and the smooth machined forms of the mass market. However, studio-crafts do not reinforce mass-market design but compete with it as it is made out of values and lifestyles antagonistic to those projected by Design Art. Potentially this could be the source of a new art niche competing with design to serve the function of giving people functional items for domestic life.

These crafted items are freed from price competition since they are made by people who do not need to make a living selling them. Their makers can feel free to indulge their own creative process and take their time, rather then primarily making things which will sell. Thus the economic pressure on them is different from that on Design Art. They do not need to exploit a mass market. These are sold on aesthetic grounds, and are made for self-fulfillment. These are not sold as throwaways or designed for obsolescence. They are meant to be kept. The craftsmen don't have to make as many as the manufacturer does because people consume less of them. This means that where people had been drinking out of throwaway cups they now use a studio-crafted one, and so do not throw it away but cherish it as a one of a kind hand-made item. This cuts against the current ideology of design marketing, namely designing for obsolescence. People might be influenced by studio-craft to no longer want to throw away items. This is a threat to design.

When we compare the life history of design to that of Fine Art, we see that design is about where Fine Arts was in the Renaissance. Design has only been a clearly distinct art profession since the 1930s. Fine Art is five hundred years old, Popular Art is two hundred years old, and Design is only approximately sixty years old. The extreme youth of Design Art shows in the flux of its ideologies. In its old age, Fine Art has seen several stages of ideology — imitation, expression, aesthetic formalism, and so on. Design is just forming its first set of ideologies. Whereas Fine Art is losing its power, and Popular Art is fully devoting itself to developing its power, Design Art is just discovering its power.

CHAPTER 5

∽

Advertising

ADVERTISING ART IS SURELY the most common form of art we see today. We see it on billboards, the walls of stores, in magazines, in newspapers, and on television. Advertisements are everywhere. Advertisements are the most contemporary art form, always being updated. Whereas the Popular Art images we see are often several years old and the Fine Art images we see are often hundreds of years old, advertisements tend to be only months or weeks old. Advertisements play for a few weeks or months and then are changed. In the advertisements people are shown looking completely contemporary wearing fashionable winter clothes in the winter, and fashionable summer clothes in the summer.

Advertising's goal is to cause us to act. It promotes something and asks us to spend money, practice safe sex, or reelect a congressman. The power of advertising is strong in Western culture. Advertising uses both the power of Popular Art as well as that of Design Art to shape people's desires and commitments. It is used to give us vicarious experiences as well as to package products and shape the consumer's personal identity.

Advertisements as we know them today didn't start until after the 1880s. Before that, the manufacturers and shops put out product announcements, but these were mostly information, not persuasion. Advertising as we have it today really depends upon the existence of a mass market and mass media. Advertisements and the mass-media, mass-market culture arose from the changes in manufacturing, transportation, and communication caused by the Industrial Revolution.

1. THE CULTURAL CONTEXT GIVING RISE TO ADVERTISING

The Industrial Revolution and Advertising

The values needed to support industrialization are the same as those supported by advertising. Industrialization cannot go forward if people want to remain where they are, doing things in traditional ways. The values associated with industrialization are the desire for material progress, the acceptance of social mobility, and the acceptance of new ideas and technologies. Advertising does promote material progress, social mobility, and a willingness to try new things. For industrial development to go forward, people needed to be willing to abandon traditional culture and class structure for the new lifestyle and professions of industrial life. Thus, advertising has been a progressive and useful force for change.

As people moved into cities and began living in small nuclear families with the Industrial Revolution, their access to advice from the extended family and local culture decreased. Such things as whom to marry, what religion to believe, what lifestyle to lead had in the past all been decided or assimilated from the extended family and local culture. After the Industrial Revolution, people needed to decide such things for themselves. The family was turned inward upon itself; it was isolated from the old and from the larger clan membership. It had to depend upon itself for everything. People were now isolated from the old people and traditional culture, and the society pressured them to forget how problems had been solved in the past and solve them in a new modern way. People now had a need for advice, which the advertisers and mass media tried to fill.

Along with the Industrial Revolution and the changes that came with it in the patterns of life, came a change in the function of the family, and a change in the amount of leisure time that people enjoyed. The family was no longer a productive economic unit — the goods and services that it provided in the past were now produced by mass-market manufacturers and businesses, or made quicker by domestic machines. People no longer worked the fields together as an extended family, or gathered and chopped wood together, or milked cows together, or picked and canned food together, or did spinning and weaving and sewing together. Instead, people now had leisure time to spend together. They spent vacation time and the weekend off from work with the family. Here, too, was a need that the manufacturers and businesses and their communicators, the advertisers, filled. They showed people how to use their leisure time. They supported the development of the entertainment industry, mass-media television, radio and movies, and produced consumer items for leisure.

With the Industrial Revolution people's lifestyles changed. People moved to the cities to find factory jobs away from their farm communities and extended families. As we said in the last chapter, their craft skills became obsolete and they began to have well furnished houses and use labor saving devices. Since they no longer knew how to make the things they used, a further function of advertising (along with word of mouth and such things as "consumer reports") was to tell them the features and advantages of one product over another. Advertising told them how to use products, and who uses those products.

Advertising is an art form that is uniquely entwined with our economic system. Businesses and manufacturers pay artists and copywriters to produce advertising, and pay the mass media to distribute advertising. At the present time, advertising stands between the overproducing manufacturer and the already product-saturated market. The basic post-industrial revolution lifestyle is now the only lifestyle most people know. The market is already saturated with products. Products compete with one another for the consumer's attention. For example, an advertisement explains why one brand-name headache pill is better than another. The advertisement must make one brand more attractive than the competitors'. Since the market is already saturated, advertising serves the function of stimulating the market. It advocates that people get involved in the economic life of the nation by buying products and thus, continue the momentum of industrial production. The manufacturer or business person has something to sell, and advertising is a way of telling people about it.

Advertising as Part of the Design Cultural Niche

Advertising is not its own cultural niche, but a specialty of Design Art which is concerned with marketing Design Art objects. Indeed there is only a thin line between graphic designers and advertisers. Graphic designers inform, whereas advertisers persuade. Graphic designers make such things as signal systems at airport terminals, signs, and brochures. They present information in a clear and readable fashion. Advertisers present information to increase the attractiveness of a product and cause desire in the consumer.

Like other specialties of design, advertising is anonymous art, and there are no singular creators. It is made by group effort. It does not show the subjective perspective of some genius artist. This came about through the conscious choice of advertisers. In the 1920s there was disagreement among advertisers themselves about whether advertising should be more like Fine Art — full of artistic value and signed by the creating artist — or only a tool for selling products. Some argued that if advertisers tried too hard to make their work look like art they would be sacrificing its power as a selling tool. The viewers should not look at the advertisement and admire the art, but should look at the advertisement and admire the products advertised. It would be confusing for the consumers to see different advertisements for different products all signed by the same people, they felt (Marchand, 1985). Advertising artists should concentrate on techniques that maximize sales rather than trying for public recognition and admiration for their creativity, and the *artiness* of their work. Here advertising artists, like other design artists, choose to step into a workshop situation to maximize the transparency of their art. They choose to forgo expressive individuality, making the opposite choice from Fine Artists, who in the Renaissance chose to leave the workshops to assert their individuality.

Typically, the group that makes advertising includes: slogan makers, art directors, advertising agencies, and manufacturers. Many skills and mentalities combine, and many different purposes blend together into the picture and text that make up an advertisement. The effect of the art is calculated in advance. The art is commissioned for a specific purpose, as was the workshop art before the Renaissance.

Like Popular Art and Design Art, an advertisement is not a unique object. It is just another rendition on a basic theme. Where a copy of a work of Fine Art is a "fake" or only a "print," the copy of an advertisement is another advertisement of equal value. The advertisement is evaluated on how well it functions, that is, how well it sells the product, not on the virtuosity displayed in its line and form, how unique it is, or how expressive it is of the emotions of its creator.

Unlike other Design Art, advertising is distributed through the mass media as well as on the mass market. Where the general function of design is to make useful and attractive objects, the function of advertising is creating desire for those objects. Advertising is the marketing end of Design Art. It creates desire for a product by adding value to it in the form of a Popular Art image. The advertiser has a dual function. On the one hand, advertising functions to give the consumer desires which can only be satisfied with consumer products, and on the other hand, the advertiser must keep track of what people want to see and what they will buy in order to help the manufacturer make products that will sell. Thus, the advertiser keeps track of the needs and desires of the consumer as well as projecting to the consumer what the manufacturer has to sell.

As we will discuss, advertising connects the Popular Art vicarious experience with the intensification of personal identity of Design Art. In that way advertising is like Popular Art as well as Design Art. Advertising uses the devices of Popular Art on the mass media to project a product image and to create desire for the product. Then the advertising image appears on the product as well to reinforce the identification between the media image of the product and the product itself. Thus, functionally advertising is distinctly different from both Design Art and Popular Art. Advertising shares properties with both, and mediates between them. As packaging, advertising is Design Art, but as image, advertising has a lot in common with Popular Art.

2. ADVERTISING AND THE POWER OF POPULAR ART

Stylistic Conventions

Advertisers look for a style which works best to get their message across. Like Fine Art and Popular Art, they are concerned with discovering stylistic conventions. The advertising artists by and large have art educations where they absorbed Fine Art technology. Between 1920 and 1940, just as the other designers were experimenting with adding modernistic aesthetics to functional form, advertisers were also experimenting with using modernism. Advertisers used modern styles taken from art movements like art deco, cubism, and futurism to show a modern image of motion and speed. They used modern art's license to give "expressive distortion" to exaggerate, thus giving emotional dimension and "soul" to the products (Marchand, 1985). Also, as contrasted to the old styles that had a lot of detail work of equal value, now imitating modernism, they could cut out all unnecessary details and accent the "most important selling qualities" of the product pictured. They used the modernistic

FIGURE 5.1 Advertisements using Fine Art style to add mood or style: Republic National Bank of New York (1994) uses a painting from their collection to show style and dependability. Reprinted by permission of Republic New York Corporation.

diagonal line to show a dynamic sense of movement and direct the attention of the viewer. Also, the off-center layout was better at catching the viewer's attention by showing an unresolved tension. Advertisers used oil paintings to express literary and sentimental overtones. Contemporary advertisers use Fine Art styles to add style or mood to their product (fig. 5.1).

After the 1940s, advertisers began to incorporate more photographs into advertising. Like the other designers who began using Popular Art imagery in figurative decoration, advertising artists also moved towards Popular Art and away from modernism. Advertising artists were searching for a style with transparency. By making the art anonymously they had eliminated any lack of transparency introduced by seeing the personality of the artist in the advertisement. But some wanted a style which did not show the touch of any artist at all in the advertisement. They were looking for a style that allowed the viewer to look at the subject matter and not notice the art technique at all. The advertising artists decided that photography would give them this stylistic transparency. This is an offshoot of the transparency of Popular Art. The viewer focuses on subject matter and is blind to form. By focusing on subject matter, the viewer can create a daydream, a vicarious experience. Advertising wanted to exploit this power by giving the advertising image the greatest non-art appearance possible.

Advertisers felt that photography had the advantage of looking like literal and objective realism but yet in fact the image could be manipulated to be just as expressive and emotional as drawings and paintings. The photographer can distort and emphasize by choosing camera angle, lens, light and shadow, as well as by making miniature scenes to photograph, and by retouching or superimposing images. Whereas a viewer looking at a drawing or painting is aware of an artist behind the work, a photograph does not give that effect. The photograph encourages the viewer to imagine that he or she is directly looking at reality without the intervention of a manipulating artist. People think that what is photographed is real. Also, a photograph is more likely to be remembered as something the viewer saw outside the advertisement than a painting is. The goal in advertising is for people to forget they saw it in an advertisement and think that they saw it in ordinary life. Thus, a photographic advertisement can act best as a reminder, a memory image that viewers can think of when they feel a desire that needs to be filled.

Advertising art shows simplified social scenes where things are shown as they should be, the homes shown are stereotyped, and the viewer's attention is directed to the foreground where the product is. Things are photographed or drawn to seem more real than life. The rain is rainier, the beach beachier than it would be in reality. Advertisements tend to flatten the visual space and be self-contained, abstracted. The place and time are "city" or "night." The places are either very iconographic — like a picture postcard of New York City, or ambiguously "your town." The time tends to be abstracted too, the birthday party, the weekend, New Year's Eve party. The advertisement relies on a shared cultural understanding with the viewer, or on basic human emotions which can be presumed to be universal.

The mass media deliver advertisement. The most recent technical achievements discovered for making advertising images involve broadcasting advertisements over television. Television is ideally suited to deliver advertising. The television can deliver the message into everyone's home. Advertisement financed television's growth, and television has acted as the best sort of delivery system for advertising. The advertisers like to sponsor shows that will be interesting enough to hold people's attention; people will stay tuned in to the show, but not so interesting that the viewers will find the advertising an annoying interruption. The shows are just the packaging, the sugar coating, to make us swallow the pill of advertising.

Television captures our attention for even inherently boring things like product advertising by making it look like something unusual is happening. To make advertisements catch our attention on television, the advertisers produce a visually dynamic series of technical events. On the average a commercial lasting thirty-two seconds will include ten to fifteen technical events (Mander, 1978, p. 305). For example, the camera zooms close and then instantly flashes to a view far away; the camera circles the product, and changes image size. The screen image is changed from one scene to another, or from one person's face to another. One image is superimposed onto another, or the screen image fades from one image to another. Words are put on the screen, or we hear a narrative voice-over, or the swell of music. Cartoon images are interspersed with photographically real ones. The screen image flits quickly from one of these technical events to another so that the viewer's attention is held just by the technical variety displayed. This produces the illusion that something unusual is happening. The advertisement looks like fast action, although in terms of content it is not.

Advertising has more of these technical events than regular programming because it has, in contrast, less real content. This sort of technology could be used to make shows more interesting, but it is very expensive. An example of a show that does use a lot of these sorts of technical tricks is *Sesame Street*, a children's show that has been the most popular show in public television for years. *Sesame Street* was originally designed and produced by ex-advertising people.

Television gives the appearance of reality, images that move and talk, but they are not reality. The people have no true life force; they are out of context, flat, object-like without presence or aura. This makes the people shown equal to objects that are shown, and in that way television becomes an ideal medium for presenting advertisements for objects. For example, dead bodies and death generally come across well on television. Death can be communicated by a single forceful image, while life takes many images, and thus, the quality of what the living thing is, may not come across at all. Products, like dead things, have no process or changing essence to them; they are static and hence can come across in single images. This fact gives the products more significance and power when presented on television against a background of television shows showing flat people than they have in real life against a background of living breathing people. Since the products have no life inherent in them, they lose nothing on the screen (Mander, 1978).

The picturing conventions we see in advertising are primarily those of the Popular Artists. Advertising art is like Popular Art in that it is structured so that the viewer's attention is directed through, not at, the art. The Popular Artist wants to enhance emotion or give rise to a vicarious experience. The advertising artist uses that emotional enhancement and vicarious experience to cause the viewer to desire a product, service, or cause enough to spend money.

The Popular Art Power of Advertising

Advertisers have changed in their view of human nature since the 1880s. At that time they thought of human nature as rational and self-interested; later they came to see the human nature of the consumer as irrational and emotional. By the 1930s advertisements had become less informative and more emotional. The success of tabloids, *True Story* magazines, and the comic pages of newspapers caused advertisers to think of the mass consumer as characterized by mental lethargy, bad taste, and ignorance (Marchand, 1985). Responding to this perception of the consumer, blatantly emotional appeals and exaggerated claims became more common in advertising. Advertisers tried to get down to the level of the consumer by giving the products a personal touch. One common way was literally by animating the products, giving the toilet bowl cleaner, or the loaf of bread, arms and legs and voice to explain to us how good each product is. This plays on the ancient tendency of seeing inanimate objects as having a life force.

The advertisers also developed "mood" advertising, and thought of advertising as creating desires. Since inner picturing is the predominant mode of thinking when having daydreams and fantasy, the copy decreased, and the images grew. Whereas text would get people to think, pictures easily bypass thinking and get people to feel and do. As we said when discussing Popular Art, critical thinking interferes with relating to art for narrative thinking.

Advertisers learned from imitating the comic pages, the confession magazines, and radio, that people respond to the quick cutting from scene to scene, close-ups, personal testimonials, and intimate drama. The comic strip was especially interesting to them since it showed how the consumer could be led to a sale one step at a time in an almost hypnotic trance (Marchand, 1985, p. 112). Thus, one way that advertisement uses the power of Popular Art is to use the identification of the viewer with the pictured consumer to give the viewer a vicarious experience of buying the product. Since we try out actions as pictures in our imaginations, advertisers can tap that by showing us pictures that play through the actions of buying and consuming. The advertisement can be structured to show the three steps of that process, namely, the desire, buying the product, and the satisfaction of the desire through the use of the product. These pictures then become visual clichés, and stimulate our basic emotions unconsciously. They give the consumer a pattern of behavior to imitate. By showing a sweaty thirsty person putting money into a pop machine to get a can of brand-name cola, then showing that person satisfied after drinking, the advertisement walks the viewer through a desire, the purchase of the product, and the satisfaction of the desire in the use of the product. The product can be bought from a pop machine or at a store and it will satisfy the "real thirst" that viewers have noticed in themselves as they contemplate the image flashed before their eyes of the sweaty-after-a-hot-run surrogate consumer really enjoying the drink advertised. It tries to convince people that they cannot fill their needs without the use of a product. Whereas we could drink water for our real thirst, the advertisement tells us that only brand-name cola will really do.

Any or all of these three steps can become the focus of the advertisement. The advertisement can show the consumer picking out the product in the store, or showing satisfaction after the product was used. Often advertisements create artificial needs. To do this they must show consumers some way that their life is inadequate which is outside the spectrum of natural needs like hunger, thirst, and so on. This sort of advertisement often works by causing anxiety. This is an elaboration of showing a desire. Instead of calling up a natural desire like thirst, the advertisement shows an inadequacy or fault that the product can cure. It tells us that people judge us by whether our glasses shine, and whether our toilet bowls are clean, and advocates that we buy brand name soap and brand name toilet bowl cleaner. It tells us that people judge us by "ring-around-the-collar dirt" and then tells us that this soap will wash that dirt away — just go to your local store and buy it in the big orange box.

In this sort of advertising, the goal of advertising becomes to create discontent in the viewer that can be momentarily satisfied only with the use of the product (fig. 5.2). The sorts of discontents that advertising can especially exploit are fear, loneliness, self-doubt, and competition (Mander, 1978). An advertisement shows a burglar breaking into a house and explains that the only way to protect your family is to buy brand-name insurance. We identify with the family in the advertisement and feel fear

FIGURE 5.2 Advertisement creating discontent that can only be satisfied with the use of the product: Coppertone Sport Sunscreen ©1993. Schering-Plough Healthcare Products, Inc. All rights reserved. Reproduced with the permission of Schering-Plough Healthcare Products, Inc., the copyright owner.

about our own safety. An advertisement shows everyone shunning someone because they have dandruff, and advocates using special shampoo. We identify with the person being shunned, and worry whether we too have dandruff. An advertisement shows Grandma getting a phone call and advises us to "stay in touch with someone we love" by telephone, thus making the viewer feel guilty for not calling Grandma, and Grandma feel bad about not getting called. In each case, the advertisement dynamically involves the consumer by making him or her feel uncomfortable in some way—lonely, fearful, guilty, or anxious—and then suggesting the product as a cure.

Another way that advertisements employ Popular Art images is by using them to add value to the product in the form of a pleasing fantasy. They appeal to our sentimentality and associate those feelings with the product (fig. 5.3). Advertising art gives people daydreams involving objects; romance comes with a bottle of wine, Christmas comes with

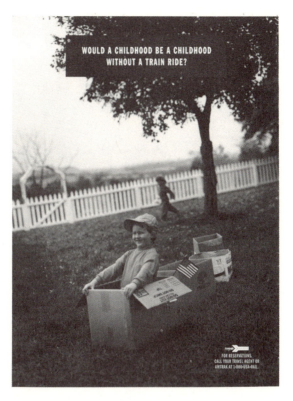

chocolate bars. The constructed fantasies reflect our desires for such things as social acceptance or romance, and show them acted out by a surrogate consumer with a product.

For example, a Hennessy Cognac advertisement in *The New Yorker* magazine is a photograph which shows a man in a swank apartment lying on a bed in loosened evening clothes. We see a woman in a see-through nightgown beyond the open door of the bathroom. On the table beside the bed are the man's keys, money, theater ticket stubs, a gold watch, and two glasses of the advertised drink. The words say "Hennessy — the civilized way to say good night." It is an after-an-evening-on-the-town scene. We could have this idealized end of a date too, just by buying Hennessy. The detail in the image allows us to think narratively in response. It presents a complete story with the product as a part of it. The image shows both the need for and its satisfaction with the product. Like Norman Rockwell art, it tells a story, and the viewer is supposed to place him- or herself in the story.

The difference between advertising art and Popular Art is that Popular Art simply presents a story with a certain emotional tone for the

| I can't believe they gave my promotion to Kaminsky. | Let him have it, I don't want all that responsibility anyway. | Besides, everyone in management develops a nervous tick eventually. | And with a reserved parking space, the boss always knows when you're late. |

| He could use the extra money, a good hair weave isn't cheap. | And a window office only means he'll have to watch the rest of us leave at five. | I can't believe they gave my promotion to Kaminsky. | **THIS IS REFRESHMENT** |

FIGURE 5.4 Advertisement showing the narrative thinking of a surrogate consumer: diet Coke soft drink. Reprinted by permission from The Coca-Cola Company.

viewer to vicariously experience; advertisements add a message by making the story to be experienced revolve around the use of a product. Thus, when we use the advertising image to structure a daydream about our life, the daydream has a product in it. Some advertisments show the consumer doing narrative thinking while consuming the product (fig. 5.4), thus reinforcing that way of thinking.

Advertisers often pick an identity for the surrogate consumer represented in the advertisement that is slightly above the true class identity of the consumer to whom they are directing their advertisement. In this way the consumer can think of him- or herself as joining the company of their betters when they buy the product. We want to impress our date with how upscale we are, and the advertisement shows us what upscale people drink, and wear and what kind of car they drive.

Advertising shows as the norm, moments of satisfaction and specialness that are rare in real life. It reminds us of those beautiful and magical moments in life that we would like to experience but rarely do, like: Christmas morning happiness, that first magic kiss, sailing on a boat with the wind in our hair. Advertising uses the special feelings people have at holidays, and the conventional symbols for Christmas, Thanksgiving, and other special occasions to enhance their products by associating the product with holiday specialness. This all works by giving

Figure 5.5 Santa Claus testimonial advertisements: a) Lands' End clothing; b) Nordic Track exercise equipment. a) Reprinted by permission from Lands' End Inc., 1989. b) Reprinted by permission from Nordic Track®.

the viewer the vicarious experience of Popular Art, but then associating the emotional tone surrounding that special occasion with the use of the product. When we think of that first magic kiss, we should think of brand-name perfume, breath mints, or shampoo.

Advertising does not so much create new heroes or social values as it reinforces ones we already have. Advertising shows us our social ideals and associates products with them. Santa Claus testifies for chocolates, cameras, sweaters, and excercise machines (fig. 5.5). Advertisements tell us that success in love, marriage, and work comes from the proper use of advertised products and let us vicariously experience that success through the art. Advertising soothes people and shows everyday man as a hero who uses a particular product. It is optimistic art in that it shows that any problem can be solved by buying the right product and achieving the right lifestyle. It focuses on the new and romanticizes the present.

The Effectiveness of Popular Art Advertising

Advertising art is more effective than Fine Art in causing action because it is supported by other institutions in the culture like the retail store and Popular Art on the mass media. Advertising has the advantage over Fine Art in that where Fine Artists speak with the voice of a single individual, at most being backed up by the ideology or movement they are a part

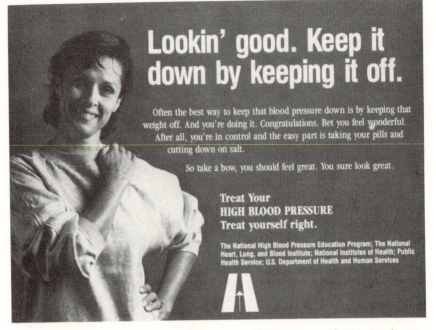

Lookin' good. Keep it down by keeping it off.

Often the best way to keep that blood pressure down is by keeping that weight off. And you're doing it. Congratulations. Bet you feel wonderful. After all, you're in control and the easy part is taking your pills and cutting down on salt.

So take a bow, you should feel great. You sure look great.

Treat Your HIGH BLOOD PRESSURE Treat yourself right.

The National High Blood Pressure Education Program; The National Heart, Lung, and Blood Institute; National Institutes of Health; Public Health Service; U.S. Department of Health and Human Services

FIGURE 5.6 High blood pressure public service advertisement. Charities and causes are sold with the same sort of images as products are.

of, advertisement speaks with a whole community of institutions behind it. An advertisement exists in a crowded world of other advertisements that compete with it for the attentions of the consumer and that repeat and reinforce its social messages and make its pictures take on a highly conventionalized look. If people wear baggy clothes in one advertisement, then they wear baggy clothes in most advertisements, on the situation comedies on television, and there are baggy clothes in stores for us to buy. If one advertisement tells us to buy underarm deodorant to prevent body odor, another tells us to buy deodorant soap, or feminine deodorant spray, all reinforcing the message that there is something wrong with natural body odors and we need a product to make us smell the way we should. Advertisements, business, and media reinforce each other. It is in part this repetitive reinforcement that gives advertising and the mass media the power to create a new consciousness, and fulfill many of the needs of religion.

Advertising is also more effective than Fine or Popular Art because we know exactly what to do in response to it. No matter how powerful a Fine or Popular Art image is, the right response to it is contemplation not action. The message in advertisement is simple: if you want happiness, to save sick children, to get rid of your headache, to have bright teeth, to get kissed, you just spend money. Charities and causes use the same sort of images as products do. There are even public service advertisments employed by the government to communicate its message (fig. 5.6). We know what to do in response to advertising art: not contemplate, but act in our own lives.

One can not only vicariously experience the advantage of some product while watching an advertisement; one can also have that product in one's own life. If that first magic kiss comes with breath mints, we can use those same breath mints ourselves to try to receive a magic kiss. Thus, advertising acts a bit like sympathetic magic. In sympathetic magic what you do in art gets done in the world — if you stick a pin in a doll, the person represented by the doll feels the pain. With advertising by using the product, you can get the good associated with the use of that product in art; thus, through the use of products, we are told, we can get in life what we see in art.

Advertising tends to present models of sentiment that our own lives cannot live up to. We cannot have the peak moments of supreme satisfaction that advertisements show; however, we can vicariously experience these moments. The moments of peak experience are exaggerated in advertisements to grab our attention and make them worthy of vicarious experience. Although the products never give us the same intense pleasure when we use them in our own lives as they give the people in advertisements, we can still feel that intense experience vicariously through advertisements. Thus, life becomes imitation art, and art becomes life.

3. ADVERTISING AND THE POWER OF DESIGN

The Brand Name and Image

Besides Popular Art functions of advertisement, advertising also has the function of projecting the product in a recognizable and memorable way. In an advertisement the product is packaged within a larger identity than only its functional identity. It is packaged in the identity of the company that produced it, normally by being displayed in some sort of container which has the company's brand name and logo on it. Thus, the Green Giant brand is on several types of vegetables (see fig. 1.5 on p. 8), and Paul Newman's picture and brand name are on salad dressing and also spaghetti sauce.

Instead of having many different makes of consumer goods, the makes get standardized under a brand name which is backed up by national advertising so that the brand name itself will be a guarantee of good quality. A brand name is the concentration of aesthetic, visual and verbal styling of the commodity into one named character. The brand name goes with uniform styling and a company "image." Companies want people to associate their brand name with the whole functional type as the product. For example, in Germany, United Fruit used a campaign that stated people should "forget the word banana, remember Chiquita" (Haug, 1986). Companies would like it if people forgot their generic words and only remembered brand names, as is already the case for names like *Kleenex* for paper handkerchiefs. Consumers forget pre-industrial technology, and use brand names. People do not remember how to make soap, or shoes. That is left to industry, and industry delivers under a brand name.

People are willing to pay more for a brand name they recognize with a reputation and advertising through national media than for a brand name that has no such reputation and media exposure, since a widely advertised brand name gives the idea that the product is respectable and reliable. People cannot see into the package, and so the picture substitutes for checking inside the package to see the quality of the product. They look at a brand-name can of peas and think of the green giant they saw on television who only picked the best peas to go into this very can. This makes them feel safe. They feel sure that inside this can will be good tasting peas.

The brand name has invested in it a national image, and its name and logo are copyrighted so that no one else may use it. The brand name becomes part of a company's capital assets. It is not unusual for one company to spend much money to buy a brand name from another successful company. Brand names appropriate and privatize words that would otherwise be in common usage, and make them into someone's exclusive property. The brand name and logo are a way of packaging a product with the values and reputation of the company that made it. The same brand name might appear on a whole series of different products all produced by the same company, so that when we intend to buy a product we look for a brand name we recognize.

Associated with a brand name is the image. The brand-name image is the total impression, the "look" of the objects, services, and facilities of some enterprise. The image for a company might include the logo, the type of lines carried, the decorations of facilities, the advertisements used, employee uniforms, or the general design of goods. Often advertisements are there for image. For example, oil companies advertise that they are concerned with the environment, hoping to counter any negative opinions people might have of them, while cigarette companies advertise that they don't really want kids to smoke.

Even politicians have an image which is the total impression they project especially through the mass media. The image in terms of advertising political candidates has two components. One is associating the candidate with images with positive emotional value, like the family dog, the American flag, and so on. These show the candidate as a person who appears to have the right virtues for the office. This continues the Popular Art idea of reflecting the viewer's worldview rather than challenging it. It creates an image of the candidate with the right symbols and slogans. The other component involves reflecting the voter back at him- or herself. They show the candidate talking to school teachers, secretaries, hard-hat workers, minorities, or senior citizens. By showing the candidate in the same image as a surrogate of whatever type of person they especially want to vote for them, the political advertisement convinces us that the candidate has that group's interests at heart. Viewers are to identify with the surrogate citizen and also vote for the candidate. Thus, in the short advertising message, too short to express or communicate any true content, the candidate tells the viewer what his or her market researchers say the viewer already believes, presents the candidate's personality, lifestyle, and family to resemble what the viewer would like someone in that office to be like, and shows the viewer images of voters backing the candidate for them to identify with. This is the same thing that advertisements for products do. They reflect the average consumer back at him- or herself, using the product.

The image gives the products, business, or politician an appearance on the same scale as the individual watching. It allows something that would be a large babble of actions, faces, departments, to have a single appearance which is coherent and easily understood.

Besides the brand-name image, the individual product also has an image. Most designers design the decoration of the product's art package as well as advertisements for that product in order to produce a calculated effect of projecting an image. A product's image might project that it is upscale, or especially targeted to women, easy to use, good for people on a diet, and so on. In some cases there are no true differences between the products behind the different images. For example, one brand of underarm deodorant is packaged in a pink flowery box, for women, while essentially the same product is packaged in a blue or black box for men. However, in other cases, the product image must act to communicate how the intended use of this product is different from that of other similar products. For example, there are several different kinds of food bars, and for each its image must project just what sort of food bar it is. To this end, one food bar image projects that its product tastes good, and in that way communicates to the consumer that the product is to be eaten as candy. Another food bar image projects being convenient to eat first thing in the morning, and in that way the image positions the product as a breakfast bar (fig. 5.7a). Yet another food bar image projects that its product is low fat and stimulates high energy, thus the image positions the bar as something to eat to obtain high performance energy before doing sports (fig. 5.7b). Thus, even though all of these bars can be eaten as snacks, they project different images not just to target different markets, but to communicate to their users their different functions.

The Advertising Package

In modern designs of products, one part of the design is the use aspect of the product, and the other is the outer look of the product. This outer look is the art package for the functional form, as we discussed in the last chapter. However, the functional form and its art package are only the product end of a series of packages designed to get the product into the hands of a consumer.

There is a layering of packaging in the design of products. The outer layer is the entertainment package that delivers the advertisement. One watches a show on television and approximately every eight minutes is shown something about headache pills or laundry soap. Read a magazine, or a newspaper, and every few pages there is an advertisement for cars, beauty aids, or food. The television show and magazine story are packages for the advertisements. They entice people to turn on the television or read the magazine so that they also see the advertisement.

Within the advertisement the product is further packaged with a slogan, a brand identity, and an image along with a Popular Art visual about the product. For example, toothpaste is advertised with a beautiful woman flashing her white teeth at a handsome man with a picture of the toothpaste box in the foreground and the slogan "cleans your teeth while it freshens your breath." The advertisement must make the box recognizable and the product desirable. Within the advertisement, besides its Popular Art enticement, the product must be displayed in such a way that the consumer will recognize it and remember it when he or she has the need. Thus, the antacid commercials that ask the question "How do you spell relief?" and then answer with the product name spelled out, are trying to form a memory bridge between desire for relief from indiges-

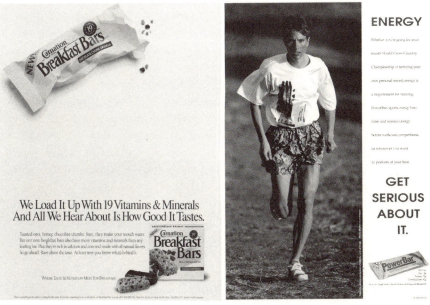

FIGURE 5.7 Bars with different nutrition images: a) Carnation Breakfast Bars b) PowerBar® energy bars. a) Reprinted by permission of Nestle Food Company, 1994. b) Reprinted by permission of Power Food Inc., 1993.

tion and the product. Also, the product is wrapped in the company identity which comes from its brand name, and image.

The product is displayed in the store inside a box, bag, plastic wrap, or can. On this, are tie-ins with the advertisement on television or in the magazine. The toothpaste comes in a tube which is sold packed inside a box with the logo, brand name, and image on it which are also shown in the advertisement. The box also functions to make the product easier to transport and stack. Inside the box is the product, itself a combination between art package and functional form. The toothpaste is white and red stripped, for example, or blue or mint green to make it more aesthetically pleasing to use.

Thus, the average design functional form has five levels of package: (1) television show, or magazine, or newspaper (2) advertisement, (3) brand name and image, (4) product box, (5) art package.

This is all needed to first get the consumer's attention (the show you watch or magazine you flip through), then create desire and display the company identity so that you recognize it (advertisement), and then make it easily shipped and recognizably displayed so that you buy it (box), then make the product good to use (art package, functional form).

Each level of packaging is needed to get the product from the manufacturer to your house. Each level of packaging is solving a different problem. The television show must get the consumer to watch a particular channel at a particular hour. The advertisement must make the product seem desirable and memorable. The brand name and image make the product recognizable. The box must be designed to protect the product, to make it easy to display and ship from the factory, as well as easy to choose at the store. The art package adds either aesthetic or Popular Art value to the functional form of the product.

Each level of packaging also ties into the level below it and above it. Advertising must *fit* the show or magazine it is positioned with. Football games carry beer commercials not commercials for lipstick; news shows carry headache pill ads not advertisements for toys. The surrogate consumer shown in the ad must match the projected consumer of the show. The advertisement must display the box with its logo, and brand name and image, and must project an image consistent with that of the company. The box must carry the advertising image, logo and brand name, and fit the product well. If the art packaging of the product is designed for children, then the box must reflect that and so on. The art package must fit the functional form and repeat the company logo from the box. Thus each level of package serves its own function, but also carries some of the function from the levels it sits between.

Like the layering of packaging in mass-market goods, computers also have layers of languages to advance from the bits in the machine to the user interface. Computers work by implementing one language in another. For example, our personal accounting system is implemented on top of an application builder like a spreadsheet or database, while that in turn is implemented on a language like PASCAL which in turn is implemented on assembly language which is implemented on machine language. Each of these languages, while having its own independent function, also functions as a support for the language above it, and is implementated in the language below it. The idea of using layers of packaging to get from one function to another is an insight shared by science, art, and engineering designers. The idea of packaging is part of the idea of the artifact which underlies design of all sorts.

Enhancing Personal Identity

Design Art, including advertising, uses packaging to enhance the personal identity of the user. Advertising does this by getting us to identify with the stereotypes shown in the ads. Except for celebrity testimonials, the figures in advertising tend to show stereotypes rather than show particular individuals. They are demographic types, for example, house-wife between 26 and 35 years old, or grandparent. Advertisers discover what the demographics (sex, age, marital status, race, religion, region, income, labor force participation) of their target consumers are and then make advertisements that appeal to that group. The people shown in advertising are highly stereotyped, presenting a social ideal as completely as possible. Advertisers want the product to be connected in the consumer's mind with a whole group or with a need or a type of occasion. They don't want to exclude anyone so they try to broaden the appeal to include a whole target group. Thus advertisements simplify, and typify, showing life worth emulating and showing people as incarnations of larger social categories.

This means that when people identify with the characters in advertisements they are identifying themselves with a group. Thus, advertising encourages us to form group alliances and identities around the use of a brand-name product. They want us to think of ourselves as the Pepsi Generation or Volkswagen owners, thus giving us a sense that we are just like others who also use the advertised brand-name product.

Media images give people a sense of national identity. By conforming to the national images people can also conform to mass conceptions of value and lifestyle. We have needs to form national identities for social mobility and to know how the better class of people behave and dress, so that we can climb the social ladder. Many of the jobs people do now are new sorts of jobs, and there are new people on the job market, minorities and women, so that the stereotypes are changing and new ones need to be formed. What successful people look like, and which brand-name products they use, help us to identify social strata in a mobile society, and help us conform to the social niche we would like to get accustomed to. We all want to be "upscale" and advertisements show us how. This allows people more upward mobility, since the mass media gives them advice on how the "better" people behave and live so they can feel more secure that they are conforming at least in appearance to the "successful" people. For example, by using underarm deodorant or designer clothes people can feel secure that they are conforming to national standards of personal cleanliness and appearance. Advertisments appeal to our identification with successful people and try to shape our sense of what successful people are like around the use of a product (fig. 5.8).

People form their identities through the mass culture, more than through the local culture and family, and in the process of doing this, people tend to adopt the prefabricated identities that are marketed through the mass media and advertising (fig. 5.9). These identities are

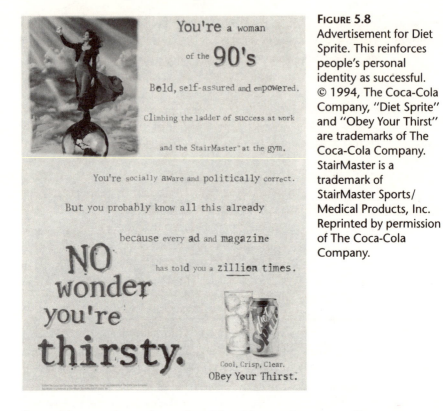

You're a woman

of the **90's**

Bold, self-assured and empowered.

Climbing the ladder of success at work

and the StairMaster™ at the gym.

You're socially aware and politically correct.

But you probably know all this already

because every ad and magazine

has told you a zillion times.

NO wonder you're thirsty.

Cool, Crisp, Clear.
OBey Your Thirst.

FIGURE 5.8
Advertisement for Diet Sprite. This reinforces people's personal identity as successful. © 1994, The Coca-Cola Company, "Diet Sprite" and "Obey Your Thirst" are trademarks of The Coca-Cola Company. StairMaster is a trademark of StairMaster Sports/ Medical Products, Inc. Reprinted by permission of The Coca-Cola Company.

formed in part through product identities, and mass-media stereotypes. Consumer goods act as an index placing their users within national and international society. For example, *neo-traditionalists* are a group formed through their consumer orientation. Neo-traditionalism began as an advertising campaign for *Good Housekeeping* magazine in 1988. Each image in this advertising campaign showed a mother with her children or child and then told the story about her job and her traditional values. The slogan at the bottom of each advertisement was "America is coming home to *Good Housekeeping*." The neo-traditional label then became a group identity label used in mass-media. According to the media image, the neo-traditionalists buy Shaker-inspired furniture, and bake bread by using a bread-baking machine. They buy farm houses in the country to retreat to from their New York City jobs and apartments so that they can feel that they are living a traditional country life, but they actually earn their living in the city. Neo-traditionalists want things like traditional weddings, even though some of them are homosexual couples. Thus, neo-traditionalists consume products with traditional motifs, and hold traditional values compromised with contemporary values (Allen, 1991).

FIGURE 5.9 Advertisement for ASICS athletic shoe. This ad exemplifies how advertisers can appeal directly to our sense of identity. Reprinted by permission of ASICS TIGER Corp.

The mass media and advertising are sculpting an image, neo-traditional, to which people can conform.

Advertising uses both the Popular Art power of vicarious experience and the Design Art power of packaging to reinforce the user's identity. Through the ability to vicariously experience what we see, we are able to make experiences portrayed on television and in the movies our own, and then by using the same products as advertised, we can enhance our own identities by packaging ourselves in terms of mass-media stereotypes. This intensifies our identities as we then become self-conscious as objects. We dress so as to project an image and put slogans on ourselves. We design ourselves and our houses to radiate an image. We have more power to do this than the pre-industrial person because we are surrounded with artifacts. Thus we can construct an image for ourselves through the use of design and the vocabulary of advertising. The mass-produced artifacts have art-packages that we coordinate into the image we project, and advertising and mass media then reflect back to us what sort of person projects the kind of image we do. Commercial products come with symbols and recognizable social status which people can use to form their own images. We get multiple media reinforcers pushing us into an image and that image is our new group identity. We are young professionals, urban poor, single mothers, neo-traditionals, or senior citizens, and so on. Through the media we see ourselves as stereotyped.

The Language of Advertising Art

All advertisements show people and things in a similar way. The emotional appeals, the poises, and expressions come in a tight collection of types giving them an iconographic sort of conventionality which makes the advertisements easier and faster to grasp and makes the messages less ambiguous. These conventions of package, image, brand name, fashion, and so on, make a language of form that we can use to communicate with each other over distance.

We use ourselves for advertising. We wear the logo of a sports team or college, or mass-media superhero on our T-shirt, hat, or jacket. Like advertised products, we put an advertising brand name or slogan on top of our art packaging of fashion. We wear product advertisements and political slogans like "Save the Whales" on our clothes. We package ourselves in the recognized language of form given by fashion so as to project our profession and class identity. We are stereotyped so that someone in Columbus, Ohio, and someone in New York City can communicate with each other and can read each other's *fashion statements*. When we paint our faces, mask our odors with perfumes, put on fashionable outfits, we make ourselves into objects which are stereotyped and easily read. It gives us a national identity, and beyond that an international identity. Fashion in the modern world serves the function of an externalized symbol system that connects people to the social world to which they aspire and individuates them in that world. Fashion gives people a sense of identity and continuity as the material possession of known brand names gives them a sense of known and ranked social status. Our outer appearance takes on a meaning in the mass-media language of form.

These idealized stereotypes then become the language of visual form. We stereotype who lives in our country. Some criticize advertising for not showing enough African-American faces, or Latino faces. They want their own ethnic group to get an equal share of the image-building force of the media. They want their ethnic group to become an element in the media language of form. The ethnic character that is not stereotyped on television vanishes from group attention, and doesn't have a group image or stereotype through which they can be identified.

Further, any message we wish to communicate can be packaged in the language of advertising. Public service announcements, for example, look just like product advertisements, and political candidates use the same language of form as insurance salesmen and retail stores. They all adopt the same language of form and project the same stereotyped public images and values.

With the appropriate packaging, we can now project ourselves as object-images. We wrap ourselves in an art package, and then become a *word* in the mass-media language of form. We dress like the stereotypes we see and are reacted to as those stereotypes. Through these stereotypes the thought of ourselves can be projected into the media by images of people wrapped in the same art packages as ourselves and we can experience what happens to them both by identifying with their art packaging, and also by wearing that art packaging ourselves, and so living in our own lives the experience we have seen projected on television. We can drive the same cars, wear our clothing and hair in the same styles, and interact with the same products and stereotypes we see in the media. This intensifies our identities, as we see ourselves as objects in the media, as well as subjects wrapped in media packaging.

The External Mind of Television and Computer

Our direct experience of our planet has been diminished (Mander, 1978). Most of us live in human artifacts: cities and within those cities, houses, and within those houses, rooms with air-conditioned or heated air, completely cut off from the non-human world of nature and the lifestyles of pre-industrial human beings. We no longer interact daily with wild animals, forests, soil, insects, and weather. Some of us can go from home to garage to car to parking garage to work place without even stepping into the outside air and weather. We are surrounded on a daily level only with things that have been planned and made by human beings. We live in Design Art.

We do not live at the same pace as nature either. We have daylight in our houses twenty-four hours a day. We don't have to experience night. We rarely see the moon or stars. We live outside the plant rhythms. We eat plants like tomatoes and oranges and cucumbers out of season. Many of us never see our food grow. The food we eat is often highly processed completed meals where we just open the package and pop it into the microwave oven. We are cut off from natural rhythms and from sensations of wind, rain, of walking in the air and experiencing the multiplicity of sound, sights, smells, touch sensations that one would feel in a natural environment like a forest.

We live in an artificial world surrounded by human mediation between our needs and the natural world of their satisfaction. We get our milk in plastic cartons from the store, not from cows. We don't walk, we drive cars when we want to go somewhere. We don't go over to people's houses to talk to them, we call them on the phone. We don't deal with things directly, everything comes to us indirectly. It is wrapped, processed, and shipped. What we know about the natural world is filtered and packaged through the media. We don't experience nature directly, we see a nature show on television. Within this artifactual world our primary sources of information about the world outside our rooms come from the mass media, primarily television. We live a sensory deprivation sort of existence, because our houses and rooms have become stimulus poor compared to the natural life of our ancestors (Mander, 1978). We have minimized external sensory stimulus and so we turn to television as the only stimulus around in a sensory deprived and speeded up life rhythm. We watch television because there are no forest creatures, threats, wind, smells, stars. One need not reckon with nature. We are bored in our safe and environmentally controlled artificial environments. Television as a flashing light in a darkened room takes over our attention. We stare at the television screen and don't experience things directly.

Television is like an external group mind wherein Popular Art and advertising play the role of thoughts. As we discussed with narrative thinking in chapter 3, people form a spatialized image of themselves to think experiences through in an inner "space." That is, we have the ability to spatialize things so as to think about them imagistically. We can imagine ourselves or others walking through events by imagining them in this inner space. We can use our inner mental space to think of ideas metaphorically, for example, ideas as objects, or time as a line. We have an inner space into which to project our thoughts, and images. With television there is now an outer "space" that serves a similar function. We experience the Popular Art on television as a narration with us in it. The television images are like daydreams to us, only the daydreams are produced by someone else. Through identification with the characters, we imagine ourselves walking through events, packaged in the media stereotypes and values. In this way, mass-media art becomes a medium for personal narration in an external mental space.

We live in human artifact, plugged into the group external mental space of television. Television gives the images; we project a forum. As we discussed, we can package ourselves and our messages in the language of form of advertising and then project them as thoughts into this mass-media group mental space. Television provides the medium, the group focus of attention, and shared style and conversational context within which these stereotyped packages can take their meaning. Within that group mental space, advertising packages messages about values and lifestyles and products in terms of brand name, image, and slogan. Thoughts are packaged so that they continue a conversation within a shared mental space. For example, one advertisement says you should wash your clothes with this brand of soap to avoid "ring-around-the-collar" dirt, then another message is broadcast into the medium that shows a car-crash dummy with a tire around its neck saying "avoid ring around the collar, don't drink and drive." The second advertisement takes its meaning by using the vocabulary of the first advertisement.

Television affects our sense of what is real and what is not. Like our own personal minds, television interprets reality. It gives us a particular slant on the family, the world, and current events. For example, it gives people the impression that there is more violence than there really is in the world around us. That which does not appear on television has no visibility in culture and so does not enter into people's thinking about events. Television uses a distorted sense of time by showing us events that took hours or even years to happen, in segments that last minutes or seconds. Events are temporally condensed on television. We also condense time when we think. When we remember something, or think through something that we expect to happen to us, we only see the high points in quick snippets. This is another way in which the images we see on television are like inner thoughts. The images we receive from television are stored in our memories undifferentiated from images of things we have personally experienced. The actions of movie heroes and advertising stereotypes which we vicariously experience as our own are also experienced as their own by everyone else tuned into that channel. In this way television becomes a personal external mental space for each of us while also uniting us all in a shared series of thoughts.

Television thus becomes a mental space akin to perception. We perceive the world through television. It becomes our eyes and ears. We get new information from it, and dreams. It allows us to perceive what everyone else who is also tuned into that channel perceives. What is shown on television then takes on reality. That is, whether the people stereotyped really are the way they are portrayed on television, or whether the news event really happened the way it is shown, we will act as though these things are real, because we all saw them that way.

Also, by being able to surround ourselves in life with the same Design Art that is projected on the screen, we can bring the mass-media experience of television into our own lives on a physical level as well. Television and Design Art allow us to share our perceptions and day-dreams with others, both while watching the television as well as when not watching television by wearing the slogans and using the products shown. What we see there becomes the outer world beyond our dark-ened rooms, and we package ourselves and our rooms to be consistent with what we see. Thus the images on television become shared cultural experiences that take on the role of metaphorical structure against which the rest of life is discussed and played.

Television is part of a new lifestyle where we do not roam the forest anymore, but sealed off from nature, we live within our own creations. Television encourages separation, by encouraging people to forsake other interactions with people for watching television. We don't interact with our real neighbors, but rather with the neighbors shown on televi-sion. We don't go to the ball game or concert or political event personally, we watch it on the screen. Thus, television both separates us and unites us. We become physically more separate and isolated, each of us sitting in our own darkened room watching television. Then we become more united as we are absorbed into the new union, the group mental space and shared experiences of television.

The television medium is being broadened and complexified. We don't all watch the same shows because there are so many choices. Thus, although television is a shared mental space, we are not really all plugged together into the same space. Some of us only watch sports and rock videos, while others only watch situation comedies and crime stories. We have cable television with all its channels, and VCRs to record shows and watch movies at home. We use the television medium to separate ourselves into groups, market niches, and stereotypes. We share an external mental space with others in the same group, but share mental space in only varying degrees with people in other groups.

We also play video games and computer games. People take home movies of their children, pets, and celebrations and play them on television. There are people working on "virtual reality" machines which project a whole world for the viewer to move around in, feeling and hearing and seeing the output of a computer program as though it were a real-life situation. For all of these modern activities, we sit passively in our temperature controlled rooms watching or interacting with flashing images on a screen. All of these activities are variations on the same theme. As we sit in low-stimulus environments we want something to do, some stimulus, some challenge. We find this stimulus and challenge by interacting not with nature, but with the man-made. We construct for ourselves alternate mental stimulants and spend our time doing things like reliving moments with our family on film, or daydreaming by watching television shows and movies, or having a video game adventure where we slay monsters by pushing a button on our video game machine.

We live within Design Art and grow external group mental spaces. We are becoming the organic self within a cocoon of artifact. Television acts as a medium for a kind of perception. We use it passively to see and hear things from the world beyond our rooms. However, besides the entertainment media, we also rely on computers to enhance our thinking. Computers not only allow us to keep written records in a memory external to any individual mind, but also allow us to think about those records in a mind external to any individual. Computers are mental processors, computing solutions to the problems we pose for them. They give us enhanced mental skills, like solving complex calculations. They keep track of information, solve problems for us, and act as a tool for us to expand the amount or quality of thought we ourselves produce. Computers also allow us to communicate with one another through electronic mail and bulletin boards, thus allowing us electronically mediated contact with people at a great physical distance from ourselves.

The computers are a form of externalized mind. They are a shared mind in the sense that we all use the same programs in our computers, and use one of a limited number of types of computers, but they are not shared mind in the sense that television is. We do not all see the same thing at the same time as we do when we are watching television.

The computers are like that part of mind which is rational, symbolic, and mathematical. Our pocket calculators manipulate numbers for us. Our home computers help us do our taxes, or help us write electronic mail messages by checking our spelling. They help us think and help us remember. We are not passively watching images when we use our computers; we are using them actively to solve problems. Where television is an external mental space that allows us to be shown images that we passively absorb, the computers are external minds in the sense that they act as additional memories and mental processors. Thus, we are growing an external group mind. It has two parts, the mass media which are perception-like, feeding us images and sounds, and the computers which are active mental processors doing rational problem solving for us. As we will discuss in the next chapter, we are adapting to this two part external mind by expanding some of our personal mental skills and shutting down others. This external mind is shaping the texture of our thoughts and mental skills. The mass media and computers are linking us together in new ways. As we will discuss, they are instrumental in shaping a new religious dimension and evolutionary stage for culture.

CHAPTER 6

The Media and the Rebirth of Mythic Culture

SINCE THE GREEKS INVENTED a phonetic alphabet and started writing, there has been growth of a logical analytical mode of thought as opposed to the ancient mythic modes of thought in Western culture. There has been a growth of science and a decline of oral tradition and mythology. Throughout the world, scientific explanations have replaced myths. Thunder is no longer thought to be the rumbling of a god, but the sound made by the physical action of electrically charged particles in the clouds. Illness is no longer thought to be caused by demons or spirits, but by bacteria and viruses. In the past people could see the significance of their lives and nature in ancient mythic terms. Much myth has been forgotten, and modern people are left with existentialist meaninglessness and despair. Although people have a need for a mythic level to their lives, the oral traditions that fed that need have been replaced by scientific secular culture that denies mythic values. There seems to be no meaning to life, no purpose or grand plan for existence from the point of view of science.

This leaves the symbols that carried the mythic values and the needs for myth free to be exploited and explored in advertising and mass-media art. Popular Art and advertising are evolving to fulfill these mythic needs. The media, television, and movies, become a medium for delivering art through the external group mental space. As this medium strengthens, a new mythic level to culture is emerging.

1. EVOLUTION OF CULTURE AND COGNITION

Three Cultural Stages

Merlin Donald (1991) has a useful theory of the evolution of human culture and cognition. Donald's idea is that from ape culture to our own late twentieth-century culture we can see three basic stages: mimetic culture, which is culture before language is discovered where communication is done through gestures; mythic culture, which is built around the skills of spoken language; and theoretic culture, which is built around the skills of written language. Each of these stages of culture is built upon the one that went before it. We also have three kinds of memory: episodic, which is the concrete memory of specific events; procedural, which is the memory of procedures, like the motions required for a dance; and semantic which is word memory. According to Donald's (1991) theory, we started with episodic memory, then procedural memory evolved with the skills of the mimetic cultural stage, and then semantic memory evolved with the skills of the mythic cultural stage. Theoretic stage of cognition has a new form of memory over and above these, namely the external memory. This is the memory in books and in computers external to the human mind. This way of looking at cultural evolution gives us a framework against which we can see the rise of a further evolutionary stage in human culture, built on top of the theoretic culture, in the media of television and computer. The external group mind we discussed in the last chapter has within it the seeds of another evolutionary stage of culture.

Mimetic Culture

Mimetic culture is human culture before language developed. In mimetic culture imitative gestures are invented which are used to represent some experienced event. The event is acted out in gestures. Such actions in a non-verbal culture are enough to allow knowledge of the event to be shared and group action to be coordinated. Such acted out events then become rituals, like in a tribal dance preparing for a hunt where someone imitates the buffalo's movement in a stereotyped way while someone else imitates the stereotyped movements of the hunter. These mimetic skills can be seen in modern culture in things like pantomime games, and mime. We use this mimetic skill when we learn through imitation, for example when we learn to do things like swimming. Children use this skill when they act out the events of the day with their dolls; if they have been taken to the doctor's office, they then take the doll to the doctor in play. In this way they are assimilating the events of the day by acting them out in mimetic play.

The use of gestural language survives into our own culture in the gestures we make when we talk, like putting our hands together when we talk about unity, or answering a question by shrugging our shoulders to express that we don't know the answer. Beside overt gestures, we also communicate our basic mental orientation through our posture. Just as a cat puts up its back in fear, and a dog wags its tail when happy, people slump their shoulders when depressed, and clench their fists or grit their teeth when angry. In religion it is often the posture and system of ritual gestures that constitute the real "meaning" of a ceremony rather than the spoken words. In this way, the mimetic body postures and gestures are still used in religious ritual. For example, when Catholics make the sign of the cross, they are grounding their faith in gestural forms like those of mimetic culture. When we stand up and put our hands over our hearts to say the pledge of allegiance we are grounding our patriotism in gestural forms as well.

In mythic cultures there are often strong remnants of mimetic culture. For example, many mythic cultures practice ritual scarification and body painting. These are used as ways to non-verbally express personal intentions and personal history (Anderson, 1990). For example, native American tribes used to paint their bodies with certain colors to indicate the intention of going to war, and other colors to indicate a celebration.

Many of the statues and images from mythic cultures seem to have the function of recording specific mimetic postures that signal a particular mental orientation and type of experience. Anthropologist F. Goodman (1986) has shown that when modern people take the postures shown in some of the statues and images from ancient cultures, holding them while attending to the fast rhythmic music of a rattle or drum, they can go into hyper-arousal trances accompanied by distinct types of experiences. The fast rhythmic music enables their layers of narrative and rational thinking to be inhibited so that they can focus on whatever thoughts arise from their body posture. The trances that people go into then display the thinking pattern that goes with that mimetic posture.

The posture and gestures produce trance experiences like turning into an animal, or hearing a prophetic voice, being healed, or taking a spirit journey. These experiments with posture suggest that many of these ancient art objects are records of mimetic cultural gestures communicating mental orientation and topic of thought (fig. 6.1).

From Mythic Culture to Theoretic Culture

From the mimetic culture humans evolved to mythic culture. This level of culture depends upon the use of spoken language. Along with this stage of culture all the skills that make speech possible were developed. When humans began to use speech, they used it for communication and story telling. To name a thing was to call its essence. Thus, in many North American Indian tribes people had secret names, and to use that name was to have power over that person. The ancient god-kings in Babylon and Egypt were said to know the true names which controlled the forces of nature.

Mythic culture developed elaborate mythological systems with stories which gave every event and object encountered in daily life a meaning. Myths preserve the cultural identities of their users. Myths are the collective digested results of generations of storytellings. They keep a remembrance of events and patterns beyond the memory of any living human. Myth governs the collective mind in such cultures. It gives social values and events significance and guides decision making. As we will discuss, contemporary mass media are the reemergence of a mythic level culture.

The next level of culture built on top of the skills of the mythic culture and mimetic culture is the theoretic culture. Theoretic culture is built around written language. In this stage, logical and scientific theories are made. These are then preserved and evolved in written language. The earliest written records we have are cuneiform writing dating back about 5,000 years in Uruk in ancient Mesopotamia. This oldest writing was used to keep lists for the purpose of trade and required a special class of scribes to read and write it. Cuneiform was not phonetic, and it was not used to write down speech, but rather to keep track of goods. The Greeks were the first in the West to use a phonetic alphabet. Around the eighth century B.C. the Greeks modified the Phoenician alphabet to permit a precise transcription of Greek sounds. While in the ancient Minoan and Mycenian civilizations only the professional scribes were literate, with the new phonetic alphabet the general population could become literate as well. By the time of the

FIGURE 6.1 The Adena Pipe, c. 200 B.C. found in Athens County, Ohio. This art shows a trance posture.

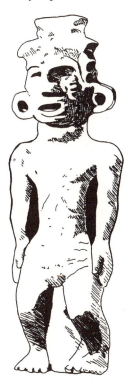

classical period, written language became almost as widely used and known among Greek citizens as was the spoken language (Vernant, 1982). Writing allowed the dissemination of knowledge that had previously been forbidden or restricted, and it became the medium for maintaining a common culture.

In the West, theoretic culture begins with these literate classical Greeks. By 480 B.C. the Greek culture had changed from a mythic to a theoretic culture. Nature and statues began to lose their animation and the gods stopped talking to people. The gods changed from being living personalities to being allegories for natural forces. The cultural emphasis in classical Greece changed from the mystical to the rational. The philosophers talked against the existence of the gods. The concept of truth changed from truth as that which is seen in a direct clear mystical vision, to that which is persuasive to the public in the way that arguments in a law court are. The political life of the cities began to use more speech and argumentation. The whole fabric of society changed, as another sort of thinking emerged.

Written language promotes the construction of logical and scientific theories about the world. Written theories can be studied and built upon. We can pass down knowledge that way to many more people than we could do orally. Writing promotes formal arguments and proofs. The kinds of constructs analogous to the myths of mythic culture in theoretic culture are theories which are systems of argued-for truth functional assertions about the world. These theories predict and explain, and exist mostly in written records. Thus with the emergence of theoretic culture, people's thinking becomes secularized.

In terms of the Greek society, for example, the mythic culture believed in a pantheon of gods and goddesses that watched human actions and caused good or bad things to happen. Herodotus (c. 484–420 B.C.), for example, thinks in the old mythic way. Although he writes that he has rejected poetry and is just telling the things that seem to him credible, he tells his history as though the active interference of gods were a fact. Herodotus still believes in living gods and spirits. For example, several times in book II of his *History* (Book II, 61 and 170) he omits the name *Osiris* from his narrative for religious reasons. At another point in his *History*, when discussing his theory that there is both a hero Hercules as well as a god Hercules, he writes: "In saying thus much concerning these matters, may I incur no displeasure either of god or hero" (Book II, 45). Herodotus not only tells his history with the gods playing an active part, but he still fears the gods and respects the secrets of their mystery cults.

Aristotle (384–322 B.C.) however, thinks in the new way. Aristotle does not fear the gods, or even believe in the gods. For example, although prophesying in dreams is given by Aristotle as one of the main experiences which support a belief in gods, in *De Divinatione Per Somnum* he completely rejects the idea that dreams come from the gods. Most so-called prophetic dreams, writes Aristotle, are mere coincidences. Further, he thinks it is inconsistent to take the sender of a dream to be a god when the receiver of the dream is not the best and wisest person, but merely a commonplace person. Aristotle rejects divine messages and divinely imparted knowledge of the future like that which runs through the history told by Herodotus. Aristotle is not afraid of the gods; they are not alive and listening the way they were for Herodotus and others still thinking in terms of the ancient mythic culture. Aristotle tries to refute the existence of the gods through rational argument. Thus already with Aristotle the theoretic culture substitutes reasoned theories for what they take to be the empty superstitions of myth.

In the theoretic cultural stage there are skills of gesture and mime, skills of speech and storytelling. Layered on those skills are the skills needed to have written language. Written language allows things to be remembered outside any individual's mind in an external memory in books and other written records. Those things that were memorized stories passed on from one generation to the next in mythic culture are written in books in theoretic culture. Once things are written, they can be analyzed, criticized, and verified in ways impossible with orally transmitted stories. Written language permits a single "true" version of the story, the written one, unlike myths in oral culture, where there are many versions of a story, and stories change over time. Writing also allows people in the past to talk to us as though they were contemporaries. Thus, we can read the words of Aristotle who lived over two thousand years ago. Aristotle's words have not changed. Spoken words are not like that. You cannot catch the words of dead people in traditional mythic culture except through communication with them in the spirit world through statues, dreams, or mediums.

The sort of thought type that goes with theoretic culture is often called *paradigmatic*. This is rational thought but not rational thought as contrasted with irrational thought, but rather rational thought as contrasted with narrative thought. Narrative thought, which is the dominate mode of thought in mythic culture, constructs stories and historical accounts; paradigmatic thought constructs theories, truth functional assertions, and logical arguments. Paradigmatic thought is used to do science. Whereas narrative thought comes naturally, paradigmatic thought is taught in schools along with reading and writing. As we discussed, paradigmatic thought, critical thought, is reinforced by aesthetic formalist Fine Art, while narrative thought is reinforced by Popular Art. In modern Western culture we use both kinds of thought, along with the mimetic skills and gestures which are held over from an even earlier cultural stage. Thus we have layered one kind of thinking and way of approaching life on top of another. As we will discuss, we consolidate the gains of theoretic culture as we move beyond it into the next stage of culture made possible by the external mind of mass media and computer.

2. THE DESTRUCTION OF MYTH

The Incompatibility Between Theoretic and Mythic Culture

Although the cognitive skills like the reading and paradigmatic thought of theoretic culture are layered on top of the speech skills of mythic culture and imitative skills of mimetic culture, there is a great incompatibility between theoretic culture and mythic culture. Theoretic culture is not concerned with significance in the same sense that mythic culture is. Theoretic culture does not look for connecting purposes and meanings, but rather for impersonal objective laws and formulas. It looks at events as information to be analyzed and generalized. The first step in the establishment of theoretic culture has been dismantling the myths. From the perspective of reason and science, myth is ignorant superstition.

As we said, the ancient mythic cultures believed that gods and spirits took active part in people's lives. The ancients thought of nature in general in more animistic terms than we do today. The ancient Greeks seem to have thought of most everything which was self-moving as inhabited by a spirit or god. For example, in his *History* (Book I, 189), Herodotus tells the story of Persian King Cyrus who had just come to the river Gyndes on his way to Babylon when one of his sacred white horses ran into the river and drowned. Cyrus believed that the drowning was caused by the river's willful insolence, and this so enraged him that he and his army stopped their march of conquest to spend a whole summer digging trenches to punish the river. To obtain revenge on the river he swore that he would break the strength of the river to such a degree that even women could cross it without wetting their knees.

From the perspective of reason and science such acts and attitudes are ignorant superstition. Rivers cannot act willfully nor can they be punished. From the perspective of reason and science, myth teaches false ideas about the animation of nature and the interference of gods. Before raw information can be used to confirm or falsify theories, it must be stripped of its mythic content. Before reason and science can work, the river must be stripped of its personality and animating will, and be viewed as mere physical water.

This process of stripping nature of myth has been going on for a long time. It was done first by the classical Greeks. As writing and the type of thought that goes with it became common, the mythic world view began to collapse. There were still myths and shrines, but the gods stopped taking active part in people's lives. The gods stopped talking to people through oracles and statues. The Greeks themselves noticed that the gods were becoming silent, that the statues no longer talked, and the oracles were no longer as accurate, and made theories to explain these phenomena. For example, in *On the Failure of Oracles* (*Moralia* 10, 415a) Plutarch (c. 100 A.D.) theorized that responses from oracles were really given by "daemons" who were semidivine beings with supernatural knowledge. These daemons, he thought, were subject to mortality and were already very old, having been giving responses since early times, and hence had declined in wisdom and accuracy and would soon not be heard at all. Thus, he resorted to a naturalistic theory for explaining the death of the god-voices rather than explaining it in mythic terms by saying, for example, that the problem was that the people were no longer good enough, the gods were angry with them, or they needed to discover a new ritual. Myth was withdrawn from nature.

Later most of the remaining pagan myths and ways of life were destroyed in the name of Christianity in the medieval period. Medieval Christianity destroyed idols and put people to death for paganism. Idols had been so widespread in the fourth century that Constantine felt the need to send out armies to smash all idols, but even in medieval Italy and Byzantium there were still a few enchanted idols who were believed to have the power to avert disaster. We hear of such idols being used as late as the fourteenth century, when for example, Pope John XXII in 1326, felt the need to denounce those who imprison demons in images through magic so as to obtain answers from them (Jaynes, 1976).

By destroying idols and forbidding their use, the Church destroyed the last remnant of cultural knowledge in Europe of the highly developed mimetic gestural language which grounded religious practices in the ancient civilizations. The medieval Church continued to use gestures like the sign of the cross within its religious ritual and thus continued to ground its own religion in the gestures of mimetic culture. However, the mimetic postures and gestures that allowed the ancient statue users access to the spirit world were forgotten.

Although the medieval Church reasserted a mythical worldview with myths and divine intervention in life, it also revered what was written in a book, not as a way of seeing, but as the absolute truth. For the medieval, every visual thing had an invisible counterpart which was its meaning in "God's" book. Nature was a living symbol of divinity. Flesh pointed to God as his living symbol. A dove meant the holy spirit, and in rivulets flowed the Trinity. Since everything came from God, everything was a symbol and had a divine meaning to be discovered. The medievals mythologized the idea of the written word into a way of seeing daily life in terms of a bigger pattern. The details of life were words being written by God. Thus the medievals saw nature and man in terms of a grand design. They still had myths, for example, the Christian central story about death and resurrection used an agriculturalist mythic theme; but Christianity substituted the word for the image and its myths were written down in a book.

With the invention of the printing press and the beginning of science during the Renaissance and the Enlightenment, the worldview of theoretic culture became strong again, and overwhelmed the medieval mythic way of looking at life. Christianity then became a target of theoretic culture's destruction of myth. The Christian stories began to be judged on the grounds of their factual truth, and treated as another set of myths to be destroyed in the name of reason and science. People felt that myths are at best only metaphorical and at worst perniciously false beliefs, so one could and should replace myths with science in order to look at the world realistically in terms of logically constructed theories. After all, the world as described by myth has within it supernatural forces and miraculous events all of which are denied by science. All such superstition should be wiped out to be replaced with a scientific and logical view of the natural world. People assumed that there is no need for myth when we have science to tell us what is true.

The Need for Myth

However, myth functions for humans in a way that science cannot. For example, according to contemporary science, we do not descend from Adam and Eve, but from animals. Science dismantles what it takes to be a false fact, that there was a primal non-animal couple from which all humans are descended. Science substitutes a complex theory about our evolution from lower animals as fact, but that leaves out the mythic function of the Adam and Eve tale. Part of the mythic function of this story is to explain that we are not animal, and have a special status in nature that makes it moral for us to eat and exploit plants and animals. This is moral, according to the myth, because animals, unlike us, do not have souls. We are special, says the Christian story; we have dominion over all the plants and animals, so we have the right to choose which animals live, and which plants are weeds to be rooted out. This mythic function is not addressed by science. Souls are not accessible to scientific discovery. Whether or not we can morally exploit animals is outside the domain of scientific reasoning. It is not fact but value. Thus some people reject the scientific truth of evolution, not because they fundamentally care about where people came from but because they do not want to give up the mythic core of the Adam and Eve story. The Adam and Eve story acts as a central myth for Christianity explaining our place in nature. Science can deny the factual claims, but that leaves a primal impulse, namely the question of our place in nature, unsatisfied. Thus, theoretic culture can substitute its theories for the myths of mythic culture, but in doing so it leaves some of the functions of myth unfulfilled.

There is still a need for myth in culture. Just as there is a place for mimetic skills in our own culture in our rituals and imitative play, there is also a place in culture for myth. Myth and science can live with each other comfortably. Myth does not need to be wiped out in order to have science, in fact we need to have both myth and science for a completely integrated culture and mind. We have a need to see ourselves within bigger patterns and to see meaning and significance in the coincidental occurrences of everyday life. We have a need to see purpose in our lives and to think of ourselves as part of a bigger plan with a personal destiny.

As Carl G. Jung (1964) said, the modern increase of scientific understanding has led to a dehumanization of natural and social forces, and people have become alienated from nature as it no longer is seen as an expression of human-like forces, but rather inhuman physical forces. The loss of a belief in gods and demons has produced a lack of awareness of the powers within human nature, and has led to an overemphasis on the conscious and rational parts of human nature to the exclusion of the feeling and intuitive parts, said Jung. The modern West is unbalanced. In modern times the intellect and the conscious will come to dominate to the exclusion of the spiritual and intuitive powers of the human personality. We have repressed many of our instincts, and so feel cut off, rootless. In the process of becoming civilized we have divided our consciousness from the deeper instinctual strata of our psyche. These strata still exist but can find expression only in dreams and myths. Archaic remnants of our biological, prehistoric past are in our dreams and myths.

Although primitive ways of thinking and being in the world are still part of us, with the growth of science, the mythic level of mind has been denied expression in culture. As a consequence, we feel rootless, ungrounded, and restless. There seems to be no meaning to life, nor any reason to believe this value system rather than that one. We live in an age where the way of thinking of theoretic culture dominates, and theoretic culture by itself is not enough to ground us in reality. Theoretic culture does not give us a way to make value choices. It does not tell us who we are, what life is all about, and what the significance or purpose of it all is. Nor can it help us see the mythic patterns of our lives. Science and reason only give us a system of objective facts; they cannot ground us in a bigger context. Thus, theoretic culture with its analysis and scientific theories does not satisfy all our cognitive needs. It does not give our everyday lives and experiences significance. It does not give us cultural identities and a sense of purpose and place in the generations of humans. It does not tell us global overarching stories that help us to connect the objects we use with significance, respect, and spirituality. It does not give us a clear sense of our place in nature. All these things are not done by theoretic culture as expressed in science and logical thought. These needs were satisfied in mythic culture but would go completely unsatisfied now if it were not for art. It is within art that these needs are recognized and addressed. A new mythic level to culture is slowly growing within the media arts. These mythic needs form a cultural function that the arts of advertising and Popular Art are created to support.

The old myths were overthrown not because people had no need for myth, but first because the myths were making claims about the natural world that then clashed with the claims of science, and secondly because people were no longer living in cultures that revolved around hunting or agriculture, so the mythic ideas lost much of their force. We need new stories to match our new lifestyle and those need to be in a medium that is compatible with theoretic culture. The new myths cannot make claims because if they make claims they compete with theoretic culture. For example, the Adam and Eve story competes with the theory of evolution. Because of this competition, the story cannot carry its mythic values. The factual claims of the story are not consistent with things we are told by the authority of science. We need stories to carry mythic values that do not compete with the beliefs of science, but rather reinforce them. Thus, both the medium for delivering mythic functions and the myths themselves need to be changed to match our new situation.

3. THE NEW MEDIUM FOR MYTHS

A Medium for Myth That Does Not Compete with Science

Contemporary culture has the beginning of a medium and stories that match our situations. We have television and movies where these stories play. The old myths conflicted with science because they were expressed as beliefs; the new myths will not conflict with science because they will be experiences, and art. That is, the old myths expressed beliefs about the natural world, spirits, magic, and life after death. They supported a worldview where spirits and gods could inhabit statues, or where divine interference in the daily lives of humans could occur. These beliefs can be expressed as propositions and refuted by science. However, once the myths have a medium of their own — videotape, movies, television —

they will be expressed as art and experience, not as claims about the natural world. After all, an experience is neither true nor false; neither is a novel, a play, or a work of visual art. Because the new medium is a medium of art, what is broadcast in that medium is judged by art standards which are outside the realm of paradigmatic thought and scientific theory.

Television art is judged on how entertaining it is, and everything on television strives to be entertaining, even news shows. Television works best to project clear overdrawn things like sports, violence, and action shows where it is easy to differentiate the good guys from the bad guys. Shows that have clear, easily grasped visuals and sounds are best. These include quiz and game shows, situation comedies, police-action shows, soap operas, shows that are not subtle, and shows with broad-band emotional content. Not only in entertainment shows, but also in the news and information programs there is a bias toward action that can be painted with a broad brush away from subtlety and complexity. News shows are art, as they select and package taped events into entertaining units. The story with a good visual image, like a statue being torn down, or a rally with people holding signs, gets more attention than a meeting where people just sit and talk. Thus news also becomes visual art.

This new mythic level to culture does not compete with science, because it carries art values and art standards, not those of science. Being entertaining is an art standard. This is the standard used to judge Popular Art. By maintaining a difference between the standards used for art and those used for science we make it possible for mythic themes to be played that do not conflict with science, but give us satisfaction for those needs science leaves untouched. That is, by making a split between science and art, we are able to split off mythic value from mythic facts. We can throw out the mythic claims about the supernatural but still keep the mythic values. Judging the shows on television by the standards of entertainment allows them to communicate mythic values about heroes, lifestyles, and ways to solve problems without communicating mythic fact. We can experience gods and demons on television without believing in their existence.

Our mythic needs are not for the *meaning* of life, which is a verbal metaphor, so much as they are for the *experience* of life. As Joseph Campbell says (Campbell and Moyers, 1988, p. 1) "I think what we're seeking is an experience of being alive, so that our life experiences on the purely physical plane will have resonances within our own innermost being and reality, so that we actually feel the rapture of being alive." This is why the media can respond to this need. The vicarious experiences we

FIGURE 6.2a Wind in your hair advertisement: Invesco Industrial Income Fund. Reprinted by permission from Invesco Industrial Income Fund.

have through art help us experience life's possibilities. Our need for myth is not a need for the gods to actually exist, but for us to experience the richness and depth of life as felt through the vicarious experience of the gods. When we see the advertisement where people are standing on a boat surrounded by a beautiful sea with the wind in their hair (fig. 6.2a), we get a vicarious experience of that thrill of life, even though we may never ourselves actually set foot on a boat. We associate wind in our hair with freedom, and that association then becomes part of the metaphorical language of advertisement (fig. 6.2b). This sort of myth-fragment does not compete with science and paradigmatic thinking because it is not propositional. It is experience. It is not true or false. When we watch the situation comedy show or movie we don't generally get assertions about the world that are there to be judged true or false; we get entertainment and experience. Advertisements like the one of the cartoon Green Giant in his valley picking only the best peas or the little cartoon elves in a hole in a tree making cookies, are merely associating the product with a

Discover the world anew...

with fresh ideas from **TRAVELER!**

Subscribe to TRAVELER today and discover the latest travel trends . . . out-of-the-way places . . . ideas for weekend or day trips . . . and much more!

You'll journey to national parks, historical sites, resorts, exciting cities, and little-known places in the U.S.A., in Canada, and abroad.

TRAVELER not only provides wonderful vacation ideas, but it also gives you all the practical information you need to plan the perfect trip! *Travel Wise*, a special section following each TRAVELER getaway, tells you how to get there . . . what to see and do . . . and where to eat and stay (with AAA and Michelin recommendations).

To order, call toll free 1-800-638-4077 *in the U.S. and Canada, Monday through Friday, 8 a.m. to 4 p.m. ET.*
Or write to NATIONAL GEOGRAPHIC TRAVELER, Dept. 01782, Washington, D.C. 20036.

Only $17⁹⁵*

for six colorful issues.

NATIONAL GEOGRAPHIC SOCIETY
Washington, D.C. 20036

* Annual rate in the U.S. In Canada, $27.20 Canadian funds or $22.75 U.S. funds. For all other countries, $25.50 U.S. funds. Please add 8% sales tax for orders sent to Maryland and 7% GST for orders sent to Canada.

pleasant story and creating desire for the product. They are not claiming that a green giant or little cookie-making elves really exist.

Mythic content is delivered through media art as an experience of metaphors and stereotypes which we can then take into our lives as Design Art. In that way after vicariously experiencing the gods on television, we can then imagine ourselves gods as we dress like them and act like them in our real lives.

The claims that are made on the media are generally couched in scientific reasoning. Advertisements say things like "nine out of ten doctors recommend," or "independent laboratory tests show," or they might run a comparative test as their advertisement, showing their product working better than some other product. The Popular Art on the media is the same way; it gives us a dream, an entertaining fantasy, and when it does purport to express a fact, that fact is presented against the background of science as the authority.

Thus the art on television does not contradict the spirit of science and theoretic culture, media art lives beside science and reinforces it by using the scientific worldview as the ultimate authority on questions of fact. But it is also independent of science by presenting fact in a highly interpreted and packaged form. The media make science fact into art. What we acquire from the media are not just factual claims, but values and experiences. Thus, unlike the old myths which presented mythic values and mythic facts, the new myths present mythic values and *science* facts.

Of course there is always the possibility that this will change, and that the media will start presenting an alternative view of the facts that does not reconcile with the worldview of science. The media might try to persuade people that, for example, aliens are among us doing experiments on people, or that ghosts really exist, through the use of personal interviews and dramatic reenactments. Thus, although the media make it possible for there to be a mythic level and a theoretic level of culture coexisting beside each other without conflict, that might change as the media mature and people's mentalities change. In the future we might find ourselves in a world dominated by a mythic worldview built on media images and values which conflict with the worldview of science.

Making Permanent Records of Visual Experience

A new "language" is being born in modern visual art. Through this language new levels of myth, significance, transcendent order, and metaphor, can be expressed. We are creating representational devices for recording visual experience into external memory, the way that writing records spoken language. In modern mass media we now learn how to "write down" visual and auditory experiences. People take home movies to vicariously experience some special event over and over again. Movies and television shows are taped and played repeatedly.

Just as theoretic culture made a new form of memory to support it in the written word, so this new level of culture also has a new form of memory, the videotaped experience. Thus, just as mimetic culture perfected a language of gestures for rituals, and mythic culture used words to communicate its stories, and theoretic culture took writing to develop its theories, new mythic culture is using videotape technology. Videotape records visual experience, like a phonetic alphabet records the sounds in speech, and can thus be used to make visual experience and its accompanying auditory experience something permanent and analyzable. Through film technology we can have an external memory that is not like an external semantic memory, like the computer memory that remembers data and facts for us, but is an external episodic memory. It remembers particular visual (and perhaps also audio) experiences for us.

These taped experiences are saved and played back to characterize the event. We see the same news film of the Kennedy assassinations, or the Rodney King beating, whenever a relevant topic occurs. Thus these fragments become the material out of which mythology is pieced together over time. These film fragments are then stitched together to make myth out of our history. As we remember our cultural history we see these images, thus personalizing the history. We vicariously experience the survivors of the Nazi death camps as we see them on film, and they become our collective experience. This view of history is limited and distorted, since it is seen only from the perspective of photogenic moments. It is mythologized history as it is history seen through art, through value, through stereotypes, and experienced photogenic images.

What the media are doing is creating a new mythic level to culture. New myths will be formed as pieced-together fragments from the permanent records of visual experience created through film and television. As we accumulate these fragments, myths are created as patterns emerge. The new myths will be history on film as the photogenic moments collected will be edited into a grand epic about our past.

When we look at classical mythology it too is made out of bits and pieces of stories. Minor gods become identified with major ones, and their stories are then put together. The gods accumulate attributes and stories as they are associated with first this, then that as their worshipers moved from this land to that land, and as events happened which enriched mythic themes. The myths are not codified coherent bodies of stories like the Christian mythology is, because they are not written but oral stories, with different versions told at different times and locations. Our own contemporary myths will be similarly accumulated bits put together to make grand themes out of recorded fragments. The most significant difference between these modern myths and the ancient ones is that whereas the ancient ones were told stories, our modern myths are videotaped experiences.

These videotaped experiences will function as myth in that they will become a body of vicarious experiences that everyone has had. This then will create a shared culture of stories that act as a metaphorical structure against which we can talk about our lives, and see the things that happen to us. The media stories are replacing the "classics" like Shakespeare and Homer, or the Bible stories, as people stop being taught these stories at school. The media stories are not taught at schools but are within everyone's cultural experience as television and movie viewers.

Further, mythic themes will be created through reinforcing patterns that run through all the film art we see, about things like how to live life and what is virtue. For example, the simple stories used by advertising to sell their products already have such themes. These are stories with a simple moral message which includes the use of the product. An example of this is the moral message that you should always keep your promises. This story line is used by various products (fig. 6.3). Another example of this is the story that people judge you by their first impression which is formed from such superficial things as whether or not you are clean shaven, used soap against body odor, or toothpaste against bad breath (Marchand, 1985). Many products use the same story line, from mouth mints for bad breath, to laundry detergent or bath soap. When so many different products use these same story lines in their advertisements, the basic moral of the story takes on a certain aura of truth and inevitability. These stories then become part of the ideological framework against which other ideas are viewed. These sorts of stories then contribute to the background of values we get from the media which then balance out the value neutral stance of science.

Thus mythic culture is reborn in a medium that does not conflict with science. It is reborn within an external memory parallel to that which supports science. In this way myth takes its natural place, not as the competitor of science to be wiped out as mere superstition, but as an art companion to science fulfilling human needs that science cannot fill.

In the ancient religions there was a *separate reality* — the other world of spirits and gods that pulled the strings making life what it was. It was from this other reality that the spirits came to inhabit statues and bring messages. It was in the other reality that our fate was decided. The myths told about that other world. This other reality looks different for different lifestyles (Goodman, 1988). That is, the habitat is mirrored in the separate reality. For the city dweller, the other reality is a mirror of the city. For city dwellers that reality is not a realm to be reached by becoming more spiritually attuned. We reach it by going down into our domestic life. The realm we reach for is the mass-media reality. The other reality that is beyond our own domestic world is the mass-media reality. It is that realm of the mass media that informs us about the impersonal national and international forces that cause things to happen. We enter that world through experiencing it vicariously, and by surrounding ourselves with its symbols, with the products we buy, and the clothes we wear. We can bring some of that world into this one in the way that

FIGURE 6.3 Advertisement for promoting cultural values. Copyright © 1990 Massachusetts Mutual Life Insurance Co. Reprinted by permission.

A promise to let you color a red rose green.

A promise that a secret whispered is as good as kept.

A promise you can always rely on me.

Nothing binds us one to the other like a promise kept. Nothing divides us like a promise broken. At MassMutual we believe in keeping our promises. That way all the families and businesses that rely on us can keep theirs.

MassMutual

We help you keep your promises.

people in mythic cultures make fetishes and good luck charms out of items with marks from the other world — like a tooth from a totem animal or a rock which seems to have an animal face etched into it. The mass media project an image of the other reality — that realm which in folk cultures is where gods live and from which the powers of the spirits emanate. The media external mental space becomes our spiritual space. This is the collective mental space where the modern gods dwell. It is outside each of us, yet it is something we share. It gives us a view of the world beyond ourselves where the true powers abide. It predicts the weather, shows world leaders, gives us advice, and shows perfect glamorized people. The gods no longer live on Mount Olympus, they live on television.

4. FULFILLING THE NEEDS FOR MYTH

New Lifestyles

Each lifestyle in human history has had an accompanying mythological theme that expresses the idea of that style of life. The hunter and gatherer societies around the world have had myths that tell of animal powers. The central mystery to their myths involved the truth that to live we must take life and that life must be replenished so that we can take it again. The hunter had to coax the animal spirits to return and let their bodies be sacrificed as food over and over again. Agricultural societies had a central myth involving the plant that died, and was buried and then was born again. Thus their myths told of a god who was sacrificed and torn apart, buried and then from the god's body, new life springs (Campbell and Moyers, 1988).

One reason that these myths have been or are being forgotten is that most of us no longer live the lifestyles which go along with these mythic themes. We are no longer living in hunter and gatherer or agricultural societies in the West so, the mythic themes which went with these lifestyles no longer speak to us. However, there is still a place for myth in culture; it is just that the old myths cannot fill that place. Myth and science can live comfortably beside each other, as we have said, but not the old myths and science. Only myths that are consistent with our lifestyle can take hold in contemporary culture to give us completion.

The big cultural idea for modern humans, like the big cultural idea preserved in myth of the agriculturalist, or of the hunter and gatherer, is about living within the artifact and within Design Art. Design ideologies are ideologies expressing this cultural idea. We are in an era of technology, machines, computers, and mass media. As we discussed in the last chapter, we live inside artifacts, cities, and within them, houses, and within the houses, rooms, far away from the natural rhythms and challenges of nature. We look out of our windows on mowed lawns or streets and houses, not wild forests untouched by human hands. Our natural needs — warmth, shelter, food — are satisfied through interactions with human beings and within human artifacts and institutions. We don't need to pray to the god of fire to keep our fires burning through the cold winter; we need to pay the gas company and the electric company. We are growing machines that expand our capacities; we are evolving machine extensions to our bodies and our minds. We are growing new machine identities. Thus, beyond themes like the human stages of life, and our personal inner journey to self-fulfillment, the primary themes we need are not about controlling the forces of the natural world, but controlling the forces of the world of the artifact, the human environment. How are we computer like? What are naturally human jobs and what are those that machines should do? We need to understand our place in the world of human-shaped matter. We need a new great mystery to structure the fundamental themes of our new lifestyles. This new mystery needs to express our relationship to our habitat, to our cities and machines, to our artifacts. The old myths have to be replaced by new ones. We have to see our humanity and its place in nature in contrast to machines. We need to reestablish our ancient "spiritual" relationships with our environment in the environment of design, computer, and mass media. We need to understand ourselves and the stages of our lives and our personal inner quests in the new world where we are surrounded by the man-made. We search for a new central mystery, and a way to spiritualize our everyday lives.

Artifact Spiritualism

As we look at people's strivings from the ancient Greek beginnings of Western culture to our own time, we observe a diminishing capacity of people to strive upward toward the spiritual. We have lost our striving toward abstract ideas or God. For example, where the medieval and Renaissance Neoplatonists projected their thoughts to God, climbing up a ladder of love through numbers or the light to the divine (see chapter 2), in contemporary culture advertising uses the Neoplatonic ladder of love to climb into the material world of products. In advertising we go from our higher feelings about social good, or love of family, down to the material plane. The ladder is used to climb down, not up. An example of this is the advertisement (fig. 6.4) that has us move from church to family to slacks. Thus we move in the opposite direction from that of the medievals. Where they projected their thoughts up to God, and saw meanings and symbols everywhere, we project our thoughts down to man-made material objects and see no transcendent meanings or symbols anywhere.

We can see the same movement from the universal idea distinct from mind to a physical sensation in the evolution of the concept of beauty. Beauty moves from being an absolute idea independent of mind in the classical Greek philosophy of Plato, to being a subjective sensation in Hume and the philosophies of taste during the Enlightenment. Thus, with the concept of beauty as well we don't reach outside ourselves to the world of the spirit; we reach inside ourselves to a private pleasant sensation without meaning. In this way our spiritual space is flattened. No longer can we go to God or the good by attending to beauty. It is a matter of taste. We cannot use it to guide us into a more spiritual approach to life.

Here, we sense how our mentality has changed from the last resurgence of mythic culture in the medieval age. We no longer try to reach a more spiritual space outside our bodies through art, even art that

FIGURE 6.4
Advertisement for
Haggar slacks. This
shows a climb down a
Neoplatonic ladder of
love: from church to
family to slacks.
MRCA, 1991 Haggar
Apparel Co. By per-
mission from Haggar
Apparel Co.

A beautiful Sunday morning. The simple joy of being together as a family.
Making time for the important things in life. These are the things that last. The things that feel good.
And once you find them, you want to hold on to them forever. Haggar has a feel for the way you live.
Maybe that's why more men take comfort in Haggar than in any other brand of slacks.
To find out where you can buy Haggar, call 1-800-4HAGGAR.

A FEEL FOR AMERICA™

serves mythic needs, but instead reach deeper into our material physical world. There is no transcendent or mystical space for art to point us toward. Thus, the yearning in us to be attuned to a more universal unity or spirituality is directed into our everyday lives and our material existence where it is structured by mass-media culture. We are grounded in the consumption of products and stereotypes portrayed in the media. Seeing our own reflection in the products and stereotypes on the screen gives us a sense of being part of bigger patterns and purposes. With only a physical approach to the spirit possible, Popular Art, advertising, and design lead us to a material spiritualism, a spiritualism of commodities.

Our cultural project is exploring the interface between man and artifact. Advertising promises us transcendence, a better life, through the use of products. Advertisers use the language of religious art to sell products.

They try to interest us in products in a religious way. For example, advertisers show a huge product with worshipping throngs around it, thus making the product seem transcendent, and awe-inspiring. Like the Egyptians who showed the pharaoh as huge with little people beside him (see fig. 1.13 on p. 31), so also the advertisers show a huge product with little people looking up at it in awe, or clustered around it expressing religious ecstasy.

Some advertisements show the product with a halo of light around it (fig. 6.5). For the medieval, light and luminosity were said to be symbols of God. God was thought of as the living light. Light was the finest and highest of substances and was the pinnacle of a hierarchy. God was the father of lights, and every physical creature contained light to the degree that it had qualities of truth, goodness, or beauty in it. In advertising halos and light shine around a product or radiate from above showing the product as though in God's light (see fig. 5.8 on p. 174), thus taking from religious art the beams of light that meant sainthood or the divine force and using them to elevate a product. The luminosity which the medievals climbed up to God, we climb down to mass market products. Advertisers do this to identify fact with value, to get a religious response triggered and associated with the product, so as to enhance the product. They show the product as containing a living light. In this way religion becomes associated with products. This goes along with the mythic need to see ourselves in terms of the artifact. We are interested in products in a religious way, because the new mythology must place us in our environment which is an environment of man-made designed objects.

Thus, where the medieval mythologized the Word, and tried to transcend the world of the flesh to the world of God, we mythologize the use of products, and try to descend into the world of material objects, of artifacts and machines. Where the medievals were suspicious of visual art because it reminded them of the pleasures of the flesh, we glorify visual art and the pleasures of the flesh. We have substituted the group mind and artifacts for God. We worship our things, and project ourselves into media art.

Our descent into the material world is completed by computers and other machines. The material world to which we sink is not the material world of nature, forest, wind, and animal life. It is the material world of artifact, of the man-made. We plug ourselves into inanimate minds, the media and computer, that we have made for ourselves. Thus we not only direct our thought down into matter, but direct down our very selves. We go out running cocooned in electronic headsets, some people wear electronic heart monitors, or even artificial hearts or limbs. We travel sitting inside our machines. We surround ourselves with machines. In art

FIGURE 6.5 Advertisement showing product with a halo of light to achieve religious elevation of the product. Reprinted by permission from Absolut Vodka.

we fantasize humans that are half man and half machine. We have movies about robot policemen, and androids, and cartoons about *transformers*, living machines that transform from one shape into another in their fight of good over evil. We have calculators and lap-top computers we can carry with us everywhere. We descend into matter to expand our capacities. We surround ourselves with a shell of intelligent machine as well as a shell of artifact packaged in Design Art. Some even talk of our descendants being intelligent machines. Whereas the cultural imperative of the medievals was to ascend to god, and the Enlightenment imperative was to understand and conquer nature, ours has to do with making copies of ourselves in electronics and solving our problems through design.

Making Copies of Ourselves in Electronics

The drive toward artificial intelligence is a drive to give our surroundings intelligence, perhaps even consciousness. We project mind outward from ourselves. We are evolving an external mind for ourselves through the computer as well as through the media. We surround ourselves not just with artifactual objects, but with artifactual minds as well. We create intelligent bank machines, intelligent telephone answering machines, intelligent cars, and intelligent cameras. We are trying to create computer programs that think so much like ourselves that we will be deceived into believing them human.

The most ancient motive for making intelligent machines is the drive to make statues that are completely imitative of human beings (McCorduck, 1979). We want to make objects that not only look like humans, but are also capable of thought and moving themselves about. We want to make a machine that thinks and feels like a human. Like the robots in the movies, we want to make a machine with a full-blown human mentality. As an art motive this is the motive to imitate. Can we make a perfect imitation of a human being in a machine? Just as the perfect imitative art of the Renaissance was painted scenes that completely fooled the eye, the perfect imitative art of the twentieth century would be computer systems that could not be distinguished from human mentalities. This sort of computer system would not just model human thought processes, but be an independent intelligence on its own.

This approach to making intelligent machines is associated with the *Turing Test*. In 1950 Alan Turing (1950) wrote a paper suggesting a test that could be performed to judge whether a machine has successfully imitated a human being. The Turing Test judges whether a machine has intelligence by putting a human interrogator in one room and in another room a machine and a human. The interrogator asks questions through a computer terminal to try to determine which is the machine and which is the human. To pass the Turing Test, the machine would have to fool the interrogator into thinking it is the human being through its typed answers to the interrogator's questions. The system must seem to have a human mentality, perhaps even responding as though it has a family and emotional life. The Turing Test requires the illusion of intelligence rather than real intelligence. Thus the Turing Test is an art standard for judging the machine's intelligence rather than a science standard.

Because of the deceptive element to passing the Turing Test, making a system that passes the Turing Test is like making illusionistic art. Indeed, we could apply just such a test to modern illusionistic sculpture. For example, there are stories told about sculptures by Duane Hanson which illustrate this Turing Test in sculpture (see fig. 2.12 on p. 70). The story is told that once at a display of these sculptures at a museum, when it came time for the museum to close, a museum guard came up to one of these sculptures and asked it to leave. When the sculpture didn't respond, the museum guard called the police to have it evicted. At another museum exhibit, supposedly, the museum guard called an ambulance for a Duane Hanson statue, because he thought it was a human who had stopped breathing. This sculpture passed an equivalent to the Turing Test. These sculptures succeeded in being completely illusionistic.

Like these sculptures, computer systems that pass the Turing Test would give the illusion of humanness. However, these computer systems would give that illusion just by generating sentences on someone's computer terminal. They would give the illusion of a mind without the help of the illusion of a body. Surely if we combined one of these Duane Hanson sculptures with a program of this sort, it would have no trouble fooling people into thinking it is human.

Another way in which we could see ourselves reflected in the machine would be by combining television skills and computer skills. Thereby we could achieve a stronger illusion of humanness. Putting television art together with computer interactive intelligence would give us an interactive image, like a computer game, with the mental depth and skills of a human being as well as the appearance of a human being. This is another way in which we might project our image into the external mind. We could make a perfect interactive human being on the screen who responds appropriately to our questions and appears in every way to be as intelligent and conscious as ourselves. Through such systems we would be attempting to put ourselves, our own minds, into machines.

Another way in which we might use the computer and television together to project ourselves into the external mind would be to become ourselves an interactive part of a living soap opera, mystery, or adventure on the screen, perhaps with other people who are also playing parts through their computer-televisions. We would then be interacting with each other in the alternate reality. This is a way we might enhance our experience of life. We would execute interactive television. We would interact with the dreams on television and thus project our own selves into the alternate reality, into the media group mind. We would thereby be projecting ourselves even further into the world of the artifact, and away from the world of nature. We would appear in each other's dreams.

5. ANOTHER DARK AGE

If we look at the cultural history of Europe from a very broad perspective, we see the Greek archaic period as a dark age transition between the ancient civilizations and the classical Greeks. In classical Greece, theoretic culture begins. However, by the medieval time, a new mythic culture was in control in what has been called a dark age between the classical world and the modern one. Then during the Renaissance and Enlightenment, with the rediscovery of Greek humanism, and the invention of printing and beginning of science, theoretic culture again asserted control. In our own time we seem to be experiencing a reawakening of the mythic level of culture. Some see this as the beginning of another dark age like the previous dark ages. This dark age would be a transitional period between the theoretic culture of the Renaissance and the next cultural stage whatever that will be.

In our contemporary times, literacy is declining. There is a rise in things like witch cults, new age religion, and various kinds of religious fundamentalism. All of these movements are to some degree ideologically incompatible with science and theoretic culture. Parts of the Western world are experiencing social chaos, with vast relocations of peoples and cultural instabilities. There are racial and ethnic tensions everywhere. We live in a world with increasing violence and social unrest. We are searching for new cultural identities. In the United States there is a growing segmentation between rich and poor, educated and non-educated. Indeed, as we discussed in previous chapters, part of the function of art in our own time has been to support social segmentation. We are going from being identified by our ethnic origins as immigrants from various parts of the globe, to being identified by new cultural categories like upwardly mobile young professionals, or neotraditionalists, or some other category. We are increasingly being classed by our consumer ethic, our relationship to values in designed products, style, and mass culture. These are often international categories. We are reshuffling in an international world culture. These new identities allow groups to form within the international culture across former ethnic lines.

Television Thought

With the rise of the media, the general population seems to have become less rational in their thinking patterns. That is, whereas, the mode of thought promoted by the written word is deductive and sequential with an avoidance of contradiction and a striving for detachment and objectivity, the approach to thinking taught by television uses short emotional chains of loose associations. "Now this" is being substituted for connections of relevance as connection between two ideas or two items of news, or news and then advertisement (Postman, 1985).

What this means is that the sort of thinking promoted by television is associational thought rather than logical thought. This is reminiscent of the thought patterns of the medievals, where, for example, four was thought to be the number of man because the distance between man's extended arms is the same as his height, thus making four points and defining a square. Four was also thought to be the number of moral perfection because, as they reasoned, there are four regions of the earth, four elements, four winds, four cardinal points, four seasons, and four letters in the name "Adam" (Eco, 1986, esp. pp. 29–39). This weak Pythagoreanism was the product of associative reasoning. Four is the number of man because it is associated with a square which is associated with man. The number four is perfect because it is associated with many perfect things including the name of the first man, Adam. The sort of reasoning promoted by the media is also associative reasoning. As we have discussed, advertising especially exploits this sort of reasoning.

Also, television information is not detached or objective, it is told from someone's perspective, as a story. Even educational shows tell a story. This entertainment storytelling mode even affects teaching, as teachers now strive to be entertaining and narrative in the classroom rather than presenting detailed carefully reasoned expositions of material. Television supports narrative thinking, and that sort of thinking is being exported outside television into the classroom.

Further the information given on television is throw-away information to be replaced the next day with new information (Postman, 1985). With respect to the information we learn from television, assumptions of coherence and avoiding contradiction have disappeared as people do not think to compare what someone said with what they are saying now. Entertainment is substituted for deductively clear reasoning as a standard of value for an utterance. Being entertaining as we have said, is an art standard. Something is entertaining when it, for example, stimulates our emotion, or gives us a pleasing fantasy to vicariously experience. The drive to be entertaining results in the media striving to fit closer to what people want. In order to be entertaining the media package their messages so that they satisfy people's needs for identity, stimulation, and myth. The media shape visual thought for their own goals, and along the way, they are causing the popular mind to drop paradigmatic thinking in exchange for having vicarious experiences of heroes, sex, violence, and shampoo.

Through mass media our concrete memories of experience, our episodic memories, are taught a language of form. We are taught to attend to our visual stimulus in a new way. We are taught to read images flashed in rapid succession and to read the stereotypes, and other parts of the language of form. The media educate our visual perception. A power of visual thought is being created by television and advertising art. This sort of thinking may come to permeate the whole culture causing everyone but a small elite to forget their paradigmatic skills. This would lead to a mythic culture wherein only a small controling elite is literate, and the rest of the culture passively consumes what this elite prepares for them.

Whereas mythic thinking skills and mimetic thinking skills are supported by internal human memory structure, this is much less true with the skills supporting theoretic culture. Children gesture and learn through imitation naturally and learn to talk naturally, but they have to be actively taught to learn reading and writing. The linear thinking pattern that goes with literacy and theoretic culture is something that gets taught at schools and received from the background theoretic culture by osmosis. It is not part of our inner natural mental development, but a product of cultural evolution. Thus, were people no longer actively taught these skills, the cultural perspective they teach would also disappear. This is what allowed the theoretic culture to disappear in the medieval period. Theoretic culture requires schooling to maintain. The mimetic culture, for example, does not reassert itself against the mythic layer because the skills of the mythic culture, spoken language and narrative thought, appear in each of us as part of our biological mental growth without active intervention from external culture. What this means is that, although we are surrounded by the powerful tools and understandings made possible only by theoretic culture, theoretic culture is fragile in that it is not part of our biological mental evolution, but our external cultural evolution. Thus, theoretic culture and thought patterns could easily be replaced by new mythic culture and modes of thought.

Need for Expert Advice Givers

Another significant way in which our mentality has become more archaic, more like that of the medievals and archaic Greeks, is in our growing dependence on external advice givers. Like the archaic Greeks and the medievals, we are becoming dependent. Where the classical Greeks found independence from the gods as they stepped further into theoretic culture, and the Renaissance and Enlightenment thinkers again found in Greek humanism an independence from divine authorities and plans, we are stepping back into dependence. We again seek the aid of external advice givers. We seek the advice of experts in child care, in marriage, in nutrition, in medicine, in finances, in gardening, in home maintenance, in every aspect of daily life. We have given up our belief that we can find happiness on our own without the help of experts.

When we ask an expert and follow his or her advice, we don't think of ourselves as responsible for the outcome. We have ceased to trust our own sense of what is right for us. We let doctors tell us about our health, and advertising tell us about our needs. If the expert who told us to do something turns out to be wrong, then we can sue him or her in court. Thus, the legal system is set up to support this attitude of dependence where we no longer take responsibility for our own decisions.

Many of us also believe that it is the government's responsibility to keep harmful influences and images out of our reach. The government censors pornographic images which it considers harmful to us and punishes us if we indulge in harmful substances like drugs. The government doesn't trust us to make decisions about such things ourselves, and most of us don't trust ourselves either. We even have laws requiring that we wear our seat belts when we drive our cars. We don't trust ourselves to guard our own safety. People think that if the law didn't tell us what was safe to do, we might hurt ourselves. Thus we are infantilized by the government. Like children we are not allowed to take risks, or make decisions about our own health, safety, or happiness.

The advice giving experts we consult are the modern analog for archaic Greek god-voices and the medieval Church. They also functioned as external advice-giving authorities. We trust what our experts say about things because we no longer trust or listen to our own selves. This need began with our change in lifestyle, and the loss of old ways and cultural knowledge. Our need for experts also comes from our isolation from nature, including our own common sense and bodily sensations. We have become cut off from nature and the past. Further, as we get most of our information indirectly from the media, we cannot discriminate reality from the non-real.

Our need for experts also comes from our changing self-image and changing identities. We don't know quite who we are or what our natures are. When we are told, for example, that our natural odors need to be covered up with perfumes, we lose touch with our sense of smell and our sense of our own rightness. When we are told that only the young are beautiful, we come to believe that there is something wrong with the natural stages of life — childhood, youth, middle age, old age, and death. We come to think of the stages of life as a problem to solve, and become out of touch with our own natures. We try to deny the natural process of aging and cease to trust the inner prompting of our bodies as they prepare us for each life stage. Thus, because we cannot trust our bodies to smell right, or stay young, or have the right cultural knowledge, we come to need advice-giving absolute authorities.

Another reason for this growing dependence is that we are developing new mental skills and redistributing old ones. We are between cultural stages. We increasingly let our electronic machines do more of our paradigmatic thinking and remembering. We are developing our capacity to vicariously experience, and expanding our capacity to comprehend the quick visual images coming across to us through the mass media. Thus our thinking skills are also disrupted, and our own thoughts do not seem as good as the thoughts being broadcast from the group mind. The mass-media dreams are clearer than our own; the information it broadcasts is better than our own; the computer remembers and calculates better than we do. The experts really do know more than we do. Our own thinking is not as good as what is being broadcast to us over the media, or what we get from the computer, and so the need for expert advice givers comes also from our sense that the group mind knows so much more than we do as individuals.

In several ways we are again in an archaic age, that is, an age in transition between one cultural evolutionary level and the next. Along with the rebirth of mythic culture comes the emergence of a new archaic mind. That is, as we adjust to the new conditions, and reassert a mythic culture to live in parallel with the theoretic culture, and adjust to the external mind of the mass media and the computer, our minds become more primitive. We are in a period between fully formed cultural levels. We are no longer squarely in theoretic culture. We are going through an archaic phase.

6. IDOLATRY

The Need for Idolatry

Idolatry is a need for art, like the needs of popular taste, for which an art cultural niche could be created. When we look over the functions for art in other societies in comparison to our own, the glaring difference is in the function of idolatry. Most cultures around the world have used art to be a doorway between themselves and the spirit world. The ancient civilizations of Egypt and Babylon, as well as the classical civilizations of Greece and Rome, used statues in temples to invoke their gods. Folk

FIGURE 6.6 *Chokwe* mask from the Zaire River Basin. The male spirit symbolic of power and riches, *cihongo*, is incarnated.

society like the Australian Aborigines and the Sepik in New Guinea and folk societies in Africa use ritualistically done drawings or carvings to call the spirits (Anderson,1990.) Art quite commonly acts as a doorway into the spirit world, or as a house for a visiting spirit.

Even though idolatry is so common in other cultures, in our own Western culture none of the art niches carry this function. There is no cultural niche of art in the West, as there is in many other cultures, which has idolatry as part of its ideological structure. We have no artist-shaman who makes art to be inhabited by spirits (fig. 6.6). We have no religious tradition that teaches how to approach art or make art so as to cause it to be inhabited. This is true not only because it was forbidden by the Church, but also because people don't remember the ancient language of gestures, so statue idols no longer signal a mental orientation to us. We cannot look at a statue and intuit from its posture what its state of mind would be and then attune our own state of mind to that of the statue as the ancients must have been able to do. A statue can call to mind a hero for us. We can stand in front of the Lincoln Memorial in Washington, D.C., for example, and think about what Lincoln would have said or done (fig. 6.7). We can fantasize him speaking through the stone. It gives us a daydream, with him as a character. However, it does not actually allow him to seem to inhabit the statue and speak to us, telling us some message. It merely gives us a daydream, not an actual independent spirit

FIGURE 6.7 Lincoln Memorial, Washington, D.C. Many treat this statue as though it holds the spirit of Lincoln. They use it to help construct a daydream of Lincoln and imagine what he might say.

presence that sees us and relates to us. All we can do now, generally, is have a vicarious experience. Using art for vicarious experience inhibits our use of it for idolatry. We cannot project someone else into the statue; we can only project ourselves or our daydream. We do not know how to use our thoughts to make art become animated with a spirit entity. We daydream and narrate, but we do not hear an external authority.

However, even though we cannot use art in this way, we still have the need for idols. People still try to use art in this way. They try to call up people through their images. We look at the picture of a loved one and try to imagine what they would say. We have statues of heroes, like Abe Lincoln, which people use to call up the hero before them. Children relate to their dolls and stuffed animals as though they had an independent life force, fantasizing adventures where the doll or stuffed animal takes an active part, and dressing them, kissing them, and explaining things to them. Thus we are still easily able to think of inanimate objects as having an independent life force. We are just not able to take that extra step of getting independent advice from the inanimate thing. We imagine that it is alive, but are unable to see it truly fill with an independent spirit and speak to us.

People's need for experts and feeling of dependence on external advice givers is also an expression of their need for idols. As we discussed, we are becoming dependent and childlike. We do not trust ourselves to know what is good for us. The mental attitude created this

FIGURE 6.8 Greek *kouros* statue c. 600 B.C., imitating Egyptian prototypes, the *kouros* holds a posture that signals a trip to the underworld. Metropolitan Museum of Art, New York.

way predisposes us to need advice-giving expert authorities who will tell us what to do. It disposes us to want idols, statues that can become animated with someone who is an adult, in relation to us, someone who knows all the answers and can guide us unerringly through our lives.

Another way in which we have a need for idols is to preserve the cultural knowledge of a previous cultural stage as we go into the next one. We need to preserve the cognitive skills of the theoretic culture in a vehicle independent of us, so that we can let go of those skills a bit and remythologize our lives.

In cultural evolution, idols can play an important part. The ancient cultures preserved the mimetic gestural skills in the representational form of their idols. The accumulated cultural experiences about exactly which gestures and postures went with which experiences were preserved within the postures, gestures, and symbols used in their cult images. Thus, their statues preserved ancient cultural skills and knowledge as their own culture changed from one stage to another. The ancient idols preserved the mimetic knowledge and thinking skills as well as the mythic insights and beliefs from the previous culture.

For example, common among the art objects found in the Archaic Greek period, besides the cult statues of gods and goddesses, were the

FIGURE 6.9 Roman period statue of Osiris. The Egyptian pharaoh god of the world of the dead has the same posture as the Greek *kouros*.

kouroi statues (fig. 6.8). These were large stone statues of nude males standing stiffly with the right leg slightly in front of the left, and their arms straight at their sides with their hands clenched in fists with the thumbs out. The early ones seem to be holding something as do the Egyptian prototypes. Their faces have large staring eyes and *archaic* smiles. Statues with this particular pose were used for almost three hundred years by the Archaic Greeks (Boardman,1978). Before that, statues showing this posture were also used in Egypt.

The *kouroi* seem to have been used as votive dedications, grave markers, and cult images (Osborne,1988). There is evidence that they were thought of as houses for visiting spirits. Since the Archaic Greeks thought that one of the souls that left the body after death could be re-animated if it were fed blood, perhaps these statues were fed blood sacrifices and used to prophesy. The posture of the *kouroi* statues was most likely thought to be the posture required for trips to and from the underworld. There are Egyptian statues of the god Osiris in the same posture (fig. 6.9). While Osiris was a god-king of the living he was associated with agriculture; later he was killed and dismembered, and then resurrected as a dead spirit to be a just and good god-king of the dead. His cult associated him with eternally happy life after death.

The idea of the *kouroi* statues might have been that by giving the spirit a stone house in the posture of Osiris, the Archaic Greeks could give the heroes embodied resurrection after death in a happy land with a good god-king, or they could use the statue to resurrect the spirit with blood sacrifices to talk to the living. F. Goodman reports (1990) that the trance that accompanies the posture of the *kouroi* statues produces the experience of being inside an opening in the earth, or a cave, in which there is the smell of blood or of putrefaction. Some trancers experience being given a message. This might be an experience of blood sacrifices and the underworld. Thus the statues are a record of the gestures which go with the state of mind and thoughts which make up the experience of going into the underworld, or being resurrected from the underworld with blood sacrifices. For the archaic the statues preserved the ancient Egyptian cultural knowledge of the mimetic skills and myths that gave resurrection to spirits.

As we leave theoretic culture for the next stage, we preserve its thinking pattern in our computers. The thinking skill that needs to be preserved in our case is rational problem solving. This is more than just reading and writing; it is the skill of paradigmatic thought for manipulating symbols and truth functional assertions in a logical manner. We are already giving over our mathematical skills to computers. Some of us don't do even simple arithmetic calculations anymore, but tend to rely wholly on our pocket calculators to do them. Thus, we make computers that are rational problem solvers and in that way we externalize reason into our machines, so we can devote our individual internal minds to something else. These computer systems could then preserve the thought skills of theoretic culture.

Engineering and computer science provide the institutional structures to discover how to structure thinking machines to fill this need. These thinking machines can be of two types. The first type is computer systems that give us help in problem solving but do not have any human-like personalities. These are the sort we already use at home to do things like help balance our check books, and spell check what we write, and at work to do things like keep track of accounts and inventories, and do mailings. There are even more complex machines of this sort that help interpret medical data, and help do computer simulations for design.

The second sort are machines that do have human-like personalities. These are systems built to pass the Turing Test which, like the ancient idols, seem to be independent intelligent personalities. Both sorts of computer systems augment our paradigmatic thinking skills, and both sorts would preserve theoretic culture should the general population cease being able to think paradigmatically or read and write. The difference in function between the two types is that the computer systems without human personalities tend to function as tools for people who still have the paradigmatic thinking skills, whereas the human-like machines could be used by people who had already forgotten those thinking skills. These human-like machines would better serve the mythic cultural function of being god-like experts.

Computer System Idols

Beyond just being perfect imitations of human beings, human-like machines would give us god-like advice. The computer system idols would act as independent authorities. They would be the ultimate experts that could serve as our doctors, tax accountants, marriage counselors, or government advisers. The advantages of machine authorities over human ones would be their "objectivity" and lack of personal agenda. We imagine that they would have no human weaknesses just human strengths. They would be ideal humans, never forgetting, never careless, and treating everyone equally, like an expert on a good day without distractions. These are the AI idols that might naturally evolve from systems made to pass the Turing Test.

The need for expert advice givers can be seen as a need to have access to the group mind, the shared collective knowledge of our culture, that we as individuals cannot know. Human experts are only in touch with their small corner of this accumulated group wisdom. The computer expert would know all the things the group knows. Thus, a computer, with its capacity for vast encyclopedic knowledge, could be the ultimate expert. It could know *everything* that was written, and if we gave it a human-like personality it could communicate whatever part of that knowledge was relevant to our situation without us having to be able to do any paradigmatic thinking ourselves. Thus, such computer idols could preserve theoretic culture and a way of thought even if the general population were to forget all those skills.

These idols might be live on the computer screen, or live on the integrated television-computer, or appear as a virtual reality image. The computer system idol would be a computer-generated human that seems to have independent will and personality. The point of making them human-like is to make them easy to interact with, especially for people with a mythic mentality. It might be someone we could fall in love with, or have as our personal companion, someone who knows all the answers, pays our bills, does our taxes, corrects our spelling, and reminds us to send a card to Grandma for her birthday. The computer system idols would always be there when we need them. They could attract good or bad fortune to us, like the ancient idols could do for their users, for example, by things like paying our bills on time, or saving our marriage through their good advice. They would have power, and hopefully be loving gods.

The motive for developing such systems is that we could not only consult these machine authorities about our problems, but also blame them if errors occur. We want to be able to say, "It is not my fault, the computer told me to do it." Perhaps we could give these expert systems bank accounts out of the profits from their sale so that they can be sued. And if they make too many mistakes, they could be banished, turned off. Further, if they are truly like human beings in their mentalities, then they would feel guilty for their mistakes, and feel joy at their successes. We already trust machines to be more accurate than human beings. The machine experts would become elevated as we accept their authority and rely on them. Then as we ourselves forget how to do the mental skills we have externalized into the machines, the machine experts would become even further elevated. The machine experts would become deified as they repeatedly give us good advice in important and complex problem solving situations. Such machine personalities would serve as modern idols. They could become unquestioned authorities on which we could depend. With a human-like machine authority, we could feel that someone in charge really knows what is being done. Unlike human beings, these computer system idols could be trusted to deal with us honestly, since they would be incorruptible by power or money. Such machines would satisfy the mythic cultural need for external authorities, for authorities from outside the competing interests of human beings, impartial arbitrators, with a god's-eye perspective.

Ancient idols were employed to give advice, cure diseases, predict the future, punish and reward their users, and bring messages from the other world. The ancients did not want idols that helped them with their taxes or with general rational problem solving. The ancients did not want a rational and literate idol. Thus, the main differences between these computer system mentalities and the idols of the ancient world are that the computer system idols are secular, not religious, so the computer system idols appear in offices not in temples. Further, they are preserving theoretic culture, not mimetic and mythical cultural knowledge, and so they are rational problem solvers. The computer system idols preserve the skills of rational problem solving for the time when we may no longer be able to use those skills ourselves. As we move into a post-theoretic stage of culture, these expert system idols will be a bridge between one stage and another. They will be grounded in theoretic culture as the ancient idols are grounded in mimetic culture. The computer system idols fit into the newly evolving mind.

7. MOVING TOWARD A FOURTH CULTURAL STAGE

The Fourth Stage of Cultural Evolution

To support another stage of cultural evolution, we need to consolidate the needs of myth and science. Theoretic culture grounds the new cultural stage, just as mimetic culture grounded the mythic. That is, it is through the type of thinking supported by the theoretic culture, and through writing, that the media and computers have come to exist. Computers do paradigmatic thinking. They are rational, literate, and symbolic. They practice the skills of theoretic culture. Thus, our computers preserve the powers of theoretic culture within them.

One part of our external mind services theoretic cultural needs, while the other services mythic cultural needs. We have new senses with television, and a new group mental space; the media provide group perception as well as dreams. We have developed a representational medium for supporting a new cultural stage, namely the external mind of television and computer. These new external mental capacities are balanced, as yet. Both the mythic worldview and the theoretic worldview are projected into the external mind. We have both rational problem solvers as well as dreams and group perception. The new stage is the stage of group external mind made possible by computer and television. The language of form in this mind is already arising in the active languages of the computer, the programming languages, and the passive representational languages of media art and advertising, and the capacity to record visual experience on film.

It is not yet clear what we humans wrapped within these external mental capacities will be like, except that at the moment the mythic point of view is reasserting itself. Also, like the theoretic culture, this fourth cultural stage of the external mind is fragile, in that it is not rooted in biological evolution but in cultural evolution. That means that this further cultural evolution could be halted at any point just by turning off our electronic machines.

Potentially, the new cultural stage supported by the external mind will express neither the theoretic nor the mythic point of view. It will be something new, transcending both. The ability to record experiences on videotape will surely have an effect on thinking patterns, just as the ability to record speech in writing did. Surely, there will be complex interactions between computer and media. But it could also be that one or the other orientation comes to dominate the external mind, flavoring the next cultural stage with myth or theory.

We are archaic in our mentality because our personal minds are in a middle phase between the new expanded mind and the old one. Like the archaic Greeks who were between the old way of idols and hearing voices of the gods, and the new way of reason, we are also in a transitional stage. A reorganization of our personal minds is occurring. Our relationship to image, language, and personal identity is in flux. This is what makes this seem like an archaic period—a time when people's thinking skills decline. Thinking skills that were so valued before, those associated with literacy and reason, are being ignored and more primitive ones exposed and worked on.

The New Bicameral Mind

The psychologist Julian Jaynes (1976) speculates that in the preclassical ancient people, the two halves of their brains did not function together in a unified manner as ours do today. In the ancient people the linear, analytical, rational "language" hemisphere, and the intuitive, synthetic, gestalting, patterning, visual hemisphere of the brain acted independently. He calls this ancient mentality the *bicameral mind*. As a result of their bicameral minds, he thinks, the ancient peoples could not introspect as we do today, and experienced auditory hallucinations of god voices which told them what to do. The voices of deities that they heard were really voices that they heard from their own other hemisphere. Bicameral humans needed to project the thoughts from the right hemisphere outside themselves, as the voice of an outer authority, in order to grasp them with their left hemisphere. As a result of this bicameralism, they were not conscious as we are today, and had no unified sense of self. Consciousness, he maintains, is very new, arising only in the last 3,000 years. Consciousness he sees as a different architectural organization for the right and left hemisphere of the brain. The characteristics of consciousness, he thinks, are self-reference, mind-space, and narration.

Consciousness, from this perspective is the mind-space created from the overlapping and integrating of the understandings from the two hemispheres of the brain.

We cannot know whether this bicameralism was literally true of the ancients; it is, however, in some sense true of us. Our minds are becoming bicameral in two ways. First of all there is a bicameralism within the external mind itself between the visual mental space of the media, and the linear, analytical rational mental problem solver of the computer. The ultimate external mind would be an integration between what are now its two independent hemispheres. If these two were to be integrated, then the television would be capable of being more interactive and the computer would be more user friendly. This would be an overlap between the art technology for creating illusion and the computer-generated problem solving. The computer could give interactive problem solving intelligence to the image and then the user could interact with the image in the way that we now interact with images in video games or computer games, or we could interact even more fully with the image as we do with virtual reality machines. If the external mind were no longer bicameral, the television and computer mental capacities would be unified. The unified external mind would have interactive advice-giving authorities as well as providing perception and dreams.

Secondly, there is the bicameralism of inner and outer mind. The external mind is public, while the inner mind is private. Although there is a continuum between them, at this point they are separate. At the moment, our inner mind is playing the role of watcher, conscious self, surrounded by the input from the outer, external mind. The external mind can still be turned off. We can still think without it. However, as the media-computer external mind grows, we feel the disorientation of bicameralism, of having "hemispheres" that don't quite talk to each other. As the external mind develops, certain skills will be given over to it. Computers will do more of our mental tasks, while we will depend more upon the media to give us information and dreams.

As we evolve culturally, the separation between the inner and outer mind could decrease until we are not bicameral anymore. Once we are adapted to it, we will be stupid when we don't have the external mind at our disposal, since we will have deposited a certain amount of the mental work we now do ourselves in that mind. As the two parts come together, some of the powers of the old way of using our minds will get lost, just as the power to hear external god thoughts has been lost, and new powers will be developed. We will take on the identity offered by the external mind. We will look at life through its eyes. We will package ourselves in its language of form. We will use its images for thought. The inner and external mind will become together just one mind, and one orientation. We will be completely rooted both mentally and physically in the artifact. We will have an inner mind and body, and the media and computer and artifact will be our outer mind and body. At that point we will have reached consciousness as part of a group-mind of some particular type, coexisting in a community of group-minds.

The new classical age, or new Renaissance will come when we come out of the darkness of bicameralism and gain self-consciousness as a coordinated inner and external mind. This will be the fourth cultural stage. Then we will decide on our group missions in our new group identities. The birth of those missions will constitute the dawn of the new age.

Bibliography

◈

Chapter 1   The Cultural-Niche Theory of Art

Anderson, Richard L. 1990. *Calliope's Sisters, A Comparative Study of Philosophies of Art*. Englewood Cliffs, NJ: Prentice Hall.

Armstrong, Robert Plant. 1981. *The Powers of Presence, Consciousness, Myth, and Affecting Presence*. Philadelphia: University of Pennsylvania Press.

Arnheim, Rudolf. 1969. *Visual Thinking*. London: Farber and Farber.

———. 1983. *The Power of the Center : A Study of Composition in the Visual Arts*. Berkeley: University of California Press.

Binder, David. 1986. "In Defence of Pictorial Mimesis." *The Journal of Aesthetics and Art Criticism* (Fall): XLV, no. 1, 19–28.

Blofeld, John. 1974. *The Tantric Mysticism of Tibet*. New York: Causeway Books.

Danto, Arthur C. 1964. "The Artworld." *Journal of Philosophy*: 571–84.

———. 1981. *The Transfiguration of the Common Place*. Cambridge, MA: Harvard University Press.

Dickie, George. 1971. *Aesthetics, An Introduction*. New York: Pegasus, The Bobbs-Merrill Company, Inc.

Edgerton, Jr., Samuel Y. 1980. "The Renaissance Artist as Quantifier." *The Perception of Pictures*, edited by Margaret A. Hagen, New York: Academic Press 1: 179–212.

Freedberg, David. 1989. *The Power of Images, Studies in the History and Theory of Response*. Chicago: The University of Chicago Press.

Gibson, James. 1966. *The Senses Considered as Perceptual Systems*. Boston: Houghton Mifflin Co.

Gombrich, E. H. 1960. *Art and Illusion, A Study in the Psychology of Pictorial Representation*, The A.W. Mellon Lectures in the Fine Arts, National Gallery of Art, Washington, Bollingen Series, 35: 5. Princeton: Princeton University Press, 1956.

Goodman, Nelson. 1976. *Languages of Art*. Indianapolis: Hackett Press.

Gregg, Robert. 1984. "Relativism and Pictorial Realism." *The Journal of Aesthetics and Art Criticism* (Summer), vol. XLII, 4: 397–408.

Hagen, Margaret. 1980. "Generative Theory: A Perceptual Theory of Pictorial Representation." In *The Perception of Pictures*, edited by Margaret A. Hagen, New York: Academic Press 2:3–45.

Hauser, Arnold. 1958. *The Philosophy of Art History*. Evanston: Northwestern University Press. (Rev. ed. 1985).

Hefferman, James A. W. 1985. "Resemblance, Signification, and Metaphor in the Visual Arts." *The Journal of Aesthetics and Art Criticism* 44, no. 2 (Winter): 167–80.

Hurlbert, Anya and Tomaso Poggio. 1988. "Making Machines (and Artificial Intelligence) See." In *The Artificial Intelligence Debate False Starts, Real Foundations*, edited by Stephen R. Graubard, 213–40. Cambridge, MA: M.I.T. Press.

Jung, C. G. 1969. *Mandala Symbolism*. Vol. 9, part 1 of *The Collected Works of C. G. Jung*. Translated by R.F.C. Hull in Bollingen Series. Princeton: Princeton University Press.

Kubovy, Michael. 1986. *The Psychology of Perspective and Renaissance Art*. New York: Cambridge University Press.

Lind, Richard. 1985. "A Microphenomenology of Aesthetic Qualities." *The Journal of Aesthetics and Art Criticism*, vol. 43, no.4: (Summer) 393–403.

Marr, David. 1982. *Vision, A Computational Investigation into the Human Representation and Processing of Visual Information*. San Francisco: W. H. Freeman and Company.

McCorduck, Pamela. 1991. *Aaron's Code: Meta-Art, Artificial Intelligence and the Work of Harold Cohen*. New York: W. H. Freeman and Company.

Mondrian, Piet. 1937. "Plastic Art and Pure Plastic Art" ("Figurative Art and Nonfigurative Art.") In *Theories of Modern Art*, edited by Herschel B. Chip, 349–62. Berkeley: University of California Press, 1968.

Perkins, D. N. and Margaret A. Hagen. 1980. "Convention, Context, and Caricature." In *The Perception of Pictures*, edited by Margaret A. Hagen, New York: Academic Press 1: 257–86.

Pollett, J. J. 1972. *Art and Experience in Classical Greece*. New York: Cambridge University Press.

Rosinski, Richard R. and James Farber. 1980. "Compensation for Viewing Point in the Perception of Pictured Space." In *The Perception of Pictures*, edited by Margaret A. Hagen, New York: Academic Press 1: 137–76.

Schufreider, Gregory. 1985. "Overpowering the Center: Three Compositions by Mondrian." *The Journal of Aesthetics and Art Criticism* 44, no. 1 (Fall): 13–28.

Suger, C. 1148. *Sugerii Abbatis Sancti Dionysii Liber De Dubus*. In *Administratione Sua Gestis*, "Of the Cast and Gilded Doors" translated by Erwin Panofsky, 47.

In *Abbot Suger, on the Abbey Church of St.-Denis and Its treasures*, edited, translated, and annotated by Erwin Panofsky, 2d ed. by Gerda Panofsky-Soergel.
Princeton: Princeton University Press, 1979.

Wittgenstein, Ludwig. 1953. *Philosophical Investigations*. Translated by G.E.M.
Anscombe, 2d edition. New York: Macmillan Co.

Chapter 2   The Fine Art Cultural Niche

Ades, Dawn. 1974. "Dada and Surrealism." In *Concepts of Modern Art*, edited by
Tony Richardson and Nikos Stangos. New York: Icon Editions, Harper and
Row.

Alsop, Joseph. 1986. *New York Review of Books* 33, no. 12: 42–5.

Beardsley, M. C. l966. *Aesthetics from Classical Greece to the Present*. Alabama:
University of Alabama Press.

Bell, Clive. 1958. *Art*. New York: Capricorn Books.

Bullough, Edward. 1977. " 'Psychical Distance' as a Factor in Art and an
Aesthetic Principle." Reprinted in *Aesthetics: A Critical Anthology*, edited by
George Dickie and Richard J. Sclafani, 758–82. New York: St. Martin's
Press.

Canaday, John. 1981. *Mainstreams of Modern Art*. New York: Holt, Rinehart,
Winston.

Cottom, Daniel. 1981. "Taste and the Civilized Imagination." *The Journal of
Aesthetics and Art Criticism* (Summer): 367–78.

Crimp, Douglas. 1985. "Appropriating Appropriation." In *Theories of Contemporary Art*, edited by Richard Hertz, 157–162 Englewood Cliffs, NJ: Prentice
Hall.

Danto, Arthur C. 1973. "The Last Work of Art: Artworks and Real Things."
Reprinted from *Theoria* 39: 1–17, 1973. In *Aesthetics: A Critical Anthology*,
edited by George Dickie and Richard J Sclafani, 551–62. New York: St.
Martin's Press, 1977.

Freud, Sigmund. 1908. "The Relation of the Poet to Day-Dreaming" from
Freud's *Collected Papers*, vol. 4. Reprinted in *Art and Its Significance, An Anthol-
ogy of Aesthetic Theory*, edited by Stephen David Ross, 492–500 Albany:
SUNY Press, 1984.

Gilbert, Katharine Evert and Helmut Kuhn. 1972. *A History of Esthetics*. New
York: Dover.

Hamilton, George Heard. l972. *Painting and Sculpture in Europe 1880–1940*, New
York: Penguin Books.

Hauser, Arnold. 1951. *The Social History of Art*. Translated by Stanley Godman.
Vol. 2. New York: Vintage Books.

Held, Julius S. and Donald Posner. 1979. *17th and 18th Century Art*. New York:
Prentice-Hall and Harry N. Abrams.

Holt, Elizabeth G., ed. 1958. *A Documentary History of Art*. Vol. 2. New York:
Doubleday Anchor Books.

Hume, David. 1757. *Of the Standard of Taste*. Reprinted in *Aesthetics: A Critical Anthology*, edited by George Dickie and Richard J. Sclafani, 592–606. New York: St. Martin's Press, 1977.

Kristeller, Paul Osker. 1961. *Renaissance Thought, the Classic, Scholastic and Humanistic Strains*. New York: Harper Torchbooks.

Levin, Kim. 1985. "Farewell to Modernism." In *Theories of Contemporary Art*, edited by Richard Hertz, 1–9. Englewood Cliffs, NJ: Prentice-Hall.

Lucie-Smith, Edward. 1974. "Minimal Art." In *Concepts of Modern Art*, edited by Tony Richardson and Nikos Stangos, 243–55. New York: Icon Editions, Harper and Row Publishers.

Lippard, Lucy. 1985. "10 Structurists in 20 Paragraphs." Reprinted in *Theories of Contemporary Art*, edited by Richard Hertz, 207–214. New York: Prentice-Hall, Inc.

McEvilley, Thomas. 1983. "Art in the Dark." Reprinted from *Art Forum* (Summer) 1983. In *Theories of Contemporary Art*, edited by Richard Hertz, 287–305. Englewood Cliffs, NJ: Prentice-Hall, 1985.

Panofsky, Erwin. 1955. "Art as a Humanistic Discipline." In *Meaning in the Visual Arts, Papers in and on History*. Garden City, NY: Doubleday Anchor Books.

Podro, Michael. 1982. *The Critical Historians of Art*. New Haven: Yale University Press.

Tomkins, Calvin. 1968. *The Bride and the Bachelors, Five Masters of the Avant-Garde*. New York: Viking Compass Book.

———. 1972. *The World of Marcel Duchamp 1887-1968*. New York: Time-Life Books.

Tolstoy, Leo. 1898. "What Is Art?" In *Tolstoy on Art*, translated by A. Maude. New York: Oxford University Press, 1924.

Weitz, Morris. 1970. "The Role of Theory in Aesthetics." In *Problems in Aesthetics*, edited by Morris Weitz, 179–180. 2d ed. New York: Macmillan Publishing Co.

Winckelman, J. J. 1764. "Thoughts on the Imitation of Greek Art in Painting and Sculpture." In *A Documentary History of Art*, vol. II, translated by Elizabeth G. Holt. New York: Doubleday Anchor Books, 1958.

Wolf, Thomas. 1975. *The Painted Word*. New York: Bantam Books.

Chapter 3   The Popular Art Cultural Niche

Armes, Roy. 1975. *Film and Reality, An Historical Survey*. Baltimore: Penguin Books.

Canaday, John. 1981. *Mainstreams of Modern Art*. New York: Holt, Rinehart, and Winston.

Campbell, Richard R. 1981. "Art World." *Columbus Citizen-Journal* (Columbus, Ohio) (December 5).

———. 1984. "It Sure Is Public, But Is It Art?" *Columbus Citizen-Journal* (Columbus, Ohio) (May 19).

Collins, Jessica. 1992. "Tax Watchdogs Take It to Art." *Insight on the News* 8, no. 5: 14–16, 37–38

Greenberg, Clement. 1961. *Art and Culture, Critical Essays*. Boston: Beacon Press.

Hauser, Arnold. 1985. *The Philosophy of Art History*. Evanston, IL: Northwestern University Press. First published as *Philosophie Der Kunstgeschichte*. 1958. Munich: Oscar Beck.

Huntington, Richard. 1986. "Starving Artists." *Buffalo News* magazine *Gusto*. January 10, Buffalo, NY.

Kouwenhoven, John A. 1948, *The Arts in Modern American Civilization*. New York: Norton and Co.

Malcolm, Janet. 1986. "Profiles: A Girl of the ZeitGeist–1." *The New Yorker*, Oct. 20, 1986, 63–64.

Peterson, Ivars. 1992. "Looking-Glass Worlds, Learning to Assemble the Machinery of Illusion." *Science News* 141, no. 1:8–10.

Sklar, Robert. 1975. *Movie-Made America: A Cultural History of American Movies*. New York: Random House.

Solomon, Robert C. 1991. "On Kitsch and Sentimentality." *The Journal of Aesthetics and Art Criticism* 49, no. 1 (Winter): 1–14.

Talor, Joshua C. 1979. *The Fine Arts in America*. Chicago: University of Chicago Press.

Tolstoy, Leo. 1898. "What Is Art?" In *Tolstoy on Art*, trans. by A. Maude. New York: Oxford University Press, 1924.

Chapter 4   The Design Art Cultural Niche

Christie, Archibald H. 1969. *Pattern Design : An Introduction to the Study of Formal Ornament*. New York: Dover Publications.

Dormer, Peter. 1990. *The Meanings of Modern Design towards the Twenty-first Century*. New York: Thames and Hudson.

Garvan, Anthony N. B. 1967. "Effects of Technology on Domestic Life, 1830-1880." In *Technology in Western Civilization*, vol. 1, edited by Melvin Kranzberg and Carroll W. Pursell, Jr., 546–59. New York: Oxford University Press.

Greenough, Horatio. 1853. "Form and Function." From *A Memorial of Horatio Greenough*, by Henery T. Tuckerman, reprinted in *Roots of Contemporary American Architecture*, edited by Lewis Mumford, 32–56. New York: Dover, 1972.

Hamilton, George Heard. 1972. *The Pelican History of Art, Painting and Sculpture in Europe, 1880-1940*. New York: Penguin Books.

Hauser, Arnold. 1985.*The Philosophy of Art History*. Evanston, IL: Northwestern University Press.

———. 1951. *The Social History of Art*. New York: Vintage Books.

Hennessey, James and Victor Papanek. 1973. *Nomadic Furniture*. New York: Pantheon Books.

Kouwenhoven, John A. 1948. *The Arts in Modern American Civilization.* New York: Norton and Co.

Marchand, Roland. 1985. *Advertising the American Dream Making Way for Modernity, 1920–1940,* Berkeley: University of California Press.

Marr, D. 1982. *Vision.* New York: W. H. Freeman.

Mayall, W. H. 1968. *Machine and Perception in Industrial Design.* New York: Studio Vista/Reinhold Art Paperback, Reinhold Book Corporation.

Miles, Charles. 1963. *Indian and Eskimo Artifacts of North America.* New York: Bonanza Books.

Mumford, Lewis. 1962. "The Aesthetic Assimilation of the Machine." In *A Modern Book of Esthetics,* 4th ed., edited by Melven Rader, 481–90. New York: Holt, Rinehart, and Winston, 1973.

Niece, Robert C. 1968. *Art in Commerce and Industry.* Dubuque, IA: Wm. C. Brown Company Publishers.

Overy, Paul. 1991. *De Stijl.* London: Thames and Hudson, Ltd.

Papanek, Victor. 1971. *Design for the Real World.* New York: Pantheon Books.

Ravetz, Jerome R. 1971. *Scientific Knowledge and Its Social Problems.* New York: Oxford University Press.

Simon, Herbert. 1982. *The Sciences of the Artificial.* 2d ed. Cambridge, MA: M.I.T. Press.

Sparke, Penny. 1986. *An Introduction to Design and Culture in the Twentieth Century,* New York: Harper and Row Publishers.

Chapter 5   Advertising

Allen, Charlotte. 1991. "The 'Neo-trads'. "*Insight in the News,* (October 14) Washington, D.C.: 10–18.

Garvan, Anthony N. B. 1967. "Effects of Technology on Domestic Life, 1830–1880." In *Technology in Western Civilization,* vol. 1, edited by Kranzberg, Melvin, and Pursell, Carroll Jr., 546–59. New York: Oxford University Press.

Haug, Wolfgang Fritz. 1986. *Critique of Commodity Aesthetics, Appearance, Sexuality, and Advertising in Capitalist Society.* Translated by Robert Bock. Minneapolis: University of Minnesota Press.

Kranzberg, Melvin. 1967. "Prerequisites for Industrialization." In *Technology in Western Civilization ,* vol. 1, edited by Melvin Kranzberg and Carroll Pursell, Jr., 217–29. New York: Oxford University Press.

Mander, Jerry. 1978. *Four Arguments for the Elimination of Television.* New York: Quill (William Morrow and Company, Inc.).

Marchand, Roland. 1985. *Advertising the American Dream Making Way for Modernity, 1920-1940.* Berkeley: University of California Press.

Schudson, Michael. 1984. *Advertising, the Uneasy Persuasion.* New York: Basic Books, Inc.

Chapter 6   The Media and the Rebirth of Mythic Culture

Anderson, Richard L. 1990. *Calliope's Sisters, a Comparative Study of Philosophies of Art*. Englewood Cliffs, NJ: Prentice Hall.

Aristotle, c. 330 B.C. "De Divinatione Per Somnum." From *Parva Naturalia*, translated by J. I. Beare, in *The Basic Works of Aristotle*, edited by Richard Mckeon, 618–25. New York: The Random House Lifetime Library, 1966.

Boardman, John. 1978. *Greek Sculpture, The Archaic Period*. New York: Oxford University Press.

Campbell, Joseph and Bill Moyers. 1988. *The Power of Myth*. New York: Anchor Books, Doubleday.

Dodds, E. R. 1966. *The Greeks and the Irrational*. Berkeley: University of California Press.

Donald, Merlin. 1991. *Origins of the Modern Mind: Three Stages in the Evolution of Culture and Cognition*. Cambridge, MA: Harvard University Press.

Eco, Umberto. 1986. *Art and Beauty in the Middle Ages*. Translated by Hugh Bredin, New Haven: Yale University Press.

Goodman, F. 1986. "Body Posture and the Religious Altered State of Consciousness: An Experimental Investigation." *Journal of Humanistic Psychology* 26, no. 3 (Summer): 81–118.

———. 1988. *Ecstasy, Ritual, and Alternate Reality, Religion in a Pluralistic World*. Bloomington: Indiana University Press.

———. 1990. *Where the Spirits Ride the Wind* . Bloomington: Indiana University Press.

Herototus, c. 445 B.C. *History*. In *Herodotus, Thucydides*, translated by George Rawlinson. Chicago: Encyclopeadia Britannica, Inc., 1952.

Jaynes, Julian. 1976. *The Origin of Consciousness in the Breakdown of the Bicameral Mind*. Boston: Houghton Mifflin Co.

Jung, Carl, G. 1964. "Approaching the Unconscious." In *Man and His Symbols*, edited by Carl G. Jung, 1–95. New York: Dell Publishing.

Osborne, R. G. 1988. "Death Revisited: Death Revised." *Art History* 11, no. 1 (March): 1–16.

Panofsky, Erwin. 1979. *Abbot Suger, on the Abbey Church of St.-Denis and Its Art Treasures*. Edited, translated, and annotated by Panofsky, 2d ed. by Gerda Panofsky-Soergel. Princeton: Princeton University Press.

Pollett, J. J. 1972. *Art and Experience in Classical Greece*. Cambridge, Great Britain: Cambridge University Press.

Postman, Neil. 1985. *Amusing Ourselves to Death, Public Discourse in the Age of Show Business*. New York: Penguin Books.

Turing, Alan. 1950. "Computing Machinery and Intelligence." *Mind*, 54: 236.

Vernant, Jean-Pierre. 1982. *The Origins of Greek Thought*. Translated from French. Ithaca: Cornell University Press.

Index